11·2009

TO ROBIN & STEVE —

No MATTER WHICH PATH
WE WALK IN LIFE, THERE IS
ALWAYS VALUE WAITING TO
BE DISCOVERED.

MAY THIS BOOK INSPIRE
YOUR JOURNEY & FUEL YOUR
DREAMS OF THE POSSIBLE.

My VERY BEST,

# A Deliberate Pause

Entrepreneurship
and its Moment in Human Progress

# A Deliberate Pause

Entrepreneurship
and its Moment in Human Progress

## Larry Robertson

New York

# A Deliberate Pause
## Entrepreneurship and its Moment in Human Progress

ISBN: 978-1-60037-652-8 (PB)
ISBN: 978-1-60037-653-5 (HC)
Library of Congress Control Number: 2009929152

1. Entrepreneurship (Business).  2. Leadership.  3. Social Psychology.

Printed in the United States of America

# MORGAN · JAMES
### THE ENTREPRENEURIAL PUBLISHER

Morgan James Publishing, LLC
1225 Franklin Ave., STE 325
Garden City, NY 11530-1693
Toll Free 800-485-4943
www.MorganJamesPublishing.com

In an effort to support local communities, raise awareness and funds, Morgan James Publishing donates one percent of all book sales for the life of each book to Habitat for Humanity. Get involved today, visit **www.HelpHabitatForHumanity.org**.

*To my readers…*

This book is your invitation and your compass to the journey we all must take. Don't just be a passenger – grab the tiller!


*To my mom…*

You always believed I had a book in me and pushed me to bring it out – here it is.


*To my family, all…*

Who gave me what I needed to write that book – your support, confidence, honest critique, and unconditional love – thank you.


*To Kai…*

My wise counselor and advisor; patient, precise, and spot-on editor; and the greatest partner anyone could ask for – you made it work.


*To Noah and Ella…*

The clay that is the future lies in your hands – sculpt a masterpiece.


*And to Bill Gorog…*

Who first showed me a better way and a better reason to be successful – you are not forgotten and live on in many.

# Contents

# Introduction: Hero, Villain, or Something More?

*"The hardest work and the greatest opportunity is a much less visible part—how we think about what we do and who we want to become. That inner landscape is something that usually gets left out of conversations."*

- Jeffrey Hollender
Founder, Chief Inspired Protagonist
Seventh Generation

In October, 2008, a survey was commissioned by the Kauffman Foundation, one of the largest foundations in the United States and the world's largest devoted to entrepreneurship.

This proved to be no ordinary time to commission this survey. The U.S. economy had just fallen off the precipice into arguably its worst downward spiral in its 232-year history. The nation stood on the eve of an historic presidential election, one in which its citizens would not only decide the next president, but the direction of the country. More, a century of industrialized growth and big institutions was showing signs that the old ways, economic and otherwise, just weren't working anymore.

Researchers hired by the Kauffman Foundation studied what people thought the new president and the government should do—and sought opinions as to who would carry us out of this crisis.[1] Of nearly a thousand registered voters surveyed, a whopping 70 percent said they believed the health of the nation going forward depended on the success of entrepreneurs, and 80 percent wanted to see the government use its resources to actively encourage entrepreneurship in

America. By a two-to-one margin, respondents said they were looking to business leaders—not government officials—to lead the way out of the economic morass.

But did they have any idea what they were talking about? A *Washington Post* article that appeared shortly after Kauffman's survey results were released made me scratch my head.

In December 2008, the rich and famous took center stage, not as heroes but as victims, as noted in this article titled "One Name Stands Alone in The Grand Scheme of It All."[2] Bernard Madoff, it reported, had allegedly bilked the likes of Steven Spielberg, real estate magnate Mort Zuckerman, a U.S. senator, and even some of Wall Street's elite fund managers out of $50 billion—billion with a B—in what was immediately labeled as a Ponzi scheme. But rather than recount the financial devastation of this news or discuss how Madoff had fooled so many smart, trusting people (as other media sources were doing), this article focused on the nature of the scheme and the iconic figure behind its name: Ponzi.

Born in Italy around the dawning of the 20th century and immigrating to the U.S. in 1903, Charles Ponzi gave his name to a form of fraud in which, as the *Post* article defined it, "belief in the success of a fictive enterprise is fostered by the payment of quick returns to first investors from money invested by others" who come into the scheme later on.[3]

A cascading list of characteristics describing Ponzi ranged from the admirable to the reprehensible: charismatic, charming, yearning for power, hungry for riches, self-deluding, and a screw-up. Smack dab in the middle of these, Ponzi was described as *entrepreneurial*.

Could this be the same kind of person that, a century later, citizens were looking toward to save their country? How, I wondered, could we keep such opposing images about one type of person in our heads at the same time seemingly unaware of the contradiction? It was as though the hero wearing a white hat quickly jumped into a phone booth to exchange it for a black one. These hero-villains seemed to amount to (as they say where I come from) all hat and no cattle.

## Contradictory Characteristics

But I knew better. When the Kauffman survey and the *Post* article evoked these images, I was already used to the contradictory characteristics tied to the term "entrepreneur." Moreover, I was already motivated by the choice I'd made four years earlier to correct misconceptions and put common impressions of entrepreneurs on the right track. In reality, I'd concluded I had "no choice" but to do so.

Let me explain.

For more than two decades, I have worked and lived in what I've come to call the entrepreneurial universe. I have been moving through this universe filling a variety of roles—advisor, investor, employee, founder, community leader—often, more than one at a time. I've served for-profit and nonprofit organizations, large and small, successful and less so.

During this time, I have come to know what many residing inside this universe—and countless others operating outside it—would acknowledge if they looked closely: At the starting line of all forward movement, at the nexus of change itself, at the wellspring of human progress, there are always entrepreneurs. The same ones may not be present at the end, but they're always there at the start.

I've come to know that the truest entrepreneurial minds are neither heroic nor demonic, wearing neither white nor black hats. They are, however, people who clearly and confidently believe in a better way to help humanity. They commit themselves fully to catalyzing the change they know must occur. They believe they have "no choice."

People who have this mindset are rare, but not because they possess an uncommon genetic attribute. It's because so few people are aware that an entrepreneurial mindset is available to *anyone*, and because precious few choose to practice it. It is in the process of thinking entrepreneurially that practitioners refine their ability to see *something more*, something better, for humankind.

## A Different Version of the Story: the Truth

Part of my choice to set straight the misconceptions about entrepreneurs was drawn from the knowledge that the best entrepreneurial minds take a form that's quite different than our stereotypes would lead us to believe.

Consider John Wood. John established Room to Read, a venture that seeks to improve literacy levels for 10 million people. (All those "people" happen to be kids, which makes his vision all the more impressive.) John holds up as hero and challenger Andrew Carnegie, the Scottish-born industrialist, businessman, and philanthropist who built what became U.S. Steel as well as financed 3,000 libraries that bear his name. John declares he wants to "out-Carnegie Carnegie," an audacious statement in its own right.

Audacious, that is, until you consider that in its first half dozen years of existence, John's Room to Read organization had a faster growth rate than Starbucks did within six years of going public—a comparison John readily shares with skeptics. His vision, his accomplishments, and his determination seem in keeping with our heroic impressions.

Yet, Room to Read is a nonprofit. True enough, in its first six years, it created incalculable value by establishing 3,300 libraries and 300 schools, and distributing more than two million books to children. And the organization continues to provide books, instruction, and scholarship to kids who previously lacked access to any vital tools of progress and survival. In addition to the immense value it delivers, Room to Read is a financially sound venture.

But if the dominant impression of an entrepreneur is one who is profit-driven and greedy, and John's primary goal isn't to make a profit, should he be excluded from the conversation about entrepreneurship?

How about Robin Chase, the woman who conceived and built Zipcar, a for-profit company that made real the unheard-of idea of renting cars by the *hour?*

Zipcar has caught on like wildfire in numerous American cities. Besides being a highly successful business, Zipcar is radically changing the landscape of public transportation in those cities. Yet after a few years, Robin turned control of her company over to others—first figuratively and then literally. She put its fate in the hands of the *customers* and took her cues for company direction from them while she was still in charge. Later, she voluntarily stepped out of the leader role, even though she was considered effective.

Where is the ego and desire for control we attribute to the entrepreneur?

In some ways, Dr. Muhammad Yunus has topped all others in defying the entrepreneur stereotypes. Here's a man whose organization broke all the rules of economics and logic, first by thinking his greatest market lay outside the world's leading economies and countries, and then by making his customers the poorest of the poor.

But Dr. Yunus didn't stop there. (In fact, he never seems to stop.) His model wasn't just to make customers out of the poorest of the poor; it was to lend them money, ultimately billions of dollars. Surely this describes a madman, not a greedy, profit-driven entrepreneur. No bank or economist would be this foolish, or so we might assume. But Dr. Yunus *is* a Ph.D. economist. And his core business, the Grameen Bank, *is* a for-profit bank. To carry his "fantasy" further, Dr. Yunus's return goal for this venture is to foster peace and opportunity, and encourage humane treatment of others.

Despite being the antithesis of commonly accepted impressions of entrepreneurship, Grameen Bank has had a 95 percent average payback rate on its loans for nearly three decades running—more than any other financial institution in the world can claim. And while Dr. Yunus would tell you his goal of peace is far from being fulfilled, in 2006, he was honored with the Nobel Peace Prize—a measure that indicates his venture produces value far beyond profit and higher than anyone ever expected.

## What's Going On Here?

These examples don't sound like the images of entrepreneurship we expect. So, are John, Robin, and Dr. Yunus entrepreneurs? Is an elementary school teacher in Los Angeles an entrepreneur? What about a lawyer? A photographer? A board game maker? An author? An investor who puts money in non-profits but doesn't expect monetary returns? Does it matter? It matters more than you might think and for reasons you might not expect. And the lessons within these and countless other stories—lessons that rarely make it into mainstream conversations—are where the true meaning of entrepreneurship lies. As you will see throughout this book, pausing to seek out this meaning and answering the question "why" matter most of all.

Because of the confusion around the terms "entrepreneur" and "entrepreneurship," because of the human progress people like John and Robin and Dr. Yunus catalyze, and because the world's challenges and opportunities will only increase, I felt an unavoidable need to take stock. I needed time to see the bigger picture differently than ever before—to study, analyze, and communicate about the true role of entrepreneurship in moving our world forward. *A Deliberate Pause: Entrepreneurship and its Moment in Human Progress* is the result. As you read it, I encourage you to stop and purposely take a fresh look at the world, too.

## Why This Book Had to Be Written

While strongly believing that common impressions of entrepreneurship were wrong, before this book I had only directed my efforts to change those impressions toward a limited audience—my clients, partners, and small localized groups of entrepreneurs. Then two dramatic shifts caused me to strike more boldly: the rise in use of the Internet and the accompanying surge of new start-up companies.

The good news brought about by these shifts was that, every day, more and more minds were being opened to a different way to operate in the new world heralded by the Internet. The bad news was that having an idea and then quitting one's job to start a new venture became synonymous with being an entrepreneur. People assumed that creativity and breaking with the old *by themselves* equaled entrepreneurship. They never stopped to understand what entrepreneurship was all about. Instead, many ran blindly forward to be part of this *new, new* way of doing things. Most failed. Still, doing other than acting lemming-like left many others feeling "on the outs" or even stupid. Confusion and complicity arrived. But like the members of the royal court and the townspeople in the fable *The Emperor's New Clothes*, no one wanted to admit *not* understanding this wave of the future called entrepreneurship—at least not openly.

During the years when the Internet bandwagon was picking up speed, I spoke to groups of hundreds of self-proclaimed entrepreneurs as well as those who wanted to make their own fortunes investing in them or advising them. Most assumed that being an entrepreneur was all about the money, both making it and attracting it to start a new venture.

As a result, I was often asked to speak *narrowly* about raising money for new ventures rather than *expansively* about the concept of entrepreneurship. I did the opposite. On such occasions, I spoke mostly about the dynamic of entrepreneurship—why having a new idea wasn't enough, what was needed to made ventures work, and why one individual wasn't sufficient for creating lasting success. I would typically spend 45 minutes of my scheduled hour talking about knowing yourself and your venture inside and out, and only 10 or 15 minutes talking about funding a venture.

After my talks, droves of "townspeople" pulled me aside to learn more about this "new set of clothes" called entrepreneurship—something they were already supposed to know. I couldn't ignore their demands to know more.

In hindsight, I see that this approach to helping others understand entrepreneurship—relying on my own expertise and reaching people in limited ways—was counter to entrepreneurship itself. What was needed was a step back from the status quo to see it anew, to look for new patterns and new possibilities. And if I were to help others understand the concept, I could no longer do it in onesie-twosie steps—client by client, talk by talk—and *hope* to change the way we collectively looked at entrepreneurship. That's what was needed and it required a seismic change that could only be achieved through a comprehensive, broad-reaching, and new approach.

In short, I needed to take an *entrepreneurial* look at entrepreneurship, one that did not cling to traditional ways of viewing it and therefore allowed all of us to see something more.

## Three Traditional Ways of Viewing Entrepreneurship

Three customary ways of viewing entrepreneurship have consistently plagued how people have formally regarded entrepreneurship. First, more often than not, **we seek the formulaic answer**. We live in a world that loves recipes and craves a Top 10 list. "Just tell us how to do it," seems to be the mantra.

It should be obvious why this approach doesn't work with entrepreneurship. If entrepreneurs are those who break new ground to catalyze change, then by its very nature, what they set out to do hasn't been done before. No preexisting formula exists if you want to create something new.

The second problem is concluding that, formula or not, **entrepreneurship takes a single form or falls within a single profile or story** like *Joe's Entrepreneurial Success*. Biographies like these and profiles of organizations can make fascinating reads and offer great insights, yet are too often interpreted as representative of what entrepreneurship is. But they *can't* be representative; every story is unique.

This dilemma becomes even more apparent when realizing that entrepreneurship as a mindset can be applied anywhere—in organizations from one to a thousand, in product or service formats, in nonprofit and for-profit structures, in any industry or topic area where making change for the better motivates people. Which leads to the third problem: **looking to only one source to understand what entrepreneurship really means, how success is defined, and what makes change last.** Concluding that entrepreneurial success hinges on one idea or the actions of a single person, for example, amplifies this error in thinking. Similarly, it's misleading to assume that value can take only one form, or that value and success can be fully measured at a single point in time.

## *An Entrepreneurial Look at Entrepreneurship*

Because logic dictates that gaining a fresh understanding of entrepreneurship requires breaking with customary approaches, *A Deliberate Pause* takes an entrepreneurial look at entrepreneurship. In doing so, it leads us to viewing the world differently.

Specifically, *A Deliberate Pause* doesn't promise formulas. Nor does it look to a single story or one organization, person, geography, role, or perspective to draw its lessons from. Rather, *A Deliberate Pause* reveals patterns across entrepreneurship in its various forms. These patterns explain a common framework that's present in all lasting entrepreneurial pursuits. And this framework embraces the whole entrepreneurial universe to yield a fresh perspective. Only with such an approach can we hope to reveal the true power of entrepreneurship and increase the frequency of its use and the odds of its success.

How was this accomplished? For *A Deliberate Pause,* I interviewed more than 200 individuals whose experiences encompass a full range of profiles and perspectives that make up the entrepreneurial universe. These interviewees are part of the conversation you have now joined by choosing to read this book. I call them contributors. They cross boundaries defined by industry, tax status, definition of value, geography, gender, and other limiting demographics. Many are, of course, entrepreneurs. Just as important, they are investors and donors, advisors and teachers of entrepreneurship, with several filling more than one of these roles. About half come from the nonprofit world; nearly one-quarter are female; roughly one-fifth are minorities or immigrants.

As you will see, these entrepreneurial contributors belie the stereotypes. They know what makes entrepreneurship work and they eagerly shared what they've seen and learned. When you meet them on these pages, you no doubt will recognize some names from news headlines and others associated with whatever slice of the world you inhabit. Many will be new to you. But regardless of role, background, notoriety, or geography, all of them feel deeply passionate about entrepreneurship. Individually and together, they have a great deal to teach from their own ventures, from advising others, and simply from inhabiting the entrepreneurial universe.

One thing is clear: What these exceptional, thoughtful individuals contribute about entrepreneurship isn't commonly taught in business schools or noted in trendy business books. This book relates what these veterans and advocates of the entrepreneurial universe believe should be known and talked about *but isn't*. Their stories allow you to understand *who* is behind the powerful force of entrepreneurship, *how* they go about doing their work, and *why* they do what they do despite the odds and setbacks.

What's in it for them? They want millions more people to understand entrepreneurship better because they know the benefits will accrue to humanity's progress. And they know it's time to put that understanding into action.

## A Framework to Follow

When you look at something in a different way, you can't help but learn and advance your thinking. Both are empowering. This book represents an entirely new view of entrepreneurship and a capacity to apply it anywhere in your world. The many lessons in this book are delivered within a framework of four parts.

Part I, ***Entrepreneur,*** offers a view of this contradictory character called an entrepreneur. It serves to unwind your preconceptions and give you a clear view of what an entrepreneur is, why the dominant myths about them are simply false, and where entrepreneurs fit into the more important dynamic of entrepreneur*ship*.

Part II, ***Entrepreneurship***, builds on your newfound sense of who entrepreneurs are, then reveals their relative importance to the larger ecosystem that makes entrepreneurship work. You will learn that creating community is a powerful, necessary force in entrepreneurship that brings forth lasting change.

Having a clear sense of *who* is behind entrepreneurship begs the question of *how* entrepreneurs do what they do. Part III, ***Perspective and Discipline***, takes you there. You'll see that the tales about entrepreneurs focus on the beginning and the end of their stories, but in reality, it's the middle part that makes all the difference. Part III explores the fundamentals—for both the individual entrepreneur and the ecosystems they spawn. It also explores oft-overlooked distinctions between evolution and growth, and rights the assumed roles of failure and sacrifice in successful entrepreneurship.

*Why* entrepreneurs (and those they attract and inspire) do what they do follows from the lessons of *who* they are and *how* they operate. This becomes the focus of Part IV, ***Reward and Reason***. By the time you reach it, you won't be surprised to learn that value and success in entrepreneurship differ vastly from common assumptions—at least for those ventures that make real the changes they seek and have lasting impact. You'll also discover there's *something more* to the who, how, and why of this powerful force called entrepreneurship. And you'll see why the importance of *always asking why* never fades.

After each part, you'll find a literary version of a deliberate pause in the form of a familiar parable that expresses lessons in a story-like way. Each of these parables invites you to directly reflect on what you have just learned. Be sure to take a deep breath and read them from a fresh perspective.

As you read, you'll learn about the people who generously contributed to *A Deliberate Pause*. You may want to look back on these contributors and their stories after reading the whole book. To facilitate that, at the beginning of each chapter I have provided a brief overview of relevant credentials for those quoted or referenced in that particular chapter. Then at the end of the book, you'll find a complete list of contributors and a more expansive breakdown of who they are and what they do. (For readers who are sticklers for details, I have not included every act, role, or recognition associated with each contributor; that simply would be impossible. The notations about each were accurate at the time of my interview, but as entrepreneurially minded people tend to do, many have added to their impressive records since.) Please know that *every* interviewee contributed to *every* chapter, for *A Deliberate Pause* presents a view of the patterns that lie *across* these contributors—indeed, across all entrepreneurship.

At the end of each chapter, you'll also find a list of Recommended Resources that have influenced my thinking over time. I've summarized the importance of these resources to my own thinking and briefly explained why, if you seek them out, you too may gain a deeper insight into the concepts presented in the chapter itself.

## The Absolutely Right Title

What does the title *A Deliberate Pause* represent? To me personally, it symbolizes the most valuable lesson I've learned—that a deliberate pause *is* entrepreneurship. It's taking a break to consider new possibilities; it's a way of slowing down in order to move forward.

Yes, a deliberate pause refers to a *moment*—an increment in time—but this kind of moment for pausing and reflecting connotes so much more. It encapsulates both how entrepreneurship works and what it can bring about in the world. It's about identifying momentous changes that will ultimately benefit humankind. It's no coincidence that *moment* also means *importance*.

In effect, you're taking a deliberate pause by reading this book and contemplating its concepts. That's how a deliberate pause operates; it draws you in to think about issues of consequence to you. You might even find yourself shifting from being an outside observer to a catalyst for meaningful change.

Let me share how this phrase evolved as absolutely the right title for me.

In researching *A Deliberate Pause*, one of the people I came to know and respect was Danny Warshay. Danny is co-founder of Clearview Software and Health Business Partners, along with numerous other ventures. (He constantly sees new possibilities that must be realized.)

Beyond the companies he has founded, Danny has played a critical role in establishing the entrepreneurship program at Brown University, plus he sits on numerous boards and operates the investment group he founded called DEW Ventures.

As we talked about this book, Danny freely shared about his many activities. Periodically, he would say ". . . and then I took a break for a bit." These references to his breaks sounded almost reverent, their tone one of respectful reminiscence. When I asked him to elaborate, he said, "Things happen naturally if you give them space to develop. Things are there to be seen if you give yourself a chance to see them. I believe in deliberate pauses to clear your head, reflect on the past, and reflect on the future."

As my interviews progressed, I heard other successful entrepreneurs saying similar things. For Brad Barnhorn (CEO of Global NutriFoods and founder and former CEO of Fantasia Fresh Juice Company), his backpacking sabbaticals function as a deliberate pause. That's when he hones and rejuvenates his comfort with "the unknown, uncertainty, and the ability to make quick assessments." What he brings back helps him navigate the entrepreneurial landscapes he repeatedly returns to.

Carter Cast (co-founder and president of walmart.com and Blue Nile) periodically allows himself time for deep personal reflection. He sorts out where he's been, where he stands, and where he should be headed. It's his way of fine-tuning his filter for the next challenge.

Richard Tait (grand poo-bah—yes, his real title—of Cranium) makes "pauses" part of his daily routine. He walks where he has to go, and uses the time to give himself perspective and distance from the world he inhabits each day. "I don't look for answers during this time," he explained, "but it helps me regain my passion, and the belief that I am making a difference. That time propels me forward and builds my desire to engage."

The reality, according to Edie Fraser (founder of Business Women's

Network and co-author of *Do Your Giving While You Are Living*), is this: "We are not taught the value of stopping and evaluating where we are. We need to be willing to pause, reflect, and shift course continually. Like any other skill, the more you practice, the better you become." Yet too few people practice this skill of pausing. For those who do, it is a distinguishing point—something that moves them from being part of the pack to forming and leading a new one.

After hearing similar sentiments from the interviewees, it dawned on me what was happening. Admittedly, when I began this whole process, I was pleasantly surprised to find so many talented, respected, and busy people willing to share their time and wisdom with me. But with each subsequent interview, it became clear: Of course they were taking time to share! Of course, *they* were learning too! Their time with me was a calculated gamble in the familiar process of exchange and reflection. And by our exploring this topic, they were engaging in the very process that had allowed them to get to where they were. As Edie might put it, they were slowing, evaluating, and staying open to the idea of shifting their thinking. Each time they did this, they were also training themselves, refining their patterns, and making this process a next step in their entrepreneurial evolution.

And it occurred to me that, in taking the time away from my own thriving business and other life commitments to research and write this book, *I* was taking a deliberate pause. My learning and training and refining would also evolve in the process. Suddenly, the pattern clearly formed in my mind. Entrepreneurship itself is an act of a deliberate pause. It's a time to look at what *is* in an effort to see *what could be*.

Within entrepreneurship, the pause constantly repeats in endless forms. It's a central theme that consciously and subconsciously returns to create the most successful entrepreneurial efforts. It's a new beginning—at the start of a venture, the dawning of a new day, or smack dab in the middle of either. "Every new beginning starts from another beginning's end," as first-century philosopher Seneca once said, "On and on it progresses, and as it does, so do we."

Specifically, taking a deliberate pause allows you to pull back from what you *do* and even what you *think* to see what's important in the larger sense. It's an act of refinement and focus, a time to rebalance perspective with discipline. Far from slowing you down, over the long haul, a deliberate pause enables you to travel more proficiently along the entrepreneurial path.

## Human Change and Forward Progress

Sometimes it takes a pause to even recognize what's going on. Other times it's all too obvious. In the second decade of the 21st century, our social structures and ways of living are coming under increasing risk of breaking down completely. Our economic engines are showing signs of faltering. Our natural environment warns us of a need for diligence. Simply put, in combination, the impact of our crumbling social, economic, and environmental systems presents a threat to everything that allows us to be human in the first place.

Thankfully, our species doesn't give up easily. A stubborn lot, we humans have the unique ability to listen to doomsday bells and hear a harbinger of opportunity. It's both a calling and a warning. Before long, one of us always steps forward to lead others in making profound changes.

Now is that time. But relying on a select few to lead is no longer enough. The fundamental message of this book is clear: We must not only change the way we do things; we must learn *how* to change in better ways—to think as changemakers do, entrepreneurially, even if we let others lead. Catalyzing change, after all, is what makes us most human in the first place. It is what distinguishes us from other animals. As Dr. Yunus told me, "What distinguishes humans from other life forms, one thing at least, is entrepreneurship. Entrepreneurs are always striving for better and always adjusting themselves. It is in every human being and everything human." That's why we need entrepreneurship as never before.

Entrepreneurship taps into the *possible* as it helps manage the *unwanted*, the *improbable*, and the *difficult*. Yes, it will take all that entrepreneurship has to offer to address the challenges facing the world today. Yet it is the fountainhead of the solutions we must create.

As participants in this conversation, as members of the human race, let's take a pause—right now and often—to integrate our patterns and thinking. When we do, entrepreneurship will more easily and naturally assume its rightful place in our advancement as people.

## An Invitation to You

You have an important choice to make about pausing to read this book in a deliberate way. Genuinely doing so can help you advance from where you are in your understanding of entrepreneurship to achieving *something more*.

Composer Igor Stravinsky once said that people often fail to listen with effort; they may hear what is said, but a duck hears, too. Stravinsky always sought advancements. He wanted his music to forever be relevant, to constantly call into question everything he had done before. As remarkable as many of his works were, he had the habit of openly, often publicly, throwing past achievements out into the bright sunlight and asking *why*—why is what exists today (even what feels good, valuable, and right) the best we can do? To Stravinsky, the process of doing this presented an opportunity to be seized.

*A Deliberate Pause* represents an opportunity to be seized—and an opportunity to think.

It isn't fashioned to give you answers. It doesn't concoct a formula for successful entrepreneurship to be blindly followed. (Run from any book or conversation promising such magic bullets.) Instead, *A Deliberate Pause* offers you a framework for renewing your own thinking. It imparts battle-tested lessons gleaned from those whose thoughts and actions have shaped our world. It gives you a window through which you can see what's possible. And then it invites you to look for yourself—deliberately.

"We are in a really unique time for opportunity," said Spencer Beebe, co-founder of Conservation International and founder of Ecotrust. "But it is a time in which we are witnessing system failure on many levels. So much of what we hold so important is threatened right now, and our institutions are not equipped to meet such challenges." Still, his view is not dark. "The one resource we have not yet made good use of is the pure resourcefulness and creativity of the human mind," he said.

You've come this far. Right now, you stand at a window that's wide open, shutters flung back. Have a look—a deep, long look at entrepreneurship through the eyes of *A Deliberate Pause*. Whether you agree with me or not, I feel confident you will be better off because you've consciously examined this view of entrepreneurship and contemplated its moment in human progress.

## Recommended Resources

### *The Tipping Point* – Malcolm Gladwell

You've heard of this book no doubt, but have you read it? If not, do so. This book breaks down the human factors that cause an idea to go from just an idea to a takeover wave. Gladwell masterfully weaves together the seemingly unrelated that, when considered together, reveal what should have been an obvious pattern. He causes us to stop, look at things differently, and think.

### *The Five Temptations of a CEO* – Patrick Lencioni

Patrick Lencioni takes us out of our routine view of the world by placing us, well, right smack dab in our daily routines but while walking in someone else's shoes. In this modern-day parable, a CEO riding the train home one night sees why he is failing to evolve. Lencioni gives us a new window for us to look—if not leap—through.

### *Ishmael* – Daniel Quinn

"Teacher seeks pupil. Must have an earnest desire to save the world. Apply in person." To sign up to become the student offers a unique concept. To take this enlightened, challenging, hard look at ourselves is even more amazing—and rare. As one reviewer put it, "From now on, I will divide the books I have read into two categories: the ones I read *before* Ishmael and those I read *after*."

### *1491* – Charles Mann

While the book *Ishmael* puts weight on looking *forward*, this book *1491* reminds us to look *back* with an equally open and questioning mind. A quick view in the rearview mirror doesn't always reflect what was. Mann shows us that our storied view of the world before our time has little correlation to reality. (The year 1491, the year before Columbus set foot in North America, defines the point from which we often mark the history of the Americas, assuming nothing major occurred prior to 1491.) In fact, he proves that if we fail to learn from history, we are doomed to repeat it. And we may already be doing just that.

***The World is Flat*** – Thomas Friedman

Gladwell may have chosen a softer topic and approach than Friedman, but they share the ability to take what the rest of us view as disparate and seemingly unrelated pieces of information, and show us patterns that we conclude should have been obvious. His lessons underscore the constancy of change.

# Part I:
## *Entrepreneur*

# Contributors to Introduction and Chapter 1

**Jeffrey Hollender**
> Founder, President, Chief Inspired Protagonist, Seventh Generation
> Co-author, *Naturally Clean* and *What Matters Most*
> Founder, Network for Learning

**John Wood**
> Co-founder, CEO, Room to Read
> Author, *Leaving Microsoft to Change the World*
> Former senior executive, Microsoft

**Robin Chase**
> Co-founder, Zipcar
> Named to *Time* magazine's *100 World's Most Influential People*, 2009
> Founder, CEO, GoLoco and Meadow Networks

**Muhammad Yunus**
> Founder, Grameen Bank and Grameen Companies
> Author, *Banker to the Poor* and *Creating a World Without Poverty*
> Winner, Nobel Prize for Peace 2006

**Danny Warshay**
> Co-founder, Clearview Software and Health Business Partners
> Founder, Managing Director, DEW Ventures
> Adjunct Professor, Co-founder Entrepreneurship Program, Brown University

**Brad Barnhorn**
> CEO, Global NutriFoods
> Board Member, Happy Planet and Harvest & Rowe Restaurants

**Carter Cast**
> Co-founder, President, CEO, walmart.com
> Co-founder, Blue Nile

**Richard Tait**
> Co-founder, Grand Poo-Bah, Cranium
> Co-founder, 13 Microsoft businesses including Sidewalk, Carpoint, Expedia

**Edie Fraser**
> Founder, Business Women's Network and Diversity Best Practices
> Co-author, *Do Your Giving While You Are Living*
> Author, *Risk to Riches: Women's Entrepreneurship in America*

**Spencer Beebe**
> Founder, Ecotrust
> Co-founder, Conservation International

**Roger Sant**

Co-founder, Alternative Energy Source (AES)

Book about Roger: *Power to People: The Inside Story of AES and Globalization of Electricity*

Chair, Board of Regents, Smithsonian Institution

**Mark Frantz**

General Partner, RedShift Ventures

Former technology advisor to Pennsylvania Governor Tom Ridge

**Ben Elowitz**

CEO, WetPaint

Former roles with eHarmony, Precor, and Bain & Company

**Allen Grossman**

Professor of Management Practice, Harvard Business School

Author, *High Performance Nonprofit Organizations*

Former President, CEO, Outward Bound

**Dan Pink**

Author, *Free Agent Nation*, *A Whole New Mind* and *The Adventures of Johnny Bunko*

Contributor to *The New York Times, Harvard Business Review,* and *Fast Company*

Former chief speechwriter to former Vice President Al Gore

# Chapter 1: An Entrepreneur Defined

*"Like navigation in unknown waters, definitions need to be distinct and unambiguous. A definition that is not precise is as bad as no definition at all."*[4]

- Muhammad Yunus
Founder, CEO, Grameen Bank
Winner, Nobel Peace Prize, 2006

As I walked to my car after meeting with a group of entrepreneurs one evening, I passed two women engaged in conversation. One woman was trying to describe someone to her friend, clearly searching for the right image to convey. Finally, she concluded, "He's a real wheeler-dealer, *entrepreneur*, on-to-the-next-thing kind of guy, you know what I mean?" This is *not* how I would have described any of the people I had just left—or for that matter any successful entrepreneur I've ever known. But her friend nodded as if the image made perfect sense. She even added, "Married to his money and his mirror too, I bet." With chagrin, I realized their words summed up the commonly accepted view of entrepreneurs many hold in their heads and use to define them.

For the most part, this conception of entrepreneurs is a vastly oversimplified stereotype. The truth is, because most entrepreneurs fly below the radar, few people ever get a good read on them. What they do falls outside the mainstream, which means they rarely get noticed and are often outright ignored, dismissed, or silenced by the majority of people. Clearly, some entrepreneurs rise above anonymity and even succeed in changing the established order, but rarely in publicly known ways. Although they may be well-known in their own worlds, the accomplishments of most entrepreneurs rarely make headline news.

When entrepreneurs do get noticed, they tend to receive more attention for their personalities or temporal accomplishments than for their entrepreneurial skills and insights. As an example, I recently came across an online forum touting itself as geared for entrepreneurs. In descriptions ironically meant as compliments, it defined them as "baby boomers who want something for nothing, spinmasters, graduates of PT Barnum's Boss School, con-men." Another popular definition goes something like this: a risk-taking maverick, brash if not arrogant, self-focused, eccentric, greedy.

Such beliefs about entrepreneurs aren't only muddled, they're flat-out wrong—and even detrimental. They mislead us to believe that the path for entrepreneurs is only available to certain personalities or motivations. We might dismiss these popular views as impressions more than official definitions but, as we will see, official definitions are no more accurate or helpful.

In both accurate and conflicting ways, most definitions of "entrepreneur" mute the value of the word. One strong sign of this is the limited value the term has to those who actually live in the very world we are trying to understand. Robin Chase, whose company Zipcar is revolutionizing transportation, called the term "entrepreneur" *uninteresting*. "But the word entrepreneur*ial*? Now *that's* interesting. It says, 'I'm going to make something happen any which way I can.' *That* word can be applied to any number of things." Robin's comments point out the ambiguity, confusion, and even negativity clinging to the term as she added, "The word entrepreneur isn't one that I enjoy being ascribed to me." Many engaged in entrepreneurship agree with her. One is Roger Sant, whose alternative energy company, AES, became better known for its inclusive culture that expected everyone to contribute to the company's value than for the man who made it happen. About the term entrepreneur, Roger stated, "I'm not sure I use it enough to define it well. I don't use it because its meaning is so unclear."

While its meaning may matter little to entrepreneurs themselves—they're mostly too busy to preoccupy themselves with definitions—it should matter a great deal to the rest of us. Why? It's important for *understanding* the entrepreneur's role in the larger context of entrepreneurship. More than that, it's important for *seeing* how the entrepreneurial mindset can advance humanity itself.

## Hard Lessons in the True Meaning of the Term "Entrepreneur"

Richard Tait has an incredibly infectious passion for entrepreneurship. He also offers some of the most important and hard-won insights about what it means to be an entrepreneur in the first place.

Richard leads the entertainment and game company Cranium, which he co-founded with partner Whit Alexander. If you've walked into a Starbucks in the last decade, you've probably seen Cranium's board games. From a baseline of zero, Cranium entered into the then sleepy board game market, rapidly ascended to the top, and revived and redefined the market in the process.

Taking a high-vantage tour of Richard's life, you might conclude that the success he and Whit experienced with Cranium would be a foregone conclusion. After all, before Cranium, Richard was part of the storied Microsoft team. In his time at Microsoft, he started and built 13 businesses, including the well-known travel site Expedia. Over and over again, Richard demonstrated his "antenna" (as he called it) for sensing opportunity and capitalizing on it. This gifted and proven venture builder could not fail. To himself and many others, Richard was the consummate entrepreneur.

But there was a catch to his apparent entrepreneurial success, one even Richard wasn't aware of. Richard had launched these 13 ventures *within* the loving arms of mother Microsoft. After leaving those arms to form Cranium, he soon realized he had little idea what it truly meant to be an entrepreneur. He had never before been out there standing on his own, with a new idea, in a hostile environment, and with only good sense and faith to carry him forward. Previously, when he'd introduced himself as "Richard Tait from Microsoft," people selectively heard the last two words of that statement—"from Microsoft." When he'd put his ideas on the table, others heard them through the filter of Microsoft's backing. They regarded Richard as envoy more than innovator. That extended to assessing risk; their confidence, maybe even some of Richard's, came from the deep pockets and security of Microsoft. For all of his background and natural inclinations, for all his great ideas and hard work, he was still an extension of a solid, safe base built on someone else's dream.

Although his idea of creating a better board game to help bring families together was bold, his leap to pursue it proved to be lonely, personally humbling, and even gloomy. Microsoft had been Richard's family, his life, and his safety net for years—far more than he'd allowed himself to realize. He'd left its safe fold feeling well versed in entrepreneurship and believing what he'd experienced was completely transferable. A crisis in confidence clouded his once-reliable antenna. "That's when I gained respect and understanding for what it meant to be a true entrepreneur."

Many, many people think of themselves, call themselves, or aspire to be entrepreneurs. Yet few are true entrepreneurs. They may exhibit characteristics of confidence, creativity, innovation, or boldness. But while often sharing similar traits, these people aren't entrepreneurs simply because of those traits. The longer those who aren't the real deal continue to think of themselves that way, the greater the potential to waste energy, lose focus, and encounter frustration—and the harder it is to actually succeed in an entrepreneurial pursuit.

Many people marching down the entrepreneurial path think, "How hard can this be?" Yet as Richard Tait's Cranium story humbly tells us, all his years of Microsoft experience didn't prepare him for what he encountered when he stepped onto the entrepreneurial path alone for the first time. If *he* had something to learn about what makes entrepreneurs distinctive, the rest of us could benefit from deeper exploration.

"There is a difference between entrepreneurs and people with entrepreneurial characteristics," said venture capital investor Mark Frantz. "That difference is critical in identifying entrepreneurs and predicting their success." Indeed, the odds of being successful in any role in the entrepreneurial universe are directly tied to knowing accurately what it means to be an entrepreneur.

## *The Power of Distinct Definitions*

At the beginning of this chapter, Dr. Muhammad Yunus's quotation pointed out the importance of clarity in definitions. This lesson is particularly important in seeking to understand the entrepreneurial universe. But to date, appreciation for this vital wisdom has been at best mixed. English speakers, at least in the United States, seem more fascinated by the ease with which words take on *similarities* to other words—to the point of being interchangeable.

But not everyone sees value in this kind of linguistic laziness. My wife, Kai, reminds me of this fact from time to time. For her, each word is important for its distinct meaning, not its overlap with the meaning of other words.

Because Kai's mother grew up in Germany, when my wife was a child, she was spoken to in both English and German. Kai can't recall which language she learned first. Yet precision in word choice is something she is fully conscious of; she is keenly aware, too, of its power in conveying precise meaning. People like Kai commonly search across languages for the best word that offers the most precise meaning. When a word's meaning is distinct and unambiguous, it becomes a powerful tool for *understanding* and *action*.

Some cultures take the importance of word choice a long way, proving the power of a word comes from its unique, precise meaning. The Inuit, for example, have several dozen distinct words for "snow," none of which means the same thing. For them, using the right word to describe a particular kind of snow conveys a full breadth of information to those who appreciate its subtle, even life-preserving nuances. One version of "snow" may require specific actions for survival; another may present a distinct set of opportunities for finding food and shelter. Each word speaks volumes about its purpose.

The term "entrepreneur" deserves its own distinction, for its potential is far too great to equate with other terms. Yet we use it liberally, even carelessly, to the point of diffusion. When we equate entrepreneurs with small business owners, for example, or use the term only to describe one who takes risk or is eccentric, we lose its crisp and critical distinction. More than that, we fail to understand how the entrepreneurship they pursue impacts us all.

## The Origin of the Term "Entrepreneur"

When seeking a word's meaning, it helps to return to its origin. The term "entrepreneur" emerged during the 18th century, a highly turbulent period of transition in the Western world. The Industrial Revolution, which began in the mid-1700s, changed the products we used, the way we created them, and where and how people worked. The American (1775-1783) and French (1789-1799) Revolutions ushered in new individual freedoms, including the opportunity to pursue ideas that could make the world better. In the short span of 100 years, cultures, social structures, and methods of governing were dramatically turned on their heads.

During this time of far-reaching shifts, some forward thinkers searched for ways to describe the people and processes they were witnessing. A logical word base to explain their efforts was provided by "entreprende," the French word meaning "to undertake, to put oneself under obligation to perform." In that era, people weren't *forced* to see the world differently; they *chose* to see it that way. And they chose to pursue their ideas and make them real. Rather than depending on someone else to make their ideas come to fruition, they relied on themselves. And their visions and impact were often world changing.

"To undertake" also means to give surety or assume responsibility. In the past, a "surety" was a personal pledge, a guarantee. Those giving it were so invested in what they promised that their word was enough for others to believe it would happen. This absolute choice and commitment has proven to be central to the true distinction of entrepreneurs who, as Roger Sant deftly described them, "won't give up until they find a way to achieve what they seek."

You may notice that the origin of the term "entrepreneur" says nothing about the form of the action or the nature of the reward that might come from an entrepreneurial commitment. Nor does it refer to the personality or type of individual who might make such a commitment. Instead, "entreprende" references the *spirit* of the undertaking. Yet in many ways, it provides a literal basis for this distinct meaning:

> to commit to *catalyzing* significant *change* in the way people think and act in order to bring *something more* to humanity, no matter what it takes. The actions that follow such a commitment are fueled by the belief that the world *needs* that change to progress, and *they (the entrepreneurs)* must make it happen.

## Commonly Accepted Definitions Fall Short

Most standard dictionaries don't offer definitions with this kind of distinction, accuracy, or applicability. Rather, they define an entrepreneur as "one who organizes, manages, and assumes the risk of starting a new business." Like those definitions derived from our impressions of entrepreneurs, this official definition is a narrow, indistinct view of what it means to be an entrepreneur.

Defining an entrepreneur as "one who organizes, manages, and assumes the risk" fails to be distinct for several reasons. In most successful ventures, entrepreneurs may take the first leap, but few are equipped to do everything required to get established on their own. The wise realize the need to spread around the responsibilities of organizing and managing to capture a full range of skill sets. More than that, the most successful entrepreneurs constantly look to minimize and spread risk right from the start. In fact, none of the experts interviewed for this book considered what they did to be characterized by unusual risk, let alone a solo act. (See Chapter 2, which discusses risk taking and acting alone.)

Common dictionary definitions also imply that entrepreneurship as they define it—the need to organize, manage, and assume risk—takes place only in the realm of business and organizations. But every type of organization, even every personal journey, encounters such demands. More, not all entrepreneurs are engaged in business or driven by profit, something the business emphasis implies.

Clearly, when we adopt commonly accepted terms and fail to

compare them to the real entrepreneurship that takes place around us, the full power of this extremely important word gets lost.

## Failing to "Listen With Effort"

If entrepreneurship is so much broader in its occurrence and relevance, why are these common definitions so business-focused and narrow? One reason is that, over time, the term "entrepreneur" has become strongly associated with economics. In a way, it seemed fated. Many changes occurring around the time the term was coined happened in the economic domain. In addition, economists have done the vast majority of writing about entrepreneurs over the past two centuries, thereby influencing its understanding from their viewpoint. But even among those who inadvertently helped skew the term's meaning, there were two important exceptions—two people who, like Igor Stravinsky, advise us to "listen with effort," not just hear what we want to hear.

Economist Joseph Schumpeter (1883-1950) was one. He placed particular emphasis on *innovation* as being the distinguishing point of entrepreneurs. But because his writings ultimately dealt with the economic impact of certain profit-minded entrepreneurs and their enterprises, his initial definition and good insights have been largely lost—a critical oversight.

While other economists focused on risk taking, profit making, organizations, and products, Schumpeter probed deeper. He spoke of the will to conquer, the impulse to fight for what the entrepreneur believed in, and the creation of major structural changes in society (not just in firms or economies) brought on not only by individual entrepreneurs but also by entrepreneurship. He even addressed the joy they experienced in the act of creation.

To him, true entrepreneurs engaged in change at a quantum level, not simply at the level of one person, one firm, one market, or even one lifetime. Schumpeter felt so strongly about the entrepreneurial spirit and its importance that he even coined his own term in his native German to express it more precisely: "unternehmergeist," meaning entrepreneur-*spirit* or *fiery soul*. Clearly, Schumpeter's observations relate more to the core of the entrepreneur as *a driven catalyst who desires to change human progress* than someone who limits activities to business or profit-making.[5]

Like Schumpeter, management guru Peter Drucker (1909-2005) has been given credit for an expanded understanding of entrepreneurs. Yet also like Schumpeter, many of Drucker's most important insights have been passed over, buried, or forgotten in favor of what he said about entrepreneurship's application to business.

Ironically, Drucker began by emphasizing areas other than profit and business. He talked about the commitment to create something new, the willingness to act, and the catalyst nature of the entrepreneur— aspects that stood out for Drucker. Entrepreneurship, he stated, was *not* a personality trait. Instead, it addressed *how* entrepreneurs took action, no matter where they took that action or how they measured its value.[6]

The degree to which entrepreneurs embrace the need for changing the human experience is central to Drucker's view of entrepreneurs. Moreover, the kind of change they bring to human progress is so vital that Drucker dispelled the myth of entrepreneurs being risk takers. In his thinking, an entrepreneur's willingness to undertake seismic change proves less risky than trying to advance by doing the same thing over and over.

Unfortunately, on-the-street uses of the term "entrepreneur" stray from these key insights. We tend to go quickly—it seems too quickly— to discuss the *ways* (risk taking and self-reward) entrepreneurs apply their mindset, the *places* (business) where they do so, and *momentary measures* (profit) of the *items* they produce. We stick mostly with the familiar or what we want to see. When we do this, we lose appreciation for the essential role entrepreneurs play as catalysts of widespread change.

### Confusing "Entrepreneur" With Other Words

It isn't only official definitions of entrepreneurs that inhibit our ability to tap into the power of the entrepreneurial mindset. Our understanding suffers from other forms of confusion. For example, although many entrepreneurs own and operate their ventures as small businesses, being an entrepreneur isn't the same as being a small business owner. And while entrepreneurs often invent, produce, and distribute new products and services as part of what they do, this doesn't mean that the term "entrepreneur" is identical with the term "inventor" or "business person." Many synonymously ascribe characteristics such as risk taking or creativity to the term "entrepreneur." Others narrowly equate it with specific business pursuits, such as being a franchisee or venturing into in a high-growth sector like technology. But used these ways, the term "entrepreneur" again takes us away from its rightful meaning as being committed to catalyze significant change.

## Proliferation of Sublabels

One prominent sign of the term's confusion has been the proliferation of sublabels such as social entrepreneur, lifestyle entrepreneur, intrapreneur (meant to distinguish one who works as an entrepreneur inside an existing company), and even co-preneur (a term that describes a couple running a business). With good intent, these adaptations are meant to identify entrepreneurship with particular applications. Yet in actuality, each sublabel *grows out of* and *adds to* our misunderstanding of the meaning of the term trying to be leveraged: entrepreneur.

The sublabel social entrepreneur, for example, was coined to differentiate ventures whose value is expressed in nonfinancial terms, something that appears to violate the profit-driven emphasis of standard dictionary definitions. Good intentions aside, this is a case of one error following another. In the process, it misses the point: if the correct core definition of entrepreneur were commonly embraced, then this one term would accurately describe *all* entrepreneurs.

This practice of sublabeling is a double-edged sword: while it allows those who use sublabels to distance themselves from the stereotypes, it also creates separation from the true meaning of "entrepreneur." The former is understandable, but the latter adds confusion and fails to embrace the critical mindset that all entrepreneurs share. Indeed, the arguments are greater for abandoning sublabeling than they are for maintaining its use. We have far more to gain from honoring what entrepreneurs have in common than diluting their value with added terminology.

## Used as a Catchall Term

Understanding suffers, too, because "entrepreneur" has become a catchall term. It is, in fact, a loan word taken from one language and moved into another with little specific translation. Not only has "entrepreneur" been "loaned" from French, it's also been "loaned" from settings in which the term is used (economics, for example) and has picked up baggage along the way. Because of this, its meaning has drifted from the *spirit* with which entrepreneurs undertake making their dreams real.

Whatever the reasons, clarity of the term "entrepreneur" has been elusive. As Ben Elowitz, CEO of WetPaint, said, "Four years ago, if you were someone who fell off a horse four times and got back on, you were just a bad horse rider. Now you're an entrepreneur."

### Last Man Standing

It is the first day of a Harvard MBA class. The subject is entrepreneurship; the audience is made up of those ready to start their own businesses and strike it rich. Eager students are sitting in the lecture hall awaiting their professor. Having made it to Harvard, these students exude an air of cockiness, a sense that their future success is inevitable. They're ready to take on the world; this class is but a stepping-stone, even an inconvenient prerequisite to their manifest destiny.

The professor enters the room and walks to the lectern. He immediately asks, "How many of you want to make a million dollars?" Every hand in the room shoots up. Unfazed he continues, "Okay. How many consider yourselves to be entrepreneurs who are capable of creating a business that can generate that million?" Nearly everyone keeps a hand up. Still, a few hands waver between up and down as they ponder the question. He proceeds, "How many have a specific idea about how you will create that business and garner your fortune?" A number of hands go down. After all, they think, isn't that why we're sitting in this class in the first place?

The professor lets the silence hang for a moment. To some, it feels like an eternity before he picks up the pace and asks, "And how many are willing to invest a million of your own money to make your million?" A wave of surprised expressions crosses the room, causing at least half of the remaining hands to go down.

He presses on, "Who is prepared to be ridiculed, humiliated, and rejected, perhaps on a daily basis—be an outcast, even among your closest friends and family members—for the nature of your idea and your stubbornness in sticking with it? Will you feel the same when you are the featured subject in the *Boston Globe* business section highlighting business failures and ideas gone wrong?" Many with their hands still up shrug off these questions with a "how bad could it really be" state of mind.

But the professor isn't finished. He adds context, uncertainties of time, probabilities, and ego to his questions.

"How many of you are prepared to spend the next eight years on your business before you even turn a profit?"

"Who is prepared to give up control of fifty to seventy-five percent of your business to a partner or investors along the way?"

"How many of you are willing to arrive at a point eight years from now and realize that your idea isn't working and you have to begin again to realize your entrepreneurial dream? Oh, and by the way, during those long years, how many of you are comfortable watching your classmates—the ones who have lowered their hands—rise through the corporate ranks to become both millionaires and CEOs in the traditional way while you still pursue your entrepreneurial dream?"

By the time the professor finishes—a mere 60 seconds after those hundred hands first eagerly shot up—only a couple of hands remain raised. Even one of the two students who still have their hands up looks unsure. Is it confidence or defiance that caused her to outlast her classmates?

What if all those who called themselves entrepreneurs heard the Last Man Standing tale *before* they chose to walk the entrepreneurial path? And what if everyone, regardless of his or her chosen path, had greater clarity about what it means to be an entrepreneur? For one thing, a lot of hands would go down. And just realizing the difficulty of walking the entrepreneurial path alone would greatly increase the odds of their success.

## Like Elvis But Without the Tassels

The "Last Man Standing" is an urban myth I was reminded of when interviewing Harvard Business School professor Allen Grossman. Yet while this story may be a myth, he, I, and others have seen many true versions of it happen in the real world. In fact, the experience is so commonplace that after a while, it plays in our heads like a medley of rock songs. Dire Straits would call it our desire to get our "money for nothin'," like the students in the class. The professorial Rolling Stones would warn that "you can't always get what you want," at least not easily. In the end, Nickelback would put this desire to grasp something great but without effort this way: "We all want to be great like Elvis, but without the tassels."

Yes, it takes a lot to acquire rewards from pursuing entrepreneurial ventures. Most people never do. Ironically, the ones who most often achieve them aren't even after the material rewards (the equivalent of sequined suits, pink Cadillacs, and even glittery tassels) most assume they are. Still, regardless of form, the rewards of an entrepreneurial undertaking can be enormous, even world changing. As *A Whole New Mind* author, Dan Pink, put it, "The very best entrepreneurs are trying to put a dent in the *universe*. They aren't tweaking; they're smashing." That possibility alone is worth getting beyond common definitions and blowing away the fog of our impressions and myths to see what truly distinguishes entrepreneurs as unique thinkers.

However, because we don't have a clear understanding of what it takes to be an entrepreneur, we tend to treat entrepreneurs in the extremes, either as a homogenous group (all are risk takers) or in the narrowest manifestations (for-profit only). This leads to sweeping generalizations and misconceptions about both entrepreneurs and entrepreneurship, none of which apply to all of them, most of which apply to none, and the vast majority of which are baseless. As a consequence, too many hands go up. Too many ventures go wrong. And too much potential is squandered.

## Guiding Question: What Makes Them Unique?

Perhaps it isn't a question of *adding* to the definition but *stripping away* from what we think we understand. Could it be that our initial definition drawn from "entreprende" is accurate all by itself? Maybe saying the act of being committed to undertaking the enormous task of pursuing a dream and seeing it through is definition enough. Maybe it isn't a precise answer or fixed definition we need but a question that guides us to better understand true entrepreneurs and the unique role they play.

I suggest the guiding question be this: "What is it about entrepreneurs that makes them unique and uniquely capable of advancing humanity?"

We won't find the answer to that question through a hard-and-fast profile or formula, or even a better definition. Ultimately, clarifying what separates entrepreneurs from others provides a good foundation, but it isn't the only insight needed to tap into the power of entrepreneur*ship*. And as you'll see in the chapters that follow, and particularly those in Part II, what matters most *is* entrepreneurship.

Still, as a reference point—and even as a warning—understanding the term "entrepreneur" can be incredibly valuable.

## Recommended Resources

### *A Whole New Mind* – Daniel Pink

The post-industrial age world ran a century or more on left-brained, linear thinking. Then at the turn of the 21st century, we drifted to the other extreme, declaring that emotional intelligence and other outgrowths of our right brain were important, too. But we all have two sides. Dan shows us how to take advantage of both and think more entrepreneurially.

### *Complications* – Atul Gawande

This book isn't about entrepreneurship *per se*. It's about hero worship, being human, and our ability to trust, all of which are fallible. Although *Complications* formally addresses surgeons and their need to stop and consider their roles, it has a strong message for all of us who share a similar need.

### *In the Heart of the Sea* – Nathaniel Philbrick

When people get in tough spots, they resort to what they know best—who they are as individuals, what they are as humans, or both. Important lessons come from such circumstances. Maybe that's why Herman Melville wrote his novel about the true story of the Whaleship Essex, which is recounted here.

### *South* – Ernest Shackleton

There is perhaps no greater story of adventure and survival than that of Ernest Shackleton, a name synonymous with ambition and vision. Much texture lies deep within this tale of how one man inspired and led all his men to survive one of the most harrowing ordeals ever recorded. Shackleton, a leader in every sense, was also a unique combination of a visionary catalyst and someone who recognized the need for discipline. As unique a visionary leader as Shackleton was, he was also humble enough to know that nothing was possible without the community he helped establish within his crew.

### *Founding Brothers* – Joseph Ellis

Some have referred to the Founding Fathers as entrepreneurs. Far more interesting is to examine how the entrepreneurial thinking of these men evolved in the pursuit of their bold vision and the challenges of fulfilling it, with (and at times in spite of) each other. Ellis does this. A masterful writer of history, he brilliantly conveys the challenges individuals and communities face after a vision is born and the first victories are won.

### *Innovation and Entrepreneurship* – Peter Drucker

If you want to taste the core of Drucker's view on entrepreneurs, this is a good place to start. Later books by him tend to assume these views. Later books about him have a tendency to overlook them.

# Contributors to Chapter 2

**Will Murray**
    Co-founder, Conservation Impact and Founder, Will Murray Company
    Former Director, The Nature Conservancy

**Rob McGovern**
    Founder, CareerBuilder
    Author, *Bring Your 'A' Game*
    Founder, President Market10 (now jobfox)

**Dipak Jain**
    Dean, Kellogg School of Management, Professor of Entrepreneur Studies
    Co-author, *Marketing Moves: A New Approach to Profits, Growth, and Renewal*
    Director, Deere & Company, Northern Trust, and United Airlines

**Mike McCaffery**
    President, CEO, Stanford Management Company
    Former President, Robertson, Stephens & Company

**Gene Kahn**
    Founder, Cascadian Farms; Founder, Small Planet Foods
    Vice President, General Mills Sustainability Council

**Jim Wrathall**
    Co-founder, ChildSecure
    Senior Counsel, Senate Committee on Environment and Public Works

**Muhammad Yunus** (See Chapter 1)

**Robin Chase** (See Chapter 1)

**Bijoy Goswami**
    Founder, Bootstrap Austin
    Author, *The Human Fabric: Unleashing the Power of Core Energy in Everyone*
    Co-founder, Aviri

**Tien Wong**
    Co-founder, CyberRep
    Ernst & Young Entrepreneur of the Year, 2001
    CEO, Opus 8

**Tracy Stone-Manning**
    Executive Director, Clark Fork Coalition

**Brad Whitehead**
    Co-founder, Core Resources and the Civic Innovation Lab
    Former Managing Director, McKinsey & Company

**Irv Grousbeck**

> Director, Center of Entrepreneurial Studies, Stanford Business School
>
> Co-founder, Continental Cable Vision

**John May**

> Founder, Principal, New Vantage Group
>
> Co-author, *Every Business Needs an Angel* and *State of the Art*

**Steve Mariotti**

> Founder, President, National Foundation for Teaching Entrepreneurship
>
> Author, *The Young Entrepreneur's Guide to Starting and Running a Business*

**Jan Bruce**

> Publisher, Managing Director, *Body + Soul* magazine

**Guy Kawasaki**

> Founder, Managing Director, Garage Technology Ventures
>
> Author, *The Art of the Start*, *Rules for Revolutionaries*, and five other books

**Charlene Drew Jarvis**

> President, Southeastern University
>
> 21-year member Washington DC City Council

**Brad Barnhorn** (See Chapter 1)

**Mike Bernstein**

> Co-founder, Simply Bits, Leapscape, and Nextrio

**Mary Naylor**

> CEO, Founder, VIPdesk and Capitol Concierge
>
> Executive Committee YPO (Young Entrepreneurs Organization)

**Laurence Gonzales**

> Author, *Deep Survival* and *Everyday Survival*

**Gene Foley**

> Former and First Chair, SBA (Small Business Association)
>
> Founder, Foley & Associates Financial Consulting

**Geoff Smart**

> Founder, Chairman, CEO, ghSMART
>
> Co-author, *Who: The A Method for Hiring*
>
> Lecturer, Kellogg and Sloan Graduate Schools of Management

# Chapter 2: Exposing the Myths of the Entrepreneur

*"The typical notion of the entrepreneur is a tale. It's not reality. There are no real heroes out there as the tales say. We mix entrepreneurs up with the Lone Ranger concept."*

- Will Murray
Co-founder
Conservation Impact

Even though confusion around our understanding and use of the term "entrepreneur" exists, we can't blame this uncertainty only on the absence of a clear, unique definition. There is a mythology around entrepreneurs that adds to the confusion and misleads people, especially those trying to build ventures on faulty expectations. The many unique forms that entrepreneurship takes belie our most popular myths about entrepreneurs.

It isn't that these myths about entrepreneurs are out-and-out lies. Like most myths, they're often based on a kernel of truth, but not the whole truth or a truth common to all those to whom these beliefs are then applied. Moreover, as myths gain power being retold and embellished, they tend not only to drift from any element of truth, but to narrow our views, focus us on the wrong things, and lead us to think that these myths, no matter how true, are representative. The myth about Flipper, the dolphin, is a great example.

## The Creation of Myths—The Story of Flipper

In the lore of shipwrecks, ocean plane crashes, and people lost at sea, recurring stories about dolphins saving people frequently surface.

These stories have their own distinguishing details, but one common element involves dolphins pushing people to land, or pushing them into currents that lead to land, or otherwise "saving" humans. The lovable character Flipper, as well as our commonly accepted views about dolphins and humans, comes out of such mythology.

*Flipper* originated as a film in 1963 and starred a heroic dolphin of the same name. This fictional dolphin helped a Florida Everglades park ranger and his sons protect the park, save vessels, and chase bad guys. Its popularity reached such heights that it spawned a TV series (with decades of reruns) as well as several remakes of the movie, the most recent in 1996, over three decades after the original.

Flipper not only reinforced his own image over time but also our misconceptions about the mammal itself. Portrayed as rescuer, hero, and friend, Flipper has helped dolphins rival dogs as man's best friend. But the image of dolphin as savior of humans is a myth. Eventually, someone researched the basis of this myth and found that dolphins simply like to push things. The object they push or the direction they push it has no particular relevance. Human rescue stories may have happened, sure, but these dolphin actions are, at best, indiscriminant and inconsistent. Who knows how many times dolphins passed by stranded humans, or worse, pushed them the wrong way? Viewing dolphins as rescuers and protectors of humans has no more basis than seeing entrepreneurs as gun-slinging mavericks motivated by pure profit.

### The Flipper Syndrome and the Entrepreneur

As with the dolphin myth, we most often look to our *impressions* of entrepreneurs garnered from stories to answer the question "who is an entrepreneur?" Since entrepreneurs frequently operate out of public view, our impressions rely heavily on stereotypes, which in turn define our expectations and too often lead us to accept rumor and myth as fact.

I think of this as the Flipper Syndrome, accepting either what we *think* we see or *want* to see as fact. As Will Murray said in the opening quotation, "The typical notion of the entrepreneur is a tale. It's not reality. There are no real heroes out there as the tales say. We mix entrepreneurs up with the Lone Ranger concept."

In my work with entrepreneurs and others who invest in them or advise them, I've heard so many rumors that, at the height of the Internet bubble when it seemed everyone began calling themselves an entrepreneur, I started including in my presentations a "Top Ten Myths About Entrepreneurs" list. But I had so many myths from which to choose—and the myth of the moment changed so often—I had to keep changing my top ten to address the latest. Sometimes these myths—you'll read them shortly—left my audience members rolling with laughter; others made them feel angry or discouraged; some emboldened them. In the end, however, these myths only cluttered the truth.

As it turns out, many myths actually emanate from each other. And frankly, discussing all of the myths ever uttered about entrepreneurs would be repetitive. It makes more sense to focus on the most pervasive and broadly applicable ones—those that show no regard for sector, size, or nature of entrepreneurial pursuit and therefore apply to virtually every entrepreneur at any point in time. They include the Risk Taker myth, the Acting Solo myth, the Motivated by Money myth, the Personality and Luck myth, and the Able to Be Free myth. When these myths are peeled away, our view of entrepreneurs gains enormous clarity.

### Myth One: The Risk Taker

More than anything else, entrepreneurs are believed to be risk takers. So I made a point of asking my interviewees whether entrepreneurs were, as a group, risk takers. Universally, they acknowledge this to be the *popular* view of entrepreneurs but inaccurate. In fact, most described entrepreneurs as risk *averse*.

The label of risk taker comes from the characters we read about in magazines and watch on TV, commented many. Think of the bootstrapping maniacal type who gives up everything, strikes it big, and gets rich. After seeing this a few times, it's easy to think all entrepreneurs are like that. But as the interviewees expanded their comments about entrepreneurs and risk, each concluded it was more of an outside view looking in—an impression but not the truth. Sure, successful entrepreneurs know what they're doing can be risky, but they minimize their view of it. Echoed Rob McGovern, founder of CareerBuilder and president of Market10, "We make a big deal about it, saying 'these people are risk takers, leveraging up their credit cards and doubling their mortgages.' It's more basic than that. Entrepreneurs know how to take *calculated* risks. It's not about being defiant; it's an ability to calculate and mitigate risk."

Like Rob, Dipak Jain emphasized that taking a calculated view of risk is a conscious act. As dean of Kellogg, one of America's top business schools, Dipak has a broad view of teaching entrepreneurship while also drawing from practical experience advising companies like John Deere, Northern Trust, and United Airlines. Looking through an entrepreneur's eyes, he said, "When I am willing to do something, I have already thought about it and thought it out. The risk is in the mind of the people I try to *convince*. The moment I take it on, I have accounted for the risk in my own mind. Risk is largely *around* the individuals and their ability to calculate honestly and completely what they are willing to do."

Rob and Dipak aren't denying the odds of successful entrepreneurship or turning a blind eye to what entrepreneurs undertake. There *is* risk in what entrepreneurs do. "You should not create an impression that risk does not exist," Dipak advised. "That shows arrogance or ignorance." But in calculating how and where risk fits in, and its relative size and importance, entrepreneurs do take a different view of risk taking. We should, too.

## How Entrepreneurs View Risk

The fact that entrepreneurs don't see themselves as risk takers but instead as risk averse quickly takes the wind out of the risk taker myth. Who, after all, is likely to know better—the person who assumes the burden of entrepreneurship every day or those who stand apart from it and observe? Drawing on nearly three decades of successfully investing in entrepreneurs, Mike McCaffery knows better than most that, "Those who do it (launch entrepreneurial ventures) don't see it as risk. They in fact think of it as *less* risky. There's only one sense of security for an entrepreneur and that is knowing what you do well and doing it."

Mike's role as a trusted steward of other people's money at investment firms like Robertson, Stephens & Company and Morgan Stanley, and for Stanford University's endowment funds, requires him to intimately assess the thinking, business models, and prospects of entrepreneurs. Both an entrepreneur's attitude toward risk and aptitude to manage it is foremost in Mike's mind. After all, he's betting on that entrepreneur's ability to mitigate risk!

Don't let the term "bet" mislead you. Investors like Mike don't deal with dice rollers, nor do they assume mythical roles themselves. They know that if entrepreneurs or those who bankroll them were true gamblers, they wouldn't be around doing what they do for long.

Without question, the people to whom Mike—and bankers and investors like him—provide capital could be considered high risk. But the entrepreneurs themselves don't see it that way. And neither do the knowledgeable people who back them. When you get in the habit of asking "why?" and feel comfortable outside the norm (as entrepreneurs are), the typical risk parameters either don't apply or they function as but one of many factors considered before taking action. The risk in an entrepreneurial venture may be higher relative to other pursuits, but it also carries lower relative importance within the venture itself. Similarly, the relevance of risk in the mind of the person who catalyzes the venture must be seen in context with the offsetting and extraordinary efforts entrepreneurs make to mitigate risk.

## Different Point of Reference

By their nature, entrepreneurs see beyond traditional boundaries, which explains why their point of reference for risk is different than for most people. What others view as unfathomable, entrepreneurs see as necessary. What many perceive as a high probability of failure and something to avoid, entrepreneurs think of as a necessary learning process toward accomplishing something greater than exists now.

Rethinking the term "entrepreneur" requires us to reevaluate, even shed, this perception that being an entrepreneur means assuming unusual or exceptional risk. While the risk taker belief may remain the view *externally*, the view held by those on the outside looking in, it tells us nothing about what goes on *internally*, inside the entrepreneur or the venture itself. Emphasizing what we *think* entrepreneurs are doing and how we *perceive* their actions rather than searching for the truth doesn't just confuse us; it can encourage those who want to think entrepreneurially to act irrationally at high levels of risk. Ironically, that would raise the odds of failing.

### Entrepreneurs Shy Away from the Term Itself

In fact, engaging in risky behavior only for the sake of risk almost guarantees disastrous consequences. To punctuate this misperception many have about entrepreneurs, in a strange twist of irony, entrepreneurs themselves frequently shy away from using the term "entrepreneur"—all out of fear of feeding this risk taker myth.

A case in point is Gene Kahn, founder of Cascadian Farms. "I don't like 'entrepreneur' as a term," said Gene, "because it connotes excessive risk taking or imprudent behavior. Entrepreneurs are risk takers because they are willing to take on an activity in every sense—they aren't just willing to run a business but to *take it on* in every sense and rethink the very foundation of it to develop something new, useful, and uniquely valuable."

Entrepreneurs live and breathe every aspect of what they're pursuing, leaving little to chance. They're fine-tuned to take calculated actions. Gene pointed out a critical distinction by saying, "Entrepreneurs are clearly working in a highly productive zone no matter what you call it. There is a difference between risk taking and rapid learning, fast failure, and knowledge creation—things that are often falsely filed under risk taking."

### Entrepreneurs Don't Let Hurdles Become Risks

It isn't just that entrepreneurs begin with less risk than we might think; entrepreneurs also proactively mitigate hurdles so they can ensure those hurdles don't become risks. In a sense, for the entrepreneur, a risk is something that's been allowed to become a *fixed* obstacle. If it can be removed, transformed, or moved around, then it no longer presents a real risk.

Whether entrepreneurs anticipate or encounter risks along the way doesn't matter. What matters is their awareness of what's happening and their quick, decisive action in response. They "get their head out of the cockpit." This phrase references a phenomenon in flying airplanes about getting fixated on the gauges *inside* the cockpit and forgetting to just look out the window.

Pilot and Senior Counsel for the Senate Committee on the Environment and Public Works, Jim Wrathall, described this concept as "always wanting to be ahead of the plane." If you ever "get behind the plane"—something that happens when you get caught up in the details without considering the context—it's almost too late. What could have been mitigated then becomes real risk. Jim has found this to be as true in the numerous ventures he has founded or advised as it is in the pilot's seat.

## Step In, Tune In, Learn, Adjust

Clearly, the way successful entrepreneurs mitigate risk isn't haphazard or reactionary; it's intentional because it's how they're wired (or more accurately, it's how they've learned to wire themselves). Given that no one ever has perfect information, some people allow that to hang them up. They're afraid to fail. But entrepreneurs don't wait for perfection. They act. And by taking action, they create opportunities to learn.

In fact, as distinct as their willingness to act is, so is their desire to learn from every action, adjust, and act again—always driving their vision forward, consistently focused on delivery. They don't speculate and create models perpetually; they step in, tune in, learn, and adjust. This cycle of acting, learning, adjusting, and acting again—over and over—gives them valuable information and insight. Every replication of the cycle begins with a pause, however grand and obvious, or subtle and second nature. They keep repeating it to mitigate risk every step of the way.

## *Myth Two: Acting Solo*

The myth of entrepreneurs as risk takers is closely rivaled by the myth of entrepreneurs as solo actors succeeding on their own. *"Damn it all to hell and get out of my way"* describes the stereotypical entrepreneur—brash, young, and fighting for success *alone,* with a flagrant disregard for everyone and everything standing in the path.

The facts simply don't support this view.

### Starts with a Willingness to Act Alone

Some myths begin from a kernel of truth and this is one of them. Without question, entrepreneurs have the ability and need to think independently and act apart from the status quo. Their willingness to see and act alone is vital to *launching* their dream. A vision and venture *begin* with the entrepreneur, but it doesn't end there.

To reinforce the importance of the willingness to act alone, consider Dr. Muhammad Yunus's pronouncement in the 1970s that he planned to eradicate poverty in impoverished Bangladesh. Nearly 35 years ago, before he had introduced the now-popular concept of micro-lending, no one would entertain the possibility of such an accomplishment—by any means. At the time (and for a long time after), his idea was considered to be sheer madness, the only deterrent most people would need to go no further and allow it to be laughed off as an outrageous joke.

But the punch line to Yunus's joke never came. In fact, he wasn't done with the telling. He wanted to go further. He planned not just to help the poor but to lend them money, an idea no banker in the world at the time (perhaps still true today) would even consider. And he wanted to lend in increments of fewer than one hundred dollars (hence the term "micro"). To most, even if the idea of lending to the poor could be taken seriously, lending in such amounts was pointless from a profitability or management standpoint. But to Yunus, it was the key to empowering the poor and enabling them to lift themselves out of poverty by starting their own businesses.

Why would this distinguished economics professor at Chittagong University, educated in the United States, and a respected citizen of the newly created Bangladesh who had fought for its freedom and international recognition, do this? Had he not been all those things *plus* a gentle warm soul, chances are he'd have been thrown out of the government, university, and commercial lending offices where he went to make his case.

But since launching Grameen Bank and his micro-lending concept, Yunus's wild idea *has* driven Bangladesh's poverty rate down to less than 40 percent from an estimated 74 percent. Moreover, it's expected to reduce the country's poverty to half its original level by 2015. This reduction has catapulted the Bangladeshi economy to become the third fastest in growth in South Asia. Its ripple effects have been enormous— life expectancy rates have risen dramatically, healthcare and education opportunities have grown, and the Human Development Index for Bangladeshis has been positively transformed.

Micro-lending itself has spread across the world like wildfire. It's now considered a vital tool in fighting poverty, even in developed countries. All these results—plus Yunus's worldwide recognition after receiving the 2006 Nobel Peace Prize—make his once-mad dream seem less outrageous. There is no question it took Yunus, the individual stepping out defiantly (and largely independently), to reach the point of micro-lending's total acceptance—as if it had always been there. But that willingness to act alone at first was not—and never is—enough.

As an idea like micro-lending becomes reality, a founder's willingness to *act alone at first* differs from *continuing to stand alone.* As Yunus said, "Community helps to encourage, enable, and value what the entrepreneur starts. If nobody notices, there is no reward for the entrepreneur, others, or the world." His experience shows that no entrepreneur achieves his or her vision alone. The solo actor role catalyzes things, but it does not become the perpetually dominant force or the ultimate key to success. "When entrepreneurship lasts," said Yunus, "what you create—the institute itself—becomes the 'person' rather than the persons who make it. It is ageless. It is a combined personality, not just one. It is a life unto itself."

## Continuing Need to Act Together

A company called Zipcar has revolutionized the way we think about transportation, both public and private. Zipcar, whose slogan is "wheels when you want them," makes getting a rental car as easy as using an ATM.

How does it work? Rather than owning a car, driving it, and maintaining it, with Zipcar, customers register as part of a community that shares cars and accesses them at predetermined locations with the swipe of a card. Easy, yes, but also revolutionary.

Robin Chase is most often credited with creating Zipcar. She catalyzed this bold vision, not by herself but with co-founder Antje Danielson and eventually Zipcar's users themselves.

From its earliest days, Zipcar made headway because it attracted the imagination and energy of others. "The idea itself came from many, many other people's ideas," Robin explained. "The execution is dramatically a community affair. At Zipcar, I'd always tell the staff that the good things happening were honestly and absolutely a result of what everyone on the team was doing well. I wasn't being politically correct; it was because everyone was a mandatory, necessary part of making it work."

Robin's comments reveal another false assumption about entrepreneurship, the belief that the entrepreneur is "king" (or "queen") for having the idea, the one idea that made it all happen. Entrepreneurship, a force larger than the entrepreneur, is about seismic change—in thinking, action, and human patterns. No one idea or person causes a tremor that great. In entrepreneurship, ideas are put on the stage by humans for the betterment of humans. When they are, each idea is vetted by humans, too. They add to it, challenge it, and take away from the idea, over and over again as each person sees his or her own version of *better*. Ideas aren't fixed. And no one idea is *the* thing. In a similar way, no one person directs where ideas go.

Honest entrepreneurs will tell you that what their venture and their vision became look nothing like they did at the start. Ever. The only way for that to happen is for an idea not to move forward. Ever.

At the seismic level of change, it isn't just a matter of entrepreneurship being bigger than the entrepreneur whose idea creates the first spark. It is, as Yunus would say, a community emerging that itself becomes the "person" rather than the individuals who facilitate change. Seismic change like the Zipcar experience derives from the sum of the parts being greater than the whole.

**Personal Evolution Required**

For this evolution from one to many to take place requires the *opposite* of self-obsession and self-reliance. Yet many entrepreneurs never grow enough personally to go beyond themselves. That kind of growth requires evolving from entrepreneur to leader, spreading responsibility and ownership, even reshaping one's ego and soul. The failure to do so commonly factors into the failure of many ventures to evolve.

The author of *The Human Fabric,* Bijoy Goswami, summarized it this way: "Entrepreneurship is an ongoing journey of more and more people. That's what's so beautiful about it. You get to do what you do well and then bring others along to be co-creators. It is not a 'me projecting out into the universe' sort of thing. The whole job of entrepreneurship is finding those dance partners and dancing well."

The original vision becomes a *shared* vision, as it did for Grameen Bank and Zipcar. If it doesn't, all too often it fades or dies. Even though an entrepreneurial vision begins with one person's belief, lasting change isn't a solo act.

## Myth Three: Motivated by Money

Most people assume that entrepreneurs are motivated by profit. Ask those who know the entrepreneurial universe and they will tell you this: It isn't money, greed, or ego that drives entrepreneurs to do what they do. Spreading and cultivating a vision of a better world and generating the value that comes from seeing that vision take form are what really drive successful entrepreneurs and effective entrepreneurship.

**Ventures Driven Only by Money are Broken**

As the co-founder of customer solutions company CyberRep, Tien Wong led his company to five straight appearances on *Inc.* magazine's 500 list, among numerous other awards. It's worth noting that *Inc.*'s list ranks for-profit companies and does so by growth rates according to financial indicators. When we encounter people who have been as successful as Tien—and see the money that has accompanied their success—it's easy to conclude that money also motivated him. But for people such as Tien, profit is a *byproduct*; it is *not* the main driver. Tien is unwavering in his belief that "any venture driven only by money is broken."

It's not that people like Tien or Tracy Stone-Manning (see her story, *Creating a Coalition Destined to Disappear*) *ignore* the profit motive or advocate others to do so. Quite the contrary. Though Tien ran a for-profit and Tracy a nonprofit, they both recognize the importance of financial stability to facilitate successful ventures. They analyze their returns on investment not because they want to get rich, but because they have limited resources and want to do the most with them. Neither loses sight of the fact that financial measures only have importance in a larger context. While valuing financial stability as one important indicator of progress and a tool for moving toward a larger mission, profit isn't the only indicator, or even always the best indicator of value.

## Value Comes Through Betterment of the World

Value is *collective measure*, one taking countless forms that, in combination, help fulfill any entrepreneurial vision. But regardless of form, value in the fullest sense of the word is best *defined* as that which supports change for the better and that which allows for human advancement.

Money isn't enough to create or measure value. Almost without exception, entrepreneurs have said that only being in it for the money never would have sustained them through all they faced. Too many times, the promise of financial rewards couldn't solve a challenge or propel the entrepreneurial vision forward.

Concluding that a driving force as shallow as money is sufficient is too easy. In fact, those who believe this have a cynical view of the world. And if we assumed money to be the main motivator when we observe entrepreneurs making a lot, where would that leave people like Tracy or Tien, Robin Chase or Muhammad Yunus? There must be something more in it for them. "Moneymaking is interesting, exciting, and people like it," Dr. Yunus once said in a *Washington Post* interview.[7] "But it's not the whole of human life. Human beings are much bigger than just being a moneymaking machine."

Not only are entrepreneurs human beings, but in some ways, they are more fully realized than others because of the way they push to change something important in the world. They are driven to do what they do more for humanity and less for themselves. In the process, they merge their goals and motivations with those of others, making their undertakings and their rewards, not just themselves, more human and more valuable.

## Creating a Coalition Destined to Disappear

If you don't live in Montana or Idaho, or you aren't an avid rafter or fly fisherman, you've probably never heard of the Clark Fork River Basin. And you certainly wouldn't assume it's a hotbed for entrepreneurship.

Tracy Stone-Manning is the executive director of the Clark Fork Coalition, an enterprise dedicated to protecting and restoring the Clark Fork River Basin, which runs from Butte, Montana, through Missoula, down to Sandpoint, Idaho. This may sound like just another environmental nonprofit organization, but its uniqueness begins with its membership. Rather than being comprised of environmentalists, the Coalition is made up of citizens, scientists, recreationalists, and business leaders.

The Coalition started in 1983 when a paper mill along the Clark River sought to loosen environmental regulations so it could dump more waste into the river. Citizens along the river opposed changing the regulation. They got organized, sat down with the mill's executives, and solved the waste problem to the satisfaction of both sides and to the betterment of the river.

More than 20 years later, the Coalition continues to fulfill its mission. It succeeds largely because its diverse members, along with Tracy and her small staff, have clearly defined the common ground they share. They understand how the health of the river benefits them all. Rather than emphasizing egos, agendas, or forms of reward, the Coalition and its contributors put in check any narrow, self-serving views. Instead, they continue to protect the environment in ways that meet every Coalition member's agenda. By doing so, businesses have renewable resources and a stable population from which to draw employees. The towns along the river basin have an asset that attracts tourists, conservation dollars, and even personal pride. Recreationalists maintain and even improve the area for the enjoyment of generations to come. And scientists gain a vibrant, natural laboratory in which to test and learn.

Coalition members have worked hard to build collective value that can't be defined by a single measure such as financial gain. The Coalition is proving that if the goal is maximizing value and sharing a common dream, then individual agendas and measures of value aren't the right focus.

This isn't the typical path for coalitions or nonprofits. Once their initial cause is over, they often spend time justifying their existence or changing the reasons for it to fit the dollars needed to support the organization. But Clark Fork isn't typical either. And much of what makes it different emanates from Tracy's unique vision.

As she sees it, if Coalition members successfully instill that larger understanding of collective value among all who benefit from it, the Coalition itself becomes unnecessary. "Disappearing" could even be considered a measure of success. This mindset and, indeed, this Coalition itself stand in stark contrast with most nonprofit organizations. In reality, the Coalition stands apart from most ventures of any kind.

Tracy sees "going away" as the ultimate realization of her vision. Her motivation clearly reflects a much larger purpose. She thinks in terms of the Clark Fork Coalition slowly erasing both the image of environmental conservation organizations and the whole idea of needing a separate organization to advocate on behalf of the environment—a truly exceptional concept. If Tracy's dream continues, each party to the Coalition will see conservation not as an issue, a burden, a requirement, or a cause, but as an integral part of the way they operate. Then Tracy's organization, job, and team may no longer exist, which suits her just fine. In the long run, it's the vision that matters—not a job or organization, not people and the funding supporting it all.

For entrepreneurship to have a lasting impact, entrepreneurs and their ventures aren't meant to last forever. If they did, how would the world ever evolve beyond them to the next level of betterment?

## *Myth Four: Personality and Luck*

People tend to see entrepreneurs as individuals whose personalities differ from their own in essential ways. So strong is this tendency to give weight to the role of personality that, over time, certain traits have become assumed proxies for entrepreneurial success.

In a similar fashion, luck is often given great weight and at times even considered *the* factor in one entrepreneur's ability to create lasting impact versus another's. Like the stone in stone soup, no single ingredient makes it the masterpiece we enjoy and even crave.

### The Relative Ingredient of Personality

If you were to scan the vast landscape of entrepreneurs, you might find certain personality traits reoccurring with regularity, but they don't indicate who's cut out to be an entrepreneur and who is not. It's like deciding certain people will play basketball well if they are tall. The trait of height says nothing about what motivates basketball players; it offers no insight into the team and environment where they play basketball; nor does it predict their odds of playing successfully because it excludes skills and talents critical to playing this game well.

Some traits, perceived or real, regularly show up in entrepreneurship, like being risk tolerant, comfortable with change, and able to stand confidently outside the norm. But how they occur and the nature of their value aren't universal and therefore don't predict their impact on the success of the entrepreneurial venture or the person behind it. Rather, these traits typically support but don't drive the entrepreneur. And they don't serve as accurate predictors of success.

Within the world of entrepreneurs lies a fine line between bold and crazy. Pity the man who tries to draw a distinction based solely on personality traits. In roles as global as managing director at consulting firm McKinsey & Company to one as local as co-founder of the Civic Innovation Lab in Cleveland, Ohio, Brad Whitehead has learned it isn't possible to judge entrepreneurs so simplistically. "The personality combination that makes an entrepreneur is a real art," said Brad. "Smart but not too smart, gutsy but risk aware, a stick-to-it nature without being stubborn, an ability to know when to change, focused without being myopic, just short of charismatic but well beyond grunt-like."

This mix becomes an art with a variable, situation-unique balance of factors playing into it. A list of stereotypical personality traits alone conveys nothing.

Are creativity and outside-the-box thinking good for entrepreneurship and entrepreneurial ventures? Of course. But do they prove to be enough to allow them to succeed? No way. Run any trait you associate with entrepreneurs by filling in the blanks. Do _____ and _____ traits prove to be enough to predict success? You'll see that a preponderance of personality traits does not a successful venture make.

A belief in the power of one's overall personality—as opposed to specific traits—is also common to entrepreneurial stereotypes. It leans on the idea that a powerful personality is enough to render (or force) success. Thus entrepreneurs are pictured as high-energy, fast-talking, smooth operators who charm everyone into following them.

But if the cult of personality sells at all, it only goes so far. If you want people to buy into a new big idea or change their priorities and values, charisma alone won't get you there. In fact, many successful entrepreneurs are mild mannered rather than possessed with the larger-than-life public persona associated with a powerful personality. If these "quieter" entrepreneurs had to rely on their personality alone to compel others, many would fail. And if slick salesmanship proved adequate, more of those who call themselves entrepreneurs in error wouldn't be failing so miserably.

The power of personality is often both *denied* as important and *blamed* as important—in the same venture and with the same entrepreneur. Dr. Muhammad Yunus experienced this quandary. In the early days of developing his micro-lending concept and establishing Grameen Bank, he was mocked for his brashness in thinking that he, one mild-mannered man, could bring about the change he sought. How could he even conceive of bank-rolling the poor? Yet, once his programs proved successful and spread, those same critics turned their words around 180 degrees. They claimed the successes he'd achieved could not have happened without Yunus's direct involvement; they accused him of creating a babysitting venture, not a banking one. Even when change becomes real, it's hard for some people to accept.

## The Fantasy of Luck

In addition to personality traits, luck is often credited to an entrepreneur's success with astonishing frequency. Entrepreneurship to some is akin to playing the lottery or blowing out the candles on a birthday cake to make that all-powerful wish.

On occasion, explaining entrepreneurial success as "luck" seems credible. The luck of timing is often cited. So is the luck of being in the right place. In reality, good timing, connections, and being on site when opportunity strikes can factor in, but no sane person ever made the decision to launch a critical venture counting on good timing, right connections, or right place as major assets. For that matter, no investors worth their salt would ever back anyone based on these factors. And no entrepreneur ever succeeded solely (or even mostly) by luck.

Yes, being lucky seems to be a convenient cover-up for what we don't know or don't want to acknowledge about success. It's easier to call entrepreneurs "lucky" than to acknowledge what elements actually contributed to their success. Of course, moments when everything aligns do occur, but these moments of serendipity are only recognized and leveraged because of the conscious actions preceding them. Luck is the product of effort and awareness.

Sure, at some level, people stay open to the possibility that life could deal them the easy card. Lighten the burden. Ease the tasks. Make advancement effortless. That's the kind of outlook promoted by fairy tales and lottery commissions. But there's no such thing as dumb luck.

## The Role of Serendipity

While we can deflate the fantasy of luck, we can't ignore the role of serendipity. Entrepreneurs may not believe in luck, but they openly acknowledge that serendipity exists.

So what is the difference between luck and serendipity? Irv Grousbeck, director at the Center of Entrepreneurial Studies and professor at Stanford Business School, explained it this way: "Serendipity is akin to being in a sailboat and getting a favorable gust of wind that moves you along a little farther and faster. It is a nice additional tailwind you didn't count on. It is not the end-all." Angel investor and co-author of *Every Business Needs an Angel,* John May, made this distinction: "There is some clear though variable element of serendipity in entrepreneurial success. You can influence but you can't control fate, timing, and coincidence. Luck, even in the greatest success, is a marginal factor and one without value. The factors around it are what define and shape things and the ones you can control."

Anyone can experience serendipity. And while it can't be controlled, you can hone your radar to see it. In a way, it comes down to a readiness to do something that "just feels right." Any moment could become one of serendipity. And such moments can just as easily fall *away* from you as fall *in* your favor. As the story goes, two people can sit next to the same person on a plane; one will come home with a brilliant idea or partnership and the other with no more than a pleasant conversation and a bag of peanuts. As Steve Mariotti, the founder and president of the National Foundation for Teaching Entrepreneurship, put it, "Luck over time is the same for everyone. Some are not ready to see opportunities, to act on them. The serendipity element depends on how the audience plays it out."

## The Similarities of Personality and Luck

Unlike the risk taker, solo actor, and motivated by money myths, those pertaining to personality and luck tend to come up in a less than all-consuming way. You'd more likely find someone referring to the first three myths as *the* factor in an entrepreneur's success than you would personality or luck. Rather, luck and personality are treated like icing on the cake; they aren't given full credit, but persistently are given undue credit for entrepreneurial success.

Many with preconceived notions of entrepreneurs can cite other myths in a similar category occupied by personality and luck. Birth order, social standing, financial wherewithal are three that come to mind. Yes, like personality and luck, these "ingredients" can factor in. But they don't make the difference between success and failure of an entrepreneurial venture. They simply aren't enough, in and of themselves, to achieve that result.

Of all these "ingredient" factors rumored to make the difference, luck and personality are the most commonly occurring and representative. But like their lesser brethren, they should be dismissed as critical factors in lasting change.

### Myth Five: Able to Be Free

Sure, people like the idea of a ready escape—quit their jobs, move to Hawaii, and sell seashells by the seashore. At least they want to remove themselves to a place where day-to-day burdens don't exist, where life isn't routine and rule-bound. So when someone appears to be unfettered by rules, it's human nature to be attracted to that lifestyle, especially when people perceive they can have certain rewards like attention, wealth, and other things they lack in their lives.

In the eyes of many, entrepreneurship equals freedom. This myth is rooted in the fact that entrepreneurs break with the status quo and appear to work for themselves. Wrap this with the image of entrepreneurs making their dreams happen and you're left with the impression of someone who's free to do as he or she wishes.

But it's a misperception that's based on two erroneous assumptions: that entrepreneurs don't have obligations to a boss, and that what they do, they do for themselves. In reality, their loyalty (and therefore their obligations) belongs to their vision of how the world could be better and their choice to make it so. And far from doing what they do for themselves, they nurture the needs of a certain segment of humanity as, for example, Dr. Yunus did setting up micro-lending for the poorest of the poor.

Clearly, entrepreneurship doesn't guarantee the reward of freedom. Moreover, an entrepreneur's work is really never done. Pursuing a vision requires perpetual motion. And while in the most literal sense, entrepreneurs don't have "a boss," they operate under the belief that their work reaches well beyond themselves. Its ultimate value lies with a "boss" of higher authority—humanity.

## Requires Sacrifice, Work, Devotion, Discipline

Yes, there *is* a certain freedom of choice that comes with entrepreneurship, but it's hinged to the continued effort and sacrifice necessary to maintain such freedom. The two work in tandem. "It's not really good or bad; it's different—both tougher and more liberating," concluded Jan Bruce, publisher and managing director of *Body + Soul* magazine. "You have a lot of freedom, *and* you are a slave."

Make no mistake about it, fostering a successful, lasting entrepreneurial way of life is hard work. Yet even the perception of living the good life causes some to plunge ahead, knowing nothing more than they've left the path they've been on. They quickly learn, as Guy Kawasaki did, that like anything worth doing, entrepreneurship takes sacrifice, work, devotion, discipline.

In his book *The Art of the Start*, Guy offered 10 points on making a venture successful. Almost from his first point, Guy shattered the illusion of entrepreneurship as a footloose walk in the park. His first commandment? Every entrepreneur should set out to *make meaning* above all else. (Make meaning? That doesn't sound easy or freeing, does it?)

According to Guy, entrepreneurs must go further, to attract others, act in concert with them, and develop a meaningful and distinct model for what they would do. They must also lay out substantive milestones, assumptions, and tasks they fully intend to deliver on. There is no "Sunday," no rest on the seventh day. "Even a born entrepreneur has to work hard to make it successful," said Guy. "Hope and prayer is not a business model."

### Entrepreneurship Made Real at Southeastern University

There is more to debunking this myth of freedom than recognizing that entrepreneurship doesn't represent an escapist fantasy. The corollary, as Southeastern University president, Charlene Drew Jarvis, stated it, is that "entrepreneurship is a run *toward* rather than a run *away* from." Charlene and her team use this mantra to guide how they teach entrepreneurship to their students.

Southeastern, located in the heart of Washington, DC, isn't masquerading as an ivy-walled school for well-to-do students from far and wide. The university serves the community in which it resides. Its students range from those who grew up in the neighborhood and came straight out of high school to local small business owners who have gone back out of necessity, not just opportunity.

Southeastern's approach to serving these students is pragmatic and smart. It's one of many universities that have developed distinct centers of entrepreneurial studies. That surprises those who erroneously think of entrepreneurship and entrepreneurial studies as the domain of the elite. In Southeastern's case, the purpose is to teach a different mindset for engaging life and business. Rather than glorifying entrepreneurship, it's put starkly into context. By applying core skills (like finance, management, and marketing), it dispels any notion of entrepreneurship as a gambler's approach, or an option for ignoring or escaping discipline. Its curriculum reflects the hard work and dedication it takes for the students to achieve their life goals.

## Ventures Based on "Walking Away From" are Bound to Fail

Discipline walks hand in hand with passionate belief—a rare combination but a necessary one. Entrepreneurs face steep odds because the entrepreneurial universe comes with no guarantees and its rewards are often elusive. A venture based on a *reaction* to something in one's life is bound to fail. As Brad Barnhorn, CEO of Global NutriFoods, has unsympathetically said, "You shouldn't pursue entrepreneurship because other things aren't doing it for you. You should do it because you're driven by something deep within." When you do, the things required to make entrepreneurship work—sacrifice, work, devotion, discipline—don't feel like the burdens many hope to free themselves from.

Freedom isn't the primary outcome sought by the entrepreneur. Echoing a familiar refrain, Mike Bernstein, co-founder of Simply

Bits and Nextrio, among numerous other technology ventures, noted that "success in entrepreneurship has a lot to do with the question of running *to* versus running *from*. If you are running from a 9-to-5 job or something you hate, good luck."

Two simple conclusions underline the points being made. One, the allure of entrepreneurship as a haven of freedom is a red herring; any hard-won freedoms are only valuable as a means to a greater end. And two, the entrepreneurial path should call to you as *the way* to reach something deep and important in your life, not as an escape route.

Certainly with great freedom comes great responsibility. But there is something more fundamental yet. As Brad put it, "If you are running to entrepreneurship, *not as a destination* or a search for some *thing* but as a result of a *mindset* that says you *must* go—despite the odds against you and for something greater than money or a guarantee—then you have just greatly improved your odds of success." It's adopting the entrepreneurial mindset that strengthens your odds of enjoying the journey and having the impact that drove you from the start.

If there's any freedom to be had, it's in having the mental and spiritual freedom to do what's right and make things better, rather than one defined by time or tangible reward. Given this, Jan Bruce's point about freedom with unavoidable commitment and responsibility suddenly becomes crystal clear.

### The Choice to See Things Differently

Anytime a closely held belief is taken away, adjusting to a new reality can be hard. If you have a pre-existing knowledge of entrepreneurship, stripping away these myths can feel unsettling. It's akin to saying that behind the white beard, Santa Claus isn't who believers trust him to be.

Yes, many really do believe that entrepreneurs are superhuman power forces (solo actors) who do what they do for financial gain (motivation). They accomplish things by magic (the force of personality or luck), and from a mere dice roll (risk taking), they live a life others only dream of (freedom). How great that would be—if only it were true.

## The Unsettling Feeling of Having Santa Unmasked

If I took that same approach to Santa Claus, my young kids and I would all be mighty unhappy on Christmas Day.

The reasons for celebrating Christmas—the festivities, brightly wrapped packages, and fairy-tale stories—are more complex than the reindeer, chimneys, and cookies-and-milk image our culture perpetuates. A much deeper force prevails for kids and grown-ups alike: *belief.*

No matter how you arrive at this conclusion as a grown-up, if you celebrate the secular aspects of Christmas, at some level (conscious or not), you do so because you *believe* it's a good thing. Likely you believe you're teaching your children about giving and wonder, about suspending reality, about embracing the magical mindset of "what if." What if people really could fly around the world? What if wishes really could be granted?

For children, believing feels easy, pure. At tender ages, their minds haven't yet put any boundaries on what's possible. Why wouldn't they believe someone could fly, or squeeze down a chimney, or grant three wishes? Any rules that stop their beliefs come much later; so does their willingness to accept those rules. Here's what I know. Belief is such a powerful force that when you believe something deeply enough, whatever *it* is, nothing can dissuade you.

It's the same for entrepreneurs.

## An Entrepreneur's View of Risk

What makes the entrepreneur's view of risk, or any other myth about entrepreneurs for that matter, different from what outsiders perceive? Let's take an even closer look at the risk taker myth and examine one critical element—the "no choice" factor—that separates entrepreneurs from others and differentiates their views.

First, risk is relative—not just to others' perceptions of what entrepreneurs do, but to what entrepreneurs actually dream of doing themselves. In their minds, any risk gets compared against the reward of what they seek to achieve.

Second, entrepreneurs consciously weigh the risks of *not* acting on their vision—the opportunity costs. They never see it as one choice among several "jobs" available, nor do they take action because someone told them they should. And their motivation for pursuing their chosen path isn't a finite reward—a salary, a net worth value, or an end point like becoming a company president or making the *Inc. 500* list of fastest-growing companies.

In actuality, entrepreneurs do what they do because they *want* to, because they believe they *need* to, because they *feel* something must change, because they *know* their actions are required to make that change. They believe they simply have *no choice.* Their conclusion is "if not me, who?"

This "no choice" factor is arguably the prime factor enabling them to move beyond an initial idea to take action, to compel and activate others to join in. They want to generate the value that results from catalyzing a vision, not just talk about it.

Contrast that to the conclusions most of us draw. We have big ideas but few act on them and fewer yet take them somewhere, engage others, and create lasting change. At play is always a sense of risk—that is, the risk of losing what we have, of assuming greater burdens, of ridicule, of many more possibilities. Risk can stop us short of action.

Not so for the entrepreneur. "It's really less about risk than you think," said Mary Naylor, the founder or co-founder of several ventures, and honored multiple times with awards for her entrepreneurial achievements. She isn't speculating; she knows the passion of her pursuits relative to the perception of risk. "That view (of me as a risk taker) is *imposed* on me by others and from *outside*. In a sense, I am *more* stable because I am controlling my own decisions." In fact, Mary and others like her, are more stable and more tuned into risk than outsiders looking in realize. Entrepreneurs are determined to *survive*. Yes, this concept of stability deserves further explanation, but understanding why entrepreneurs relate to survivors provides a helpful base.

### Survival in the Truest Sense

Laurence Gonzales, author of *Deep Survival,* knows about survivors. As an extreme adventure enthusiast and a writer for such publications as *National Geographic Adventure* and *Outside* magazines, he has studied survivors for decades. He recognizes parallels between the survivors he writes about and entrepreneurs.

Describing entrepreneurs, Laurence said, "Theirs is survival in the truest sense. Whatever form 'wilderness' may take, entrepreneurs are constantly forced to make decisions in an unknown environment—some very serious ones that may determine their fate—and do so with incomplete information and conflicting signals. In every way, they function in the opposite environment of a comfort zone."

That sounds like a risky place to be, especially by choice. But in effect, the *lack* of choice itself serves to mitigate the risk. For the many wilderness survivors Laurence has observed, they also had no choice except to will themselves to move forward, to keep a clear head, to be resourceful, to survive for something bigger than themselves. And that's the whole point about survival; no one would be mad enough to do certain things if they weren't absolutely necessary.

This mirrors what happens to entrepreneurs as they evolve to the point of feeling they have "no choice" but to move forward. It feels horrific to them *not* to address an injustice or *not* to tap into an opportunity that would make their world better. Their vision of what it should look like galvanizes them; having no choice becomes their commitment. They do it less for their own reward or well-being, and more for the well-being of humanity. Gene Foley, the first head of the Small Business Association, said it this way: "Entrepreneurs truly think and believe that humanity is waiting for them."

For entrepreneurs, risk lies in *not* acting on their "what if?" ideas. For them, alternatives to what they're pursuing carry a much higher risk than the entrepreneurial paths they've chosen.

## *"No Choice"—A Common Thread Among Several Elements*

Although this "no choice" factor obviously undermines the risk taker myth, it also contributes to the dismissal of *all* of the myths about entrepreneurs. Consider how it ties in with the solo actor and the motivation myths. When choice is based on what you must do for humanity and not yourself, any belief that you can achieve it all by yourself quickly falls away—it's simply too big to conquer solo. So, too, does the possibility that one measure alone can define motivation.

When the desired reward will be shared with many, you can't calculate or classify value by yourself.

More than representing a common thread that dispels the mythology of the entrepreneur, the "no choice" factor aligns with other lessons in this book. For example, in Chapter 3, The Entrepreneur as Change Catalyst, you'll learn that this "no choice" factor is central to one of the five elements that makes the entrepreneur truly distinct. And in Chapter 7, The Evolution from Dream to Reality, you'll discover where the "no choice" factor comes from—a deep awareness of self and extreme confidence in one's own abilities.

This point about confidence is worth a preview here.

When studying entrepreneurs leads us to that link between the "no choice" factor and self, self-awareness, and self-confidence, it shifts our discussion. Who entrepreneurs are and what they do evolve from being a gamble to becoming a certainty, even a feeling of destiny. Geoff Smart stated it this way: "With entrepreneurs, risk is about a willingness to bet on one's own talent. But to them, it feels like a sure bet."

Geoff and his team at ghSMART have helped countless private equity investors, Fortune 500 CEOs, and entrepreneurs comprehend what makes for successful leaders and thriving ventures. His company has assessed thousands of successful executives, more than half of whom Geoff considers entrepreneurs. (He has also benefited from his Ph.D. graduate work at Claremont College with management guru Peter Drucker, someone who knew a thing or two about entrepreneurs.)

Geoff has concluded that "entrepreneurs realistically assess and have confidence in their own talents, and are willing to allow their talents to be a disproportionate part of the mix. It's bounded risk." It's here the connection starts. If I, as an entrepreneur, know myself well enough to trust my own talents and intuition, then when I believe I have "no choice" except to pursue a change, its size, complexity, and initial resistance from others is relative. Rather than seeing them as impossibilities, the resistance I face and the hurdles I encounter represent *lessons* I must learn, *things* I must try, *steps* I must take. More than that, they tell me which areas to engage *others* in my vision so I can tap their abilities to jump the hurdles.

Believing they have no choice except *to do what they must* brings a whole new perspective to understanding who entrepreneurs are—and why they do what they do. This factor doesn't minimize the fallacy of the myths about entrepreneurs; it simply plays a critical role in defining these individuals and distinguishing them from others.

## Gene Kahn's Vision: No Choice for Everyone

When Gene stopped within inches of completing his Ph.D. work and began learning organic farming, he didn't know then that he'd create one of the most successful organic food companies in the world.

But that wasn't the point.

Gene *did* know he wanted to better the planet and man's interaction with it. And he knew he had no choice but to figure out how. So organic farming became his first step. But he knew there was more. After all, no one gives up years of hard work and the promise of academic tenure without cause. But in Gene's mind, there was no question. He struck out in the direction of his vision by way of organic farming, knowing he had a lot to learn.

Gene's first hurdle came when he began farming in Washington State's Olympic Peninsula. Now, anyone who knew organic farming would have told him this choice of locale was less than optimal. Maybe they did. Maybe they even called him crazy. Maybe that just emboldened him all the more. But he quickly found out why.

The soggy Olympic Peninsula has one of the highest rainfalls of anywhere in the U.S., with up to 12 feet falling each year in some areas. High rainfall means more fungus growth on fruits and vegetables. And in the absence of pesticides (a no-no in organic farming), that tends to mean lower crop yields— maybe disastrously low.

A hurdle? Yes. A risk? That was to be determined. But this much was clear to Gene: He had chosen a path to better man's relationship with the natural world that no one had been able to crack except in modest ways. For him, finding a sustainable way was a necessity. The way itself was secondary; he gave himself no choice but to make it happen.

You could call Gene Kahn stubborn, but not stupid. He knew he'd face hurdles, even if he hadn't fully internalized how hard they'd be to overcome. And the hurdles weren't just conceptual. Right from his first fungus-covered harvest, his high hurdles became challenges and temporary blind spots in his knowledge.

So Gene went to work to find ways around the hurdles, even transform them before the cement was set. He accumulated a library of every conceivable text on organics and agriculture, farming and soil content, climates, and more. (Today, he has one of the most extensive and rare collections.) He read voraciously. He talked with his community of fellow farmers, with scientists, with anyone from whom he could glean insights. Through these sources and testing new farming methods, Gene reduced the threats to ensure he could grow promising crops. More than discovering the answer, he created a new one; more than lessening a risk, he mastered it.

Over the years, Gene has repeated this process countless times. After figuring out the best way to grow organic crops, he had to get them to market while still at the peak of freshness. (Flash freezing became the answer—something mainstream food producers had used for years, but which organic growers had rejected as non-traditional while they watched their produce wither on the way to market.) Once he'd jumped that hurdle, he was challenged to get organics accepted into mainstream supermarkets. Then the hurdle became producing volume; later it became offering enough variety to win shelf space.

On and on it went. And on and on it goes perpetually. Gene kept seeing these hurdles as more detailed lessons he needed to learn to reach his goals, not as risks or reasons to give up. Time and again, he found ways to mitigate risk on the way to his fulfilling his vision.

You can be sure that people whispered behind Gene's back (if they didn't laugh to his face) because they believed the risks he was taking would break him. But Cascadian Farms has not only become a success in its own right; it has also opened the doors to having shelf upon shelf of organic foods in our supermarkets today.

Skepticism and accusations of risk taking don't end for those with big visions and no choice. Not too long ago, Gene sold the family of companies he'd created or acquired (Small Planet Foods) including Cascadian Farms to General Mills, a large mainstream food producer of such brands as Cheerios, Betty Crocker, and Green Giant. More than one of his admirers called him a traitor.

But for Gene, the move wasn't about abandoning the plan; it was part of the plan. Rather than selling to the outsider (what some viewed as the enemy), Gene was becoming an insider. He was seeking change on a larger scale, not by throwing stones but by infiltrating.

Ultimately, Gene's vision was never only about Cascadian Farms. It was about bettering the planet and man's interaction with it. By now working with a well-accepted mainstream leader in his industry, Gene is methodically moving all of us—every eater of Cheerios or peas—to one day conclude that we have "no choice" but to better the planet and our interaction with it.

## *One Last Look at a Fading Mythology*

Think back to the Flipper Syndrome. There is a randomness to the choices dolphins make about what to push. The important fact—for them and for us—is that dolphins *like* to push things. Their ability to push people doesn't mean dolphins have a penchant for saving those lost at sea. They aren't conscious or reliable heroes.

Just like we shouldn't count on dolphins for rescue, we shouldn't rely on myths to tell us the truth about entrepreneurs or their relative role in entrepreneurship. We may have a Horatio Alger desire to want every entrepreneur to be a hero and every entrepreneurial venture to go from rags to riches. It makes a good story to call someone a swashbuckling risk taker acting alone, with nothing but personality and a run of good luck to deliver freedom, wealth, and success. But believing what we want to believe rather than searching out the truth leaves us adrift with nothing but a poor understanding—of entrepreneurship or anything else.

## Recommended Resources

### *On Bullshit* – Harry Frankfurt

Plain, short, and bluntly stated, Frankfurt cuts through the crap (so to speak). This provides an entertaining look at the fine edge between hard truth and what we often embrace as reality. While comparing lying versus fibbing versus absolute BS, Frankfurt gives us a wonderful model for examining many gray areas of everyday living—and many blurred meanings we often hide or take comfort in.

### *Lucky or Smart?* – Bo Peabody

Bo Peabody has been labeled an entrepreneur and has experienced what so many entrepreneurs do—moments of both success and failure. But was his success due to luck, as onlookers often told him? No. But rather than dismiss luck altogether, he wrote this short, blunt book about the topic and argues luck's role (or lack thereof) in any venture.

### *The Luck Factor* – Dr. Richard Wiseman

Where Peabody discussed luck through the lens of his own experiences, Wiseman does a full accounting of luck, sharing his more than two decades of research on the topic. If you want facts to back up or challenge your views on luck, Wiseman offers an insightful and entertaining base.

### *The Arctic Grail* – Pierre Berton

I've never encountered such a comprehensive and dispassionate look at Arctic exploration highlighting the turn-of-the-19th-century hunger to reach the North Pole and find a Northwest Passage. While Berton's book is fascinating for this reason alone, it reveals the truth about human nature when we are challenged beyond our perceived limits. It also delves deeply into the difference between vision and reality. And it compares and contrasts those who dream with those who deliver, citing the often-shaky baton pass between dream and reality.

# Contributors to Chapter 3

**Mike McCaffery** (See Chapter 2)

**Patrick Von Bargen**
 CEO, Center for Venture Education for the Kauffman Foundation
 Founder, Executive Director, National Commission on Entrepreneurship

**P.V. Boccasam**
 Founder, President, and CEO, Approva
 Co-founder, T.I.E. (The Indus Entrepreneurs or The Innovative Ecosystems)
 Formerly with Microsoft

**Spencer Beebe** (See Chapter 1)

**Mario Morino**
 Chairman, Venture Philanthropy Partners
 Founder, Legent Technologies and Netpreneur

**Gene Foley** (See Chapter 2)

**Wayne Silby**
 Founder, Calvert Funds
 Co-founder, Social Venture Network

**Robin Chase** (See Chapter 1)

**Jeffrey Hollender** (See Chapter 1)

**Bill Shore**
 Founder, Share Our Strength and Community Wealth Ventures
 Author, *The Cathedral Within*, *The Light of Conscience,* and *Revolution of the Heart*
 Director, Timberland

**Ed Robinson**
 Founder, President, Capacity Building Solutions
 Former Chairman, Community Wealth Ventures

**Doug Davidoff**
 Founder, Imagine Companies
 Co-author, *Parenting the Office*

**Stephen O'Connor**
Founder, CEO, Group Publisher, New World Publishing
**Laurence Gonzales** (See Chapter 2)
**Ed Feeney**
Feeney & Associates
Career Achievement Award, Applied Behavioral Sciences
**Betsy Friedlander**
Principal, Willmott & Associates
Author, *How to Land Job Offers: The Art of Generating Job Opportunities*
**Caren DeWitt Merrick**
Co-founder, Vice President Marketing, webMethods
Partner, Bibury Partners investment and advisory fund
Former Director, AOL
**Ken Ramberg**
Founder, JobTrak, GoodSearch
Board of Governors, Cedars-Sinai Hospital
**Jed Emerson**
Co-founder, Blended Value
Co-author, *Enterprising Nonprofits* and *Strategic Tools for Social Entrepreneurs*
Author, *New Social Entrepreneurs*
**Dan Pink** (See Chapter 1)
**Bill Drayton**
Founder, Ashoka
Named to *U.S. News & World Report's* list of America's 25 Best Leaders, 2005
Former Consultant, McKinsey & Company
**Harry Weller**
Partner, New Enterprise Associates

# Chapter 3: The Entrepreneur
# as Change Catalyst

*"It is a very rare combination to see the future and make the future happen with an ability to communicate it in a way that gets others to sign up."*

- Mike McCaffery
Former President
Robertson, Stephens & Company

"Progress is built on the actions of entrepreneurs in the economic, social, and political spheres," said Patrick Von Bargen, CEO of the Center for Venture Education for the Kauffman Foundation. In his view, all things begin with entrepreneurs. "They are the ones who drive the change that becomes the key to success in anything." It's not that entrepreneurs possess every skill or capability required for progress to take place, but without a doubt, they ignite it.

Recall our definition that establishes a cornerstone of being an entrepreneur as "committing oneself to catalyzing significant change in the way people think and act." Entrepreneurs engage in this commitment to a degree most people would not. They possess a willingness and obligation to see their vision through—no matter what it takes—in order for the world to progress, evolve, and even survive.

Uniquely, entrepreneurs believe that they alone must take that first step toward change in their universe. In the end, it's this *change catalyst* role that distinguishes entrepreneurs from others. It defines them and their interactions with people, and sets up opportunities for us to live up to our collective human potential.

Exactly what distinguishes entrepreneurial change catalysts from others? The patterns I've observed across entrepreneurs have led me to pinpoint these five elements: *pattern recognition, action, activation of others, value creation and transfer,* and *drive.* Let's examine each of these in depth.

**Defining the Entrepreneur**
Figure 1

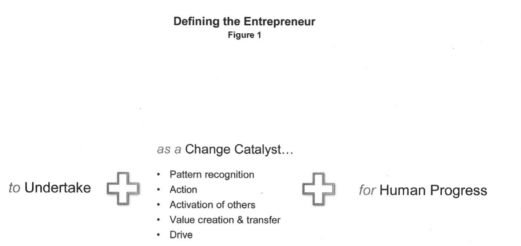

as a **Change Catalyst...**

*to* Undertake

- Pattern recognition
- Action
- Activation of others
- Value creation & transfer
- Drive

*for* **Human Progress**

## The 1st Change Element: Pattern Recognition

Although we tend to focus on the *ideas* that entrepreneurs come up with, it's their ability to recognize *patterns* that's far more important to what they ultimately achieve.

If nothing else is certain, we know this: entrepreneurs' ideas are big, bold, and new. Through their ideas, they aim to take us in new directions, shape new ways of thinking, and alter what's commonly known and accepted.

But as much as we'd like to fantasize otherwise, such ideas do not simply emerge out of nowhere. Instead, they're anchored in something the entrepreneur knows well. Lots of us understand things *well*. But entrepreneurs come to understand those very same things *differently*. Theirs is a recognition of the *possible*; ours is an understanding of the *known*. The way entrepreneurs see the world—at least that portion of the world on which they fix their gaze—stands in stark contrast to knowledge and understanding that is *common*. The entrepreneur shows us a new view.

There are no lines to box in their view and constrain it to one particular vantage point. For them, the world is constantly open to reexamination, reorganization, and improvement. As a result, they are able to see patterns that aren't obvious to the rest of us. Most people think of this as thinking outside the box; entrepreneurs regard it as a holistic sense of reality. "It's [not that] entrepreneurs are idealists," pointed out P.V. Boccasam. "They are very much realists—it's just a reality beyond our reality today." *This pattern recognition—this sense of a larger reality yet to be made real—is where unique ideas begin.*

## An Ability Born of Time and Exposure

To get a different sense of where ideas come from and how they link to one's ability to detect patterns, step outside the boundaries of contemporary conversations and consider the American Revolution.

Most Americans are taught a version of the birth of the United States that leaves us to conclude—far too easily—that it happened quickly, almost immaculately. But the choice made by thirteen distinct colonies to break away from the mother country certainly wasn't spontaneous. We mark the American Revolution as spanning the brief period from 1775 to 1783. In that short eight years, the colonies came together—without having established a means of founding, governing, or defending a new country—to take on the world's most powerful empire at the time. This hardly seems like something that could have occurred overnight—and, in fact, it didn't.

More than a century and a half separated the signing of the Declaration of Independence in 1776 from the country's earliest beginnings in 1607. For five to seven generations, decades of experience, observation, and thinking took place that shaped the way a handful of visionaries came to view their world in the years leading up to revolution. During that frequently forgotten time in history, tensions steadily built between England and her offspring. From governance to commerce to simply how they viewed the world, more and more colonists formed different views. While an increasing number felt like England's indentured servants, most colonists remained fiercely loyal to their motherland, even five generations after their ancestors journeyed to the new world. Why? Because it was what they knew. The boundaries of the box the colonists lived in made them heavily reliant on England for goods, for protection, and for leadership. Recognizing their dependencies and concluding they were tethered to the country of their ancestors, colonial leaders defaulted to working with the rulers from afar to address their grievances for 169 years. Their decision to break with England was neither easy nor impulsive.

But for some in late 18th century colonial America, the new patterns they saw emerging were simply too strong to ignore.

For one, the colonies' dependence on England for goods and commerce was not total. They traded actively—and quite profitably—with other European and Caribbean countries. And while, in practice, most still looked to England for its blessing in ruling their own colonies, the reality was different. From as far back as the first surviving colonial outpost at Jamestown, the colonists had been making their own laws. When these and other emerging patterns were recognized, an overwhelming belief that things *could* and *must* be better overtook a bold few. The lid of their box flew open and its sides fell away as they asked new questions.

Why be beholden to a king who knew nothing of their world and clearly did not have their best interests in mind?

If they could build viable communities and commerce out of veritable wilderness, what would keep them from undertaking all other tasks that any independent nation would assume?

Although the colonies had long been considered separate from each other, could they not band together to throw off the past and walk forward into a better future?

Opinions among them differed; many could not bring themselves to envision a life beyond the one they knew as English colonists. But at least 56 colonial leaders (the signers of the Declaration of Independence) resolved to create a better way. They willingly bet their lives to pursue the opportunities they saw "outside the box."

From those leaders who recognized new patterns of opportunity emerged the United States of America.

## Evolution Precedes Revolution

Beyond being outside-the-box thinkers, entrepreneurs catalyze change, often of seismic proportion. They shake up the thoughts and actions of those in the world around them. And they do it in a revolutionary way—or so it may seem.

In truth, *evolution* precedes *revolution*. Popularly, we think of revolution as sudden and momentous change in a situation. But we also think of it as total and complete change. The latter is the kind of revolution that gets attention because it sticks, not because it disrupts. A revolution that sticks has a long fuse.

Entrepreneurial actions to disrupt the status quo are far from knee-jerk ones. By the time the opening bell sounds and they leave the gates in pursuit of their vision, they've grown deeply knowledgeable and determined that *something more* is both possible and necessary. They know why, and they know where and how it can occur. As they build this deeper, more expansive knowledge base, they become resolved, convinced, committed, and therefore quite bold—characteristics that can make them appear to be disruptive revolutionists in the sudden, momentous way. But without question, they're evolving. The change they seek is total and complete.

Perhaps we shouldn't be so surprised when entrepreneurs incite revolutionary thinking and change. In a sense, entrepreneurial thoughts and actions are naturally human, based on natural human evolution.

Entrepreneurial thinkers from all ages sense this: they know that first *seeing* change and then *seeking* change isn't an impulsive exercise, but a necessary human one. As colonist Thomas Paine wrote in his famed pamphlet *Common Sense* at the height of the American Revolution, "... the cause of America is, in great measure, the cause of all mankind. Many circumstances have, and will arise, which are not local, but universal, and through which the principles of all lovers of mankind are affected."[8]

## Boundaries Made of Chalk

Entrepreneurial ideas go beyond fresh, abstract thinking and observation within the known world. "Entrepreneurial thinking is distinct less because it's thinking outside the box than it is because those who think that way don't know there *is* a box," said Ecotrust founder, Spencer Beebe. Various worlds mix and merge for entrepreneurs who barely heed existing boundaries. They don't only see unrecognized patterns in their own world; they also see patterns *across* worlds.

Consider the colonists' choice to stand united in their vision after previous generations had been anchored in thirteen different worlds. Each colony was separated geographically by boundaries. Connections outside their world were often stronger to the Motherland than among the colonies themselves. It's easy to see, for example, that Pennsylvania's colonial roots in William Penn's vision of broad religious tolerance and self-rule would have been quite different from the plantation-anchored structure with tight commercial ties to England established by Thomas Jefferson's ancestors in Virginia. Despite living in different worlds, by the late 18th century colonial leaders recognized opportunities for *something more* to be gained by tempering the lines between their worlds and changing the patterns within them. Hard boundaries that had existed for decades became more like the chalk lines on a baseball field—thin, impermanent, malleable.

"Entrepreneurs don't follow a particular line," Spencer pointed out. Instead, they take deliberate pauses, ignoring accepted constraints and searching for untapped opportunities. Doing so naturally and continually refines their ability to recognize patterns. "If I look for more, I see more" is their modus operandi.

Their refinement is constant; chalk lines are drawn, smeared or erased, redrawn elsewhere an infinite number of times. And the motivation to do so gets reinforced naturally. As entrepreneurs recognize more patterns, they delve deep to find expanding forms of value they can mine from those patterns.

## Compelled to Create New Patterns

Entrepreneurs don't only *see* differently than most people; they also *feel* differently about what they must do and why they must do it. Mario Morino, founder of Legent Technologies and chairman of the social venture fund Venture Philanthropy Partners, put it this way: "Pure entrepreneurs see things that others believe are illogical or irrational. And then they are obsessively compelled to achieve them. They must be this way to survive."

As Mario's statement implies, if entrepreneurs heeded established boundaries or even tried to justify them, they would never recognize new ways of doing things. Or if they did see them but didn't have the commitment to propel them, they might stop short of taking action to realize them.

Remember, entrepreneurs genuinely believe they see the world uniquely, that they're meant to impart their vision to the world to make it better. (Recall Gene Foley's statement in Chapter 2: "Entrepreneurs genuinely believe and think that humanity is waiting for them.") They know in their hearts they must make that change happen, especially if no one else is stepping up to the plate. Entrepreneurs are not just idea generators; they are change catalysts. They expect the world to change and are unwilling to wait for that change to happen *someday*. Calvert Funds founder, Wayne Silby, echoed this viewpoint. "Reasonable people adapt to the world. Unreasonable people expect the world to adapt to them. Hence all change and advancement in the world depends on unreasonable people."

When entrepreneurs first describe the patterns and resulting opportunities they envision for the future, others commonly judge them to be unreasonable. (That is stating kindly how initial reactions to their visions are often received.) Of course, it's natural to push against an idea that disrupts the known or feels strange, especially if its rewards are unproven and attaining them requires unreasonable effort. Most "visionaries" turn back after receiving such reactions. But as irrational or obsessive as they might appear, true entrepreneurs are compelled to follow the unlikely direction they see.

"Kites rise against—not with—the wind," 19th-century Nova Scotian shipbuilder, revolutionary, and politician William Lawrence once said. That's the way change catalysts operate. And the "no choice" factor discussed in Chapter 2 prevails.

## Chase—On to Realizing a Larger Vision

It's not the product nor the Zipcar company that matters most to its founder, Robin Chase; it's taking the first step toward broader changes that excites her. In fact, Robin left Zipcar in the capable hands of other leaders and her evangelical customers to carry that particular vehicle forward (no pun intended). She noted, "My willingness to engage in things beyond just what I'm good at—and even beyond what is known—has led to revolutionary and improbable ideas. Others didn't see what I saw because they are stuck in whatever they do or have or know. They don't see beyond their self-imposed boundaries."

Robin has moved on to realizing a larger vision as she takes on the auto and telecommunications industries and even government regulation through her ventures, GoLoco. org and Meadow Networks. These ventures seek to address transportation and climate change issues in a big way. Her new focus may seem like a huge leap forward, even away from Zipcar. But it's all part of the same vision. And it all results from her perpetually wondering if there's *more* and *better*.

Some people say unreasonable things about her latest initiatives. "They tell me, 'Robin, get off of it! It's never going to happen.' That's what they told me about Zipcar, too. But I once heard someone say that you have to take a stand, whatever happens. Taking on the improbable nature of something is a place I'm willing to go." Perhaps that's one reason *Time* magazine named Robin one of the *100 World's Most Influential People* in 2009.

Seeing the world the way entrepreneurs do and being awake to the patterns they sense doesn't come easy for most people. "We are such creatures of habit and set patterns that so much of today is what we've already lived yesterday," noted Seventh Generation's president and—as he likes to say—chief inspired protagonist, Jeffrey Hollender. But entrepreneurs so strongly feel the need to follow the patterns they see that pursuing them seems relatively easy.

No doubt such feelings drove Jeffrey from *seeing a need* for changing the way humans relate to their natural environment to *putting into action* what he calls his Precautionary Principle by starting Seventh Generation. This principle hinges on erring on the side of caution when it comes to actions that could affect our environment. Seventh Generation shows the way by providing alternatives to unhealthy, conventional household products that make it easier for us to adopt the changes Jeffrey knows are essential.

"When you see something in your life that feels wrong," explained Jeffrey, "that experience becomes a call to action. Even if you don't know what to do, you've got to do *something*. For me, certain visceral experiences have shaped my life. After seeing or feeling them, I can't reconcile *not* being involved and trying to shape things. Those who can see clearly have the most responsibility to do something with those insights."

### The 2ⁿᵈ Change Element: Action

Most people who get an idea or see an opportunity generally don't pursue it. Sure, they may act to refine it or share it with others, but most ideas end right there. Those few who proceed usually give up at the first signs of resistance or when they realize it requires sacrifice and inconvenience.

Entrepreneurs stand apart from that. They have every intention of delivering on their ideas. Their actions take the form of relentless pursuits driven by a willingness to do whatever is necessary to deliver. "The entrepreneur is a jaywalker," quipped Share Our Strength founder, Bill Shore. "He doesn't wait for the light to change. He goes his own way to get somewhere."

"Entrepreneurs are problem solvers, not just problem identifiers," said Ed Robinson, president and founder of Capacity Building Solutions and former chairman of Community Wealth Ventures. "Many people like to *plug into* a solution; entrepreneurs like to *create* the solution." They fully expect that, in taking time to first formulate and then pursue their ideas, the solutions will be theirs to develop. Taking a deliberate pause to formulate those solutions is key to the kind of fresh thinking that happens.

Again, this sense of having "no choice" about taking their ideas to fruition is a motivating force. For true entrepreneurs, turning back, stopping, or quitting is never an option.

## Starts with Disruption; Moves to Deconstruction

The combination of perspective (pattern recognition) and tenacity (action) contribute greatly to the entrepreneur's unique capacity to seed change. As noted earlier, that ability doesn't come without repercussion. Their actions often have a disruptive effect, even if their ultimate aim isn't focused on disruption but on deconstruction—turning *what is* into *what could be*.

"Entrepreneurship is a creative act. And a creative act is, by definition, disruptive," pointed out Doug Davidoff, founder of the Imagine Companies. "To get somewhere new, you have to alter, change, or even destroy what was. You do it and go through the inevitable pain because you feel others are missing something."

This describes the "catch" in the kind of action entrepreneurs take—one that many who contemplate walking an entrepreneurial path fail to calculate. In the period during which "new" is being introduced but "old" still holds sway, those whom entrepreneurs reach out to may have difficulty grasping both kinds of thoughts in their minds simultaneously. It's also hard for them to simultaneously play out both old and new patterns in their lives. Indeed, the people entrepreneurs want to influence aren't the only ones challenged by change. Most entrepreneurs themselves fail to anticipate the extent of the deconstruction, building, and rebuilding required. Often, between their great ideas and great outcomes comes great pain.

Disruptive actions also spark resistance. People may like new things once they prove beneficial, but they rarely enjoy or passively allow the known to be dismantled. Pressing through such resistance requires sheer tenacity, as the story about Stephen O'Connor reveals.

## "Getting Your Head Shot Off"—O'Connor

"You have to believe in sticking your head out… and risk getting it shot off. Then you have to stick it out again and keep going, no matter what," declared innovative publisher Stephen O'Connor.

Stephen has certainly experienced the resistance that can come with being a catalyst of change. One of his earliest experiences happened in Eastern Europe immediately after the fall of the Berlin Wall in 1989. As founder, CEO, and group publisher of New World Publishing, Stephen set out to launch three business journals in the former Soviet cities of Warsaw, Budapest, and Prague.

Stephen's prospective readers lived in a hardened, inflexible culture that had been oppressed for decades, even centuries, by social systems that were the antithesis of entrepreneurial thinking and free speech. The magnitude of change required to reshape the thinking and actions among those he sought to serve was far-reaching, almost inconceivable. After years of hiding and protecting their heads in the cultural safety of Soviet-influenced society, these people needed encouragement to stick out their own necks and follow his lead.

Stephen walked into that uncertain terrain a stranger in a strange land. Most would have called his publishing plans risky, from both a safety and success standpoint. But he knew that by establishing these business journals, he was paving a new road toward entrepreneurship, capitalism, and free markets.

While former president Mikhail Gorbachev of Russia may have theoretically approved new freedoms, Stephen was clearly testing them. In his editorials, he criticized the government for its policies constraining the free markets; in open discussions that were facilitated in his journals, readers were encouraged and guided to start businesses that would create personal wealth and break free from the old system. As a result, he and his staff members fielded objections and threats, subtle and veiled, direct and indirect. Yet he persevered to establish viable publications.

Sticking out one's neck first is often the only way for change catalysts to convince others to shift their mindsets—and the only way to shape new patterns and opportunities.

Indeed, it's that survival factor all over again—the "transformation, an attitude of commitment, not resignation" that Laurence Gonzales wrote about in his book *Deep Survival.*[9]

In taking this first action, we see the "no-choice" factor in entrepreneurship emerge yet again—that is, having no choice except to realize the change you see, to take action and to spur others to act, too. As crazy as it may sound, the true entrepreneur believes in his heart that the very survival and advancement of the species depends on it.

Clearly, many factors and supporters come into play before an entrepreneur's dream can be fully realized. But being the first to act proves that entrepreneurial ideas aren't just talk. Indeed, catalyzing the actions of *many* requires someone (often some *one*) to step forward first.

Put plainly, without action, there is no catalyst, only concept. Thoughts of resignation, turning back, or never starting simply don't occur to true change catalysts. As Ed Feeney, a pioneer in applying behavioral science to business productivity, said, "Entrepreneurs are distinct *because* they act. End of interview."

## The 3rd Change Element: Activation of Others

While entrepreneurs must be able and willing to act alone, it's their ability to involve others that separates them from would-be entrepreneurs. Successful entrepreneurship is ultimately a collective act. Of course, the individual entrepreneur's involvement must be deep, full, and personal, characterized by a wholehearted belief in the venture. But to bring that dream into reality, an entrepreneur must appeal to and engage others who also fully support the effort and indeed call it their own.

Entrepreneurs don't simply seek members to join a team. Although their ventures may employ people, attracting employees isn't enough. And although they want others to benefit from the value offered, if those they attracted aren't engaged in the vision as well as the venture, then success will be limited or short-lived. After all, a successful venture isn't built on a job posting like this: "Founder needs others to come in and do jobs he simply can't do alone; founder will pay said people to do jobs that in turn make founder a success." Entrepreneurs need those who join them to bring more than assets for growth, advice, and support. They need others to buy into the dream, become a part of it, and adopt it as their own. This is *activating* rather than *employing*; it's engaging others in shaping a vision rather than simply attracting them to the task of the moment.

It would be a mistake to interpret the intent to attract others solely as the entrepreneurs' effort to gain support for themselves and their personal agendas. This is not to say that—like all human beings—entrepreneurs don't have their own agendas or a desire to succeed. But smart change catalysts—those who seek every possible way to mitigate the risks to their success—want others to help shape and interpret the dream—add to it, build onto and off of it, use it as a seed for other dreams. In this way, they *activate* others to partner in a commitment that leads to profound change.

Betsy Friedlander, principal of the HR firm Willmott & Associates, reflected on her numerous entrepreneurial ventures this way: "I didn't always know exactly what I was doing, but I was determined, persistent, excited, and had a vision. I took what I had and jumped in." In that sense, personal passion drove her. "But," Betsy quickly added, "I always turned what I believed in 'outward' to others, being open, sincere, compelling, insightful, and making a connection to what was important to *them*."

Entrepreneurship stops being about one person almost from the first action taken toward realizing that entrepreneurial vision. Said Caren DeWitt Merrick, co-founder of webMethods, "The hardest thing is to get entrepreneurs to know when they need to make room for others. That's harder than convincing people that what you're doing has value or is just right."

Caren emphasized the importance of connecting to others as a result of her own entrepreneurial ventures, some successful and others less so. As her story (see *Making Web Technology Usable: The Aspen Effect in Action*) indicates, she certainly endorses the need to cultivate what I call the Aspen Effect.

## The Aspen Effect: Many Out of One

The white-barked, quaking-leafed "trees" named aspens are actually not individual trees at all. The stands we see of beautiful trees are an illusion. What appears to be many is actually one organism, derived from a single seedling and connected by an intricate web of roots beneath the forest or meadow floor. Compared with an oak tree that occupies its own relatively small circle of space, a single aspen stand can fill acres of space.

Entrepreneurship is like that aspen stand. What begins as one *must* become many; it *must* spread far and wide to survive. The many function as one, moving together toward a common vision, supporting one another's efforts.

Effective change catalysts must make sure this Aspen Effect occurs if they want their visions to flourish. Think of it this way: the odds are heavily stacked against one lone branch in the middle of a high alpine meadow surviving, let alone thriving. *What begins as one must become many.*

### Making Web Technology Usable: The Aspen Effect in Action

Around the time Caren DeWitt met and married her husband Phillip Merrick, she saw coming to life the very thing that attracted her to him in the first place.

Phillip is a visionary. He sees patterns and opportunities that others don't. Often his visions are so big, so new, and so revolutionary that they're hard for others to recognize, at least at first. Let me explain.

In the early days of the Internet, everyone seemed to run around willy-nilly trying to grasp the nature of its power and figure out how to generate value from it. Phillip took a different path. Instead of jumping blindly into this emerging opportunity, he stepped back and wondered *why* people were having trouble tapping into the Internet's power. How could he help those hoping to leverage this wonder and use it effectively to meet their goals?

His questions evolved into creating webMethods, one of the first businesses to integrate Internet tools with the people and organizations who wanted to use them to advance their own dreams. webMethods has proven to be one of the most successful Internet ventures of the last century, and remains a leader in shaping how people use the Internet today.

From a technological viewpoint, though, Phillip's vision was powerful but limiting. Most of the people and businesses webMethods wanted to help either weren't technically oriented or were totally new to its workings. Because the technology that fueled Phillip's vision was tough to learn, it was also tough for prospective users to appreciate its value.

That's where Caren came in.

Caren knew how to toggle seamlessly between the vision of a world yet unrealized and the reality of what needed to happen to get there. (This skill is discussed in Chapter 4.) From webMethods' beginning, she could discern both the value and return on investment that it could eventually provide. And she realized that, despite its potential, a disconnect with target customers couldn't be ignored. In fact, their investors and partners were also struggling to understand the value of what they perceived as a technical tool.

Caren changed their perceptions by telling compelling stories about the "business advantage" webMethods offered. She showed how its tools could help webMethods customers do what they were already doing only *better*. Suddenly, the technology concern fell into the background. In a way, from the customer perspective, it wasn't about technology anymore; it was about advancing their businesses. All clients really needed to know was how webMethods could revolutionize their ability to capture and win over their customers, not how the technology was designed to make that happen. Without Caren's ability to articulate its benefits, webMethods would arguably never have enjoyed its more than $1 billion in sales to date.

From Phillip's seed idea, the original tree grew and, through the Aspen Effect, spread to Caren and beyond. Her talents allowed the company to reach thousands of others who, in turn, used it not only to spread the webMethods vision, but also to fuel their own visions and dreams. Caren described the phenomenon of the Aspen Effect as "a journey you have to keep recalibrating in every season of your life and business. Seeing broader and letting go become critical skills. They allow you to do more, change the way things are, have balance, and be different." The result? What an entrepreneur catalyzes evolves into entrepreneurship. The change envisioned by one becomes real and lasting for many.

These days, Caren and Phillip advise entrepreneurs in their ventures as consultants. Said Caren, "One of our challenges is getting them to see the range of people needed to succeed and how pivotal doing so is. It's absolutely a matter of community— and community lasts." So do the entrepreneurial dreams that are firmly built on community.

Moving mountains requires embracing a dream as if it's your own. Yes, one person can have an impact on the world, but it takes many to create lasting change. It's engaging others in the vision that achieves the exceptional results associated with entrepreneurship. Spreading ownership of the dream becomes the entrepreneur's heartfelt reward.

For true entrepreneurs, the journey isn't about them. It isn't about *their* creation, *their* return, or even the achievements of *their* own lifetime and by *their* own hands. It's about activating their vision in the minds of many others.

### The 4th Change Element: Value Creation and Transfer

What do entrepreneurs recognize in patterns? What is the output they seek from their actions? What enables them to draw others into their entrepreneurial dream?

A single word answers all of these questions: *value.*

Value measures the uniqueness and relevance of what the

entrepreneur envisions; it's the driver for anyone committed to pursuing an entrepreneurial dream. Value—and the potential for expanding value—is also what allows the entrepreneurial dream to pass from hand-to-hand, venture-to-venture, and even dream-to-dream. So the entrepreneur's ability to stand back and first recognize it, then create it, and eventually pass it on is critical. Without value, the idea can never be realized.

Many people think of the entrepreneur as the single source of value in entrepreneurship. In reality, value is shaped by many contributors in a cumulative process, as Ken Ramberg (see the story *GoodSearch Makes Value Viable for Masses*) discovered. That requires entrepreneurs to clear several hurdles. The most obvious is recognizing value. But they must be able to create value too, something that is hard if not impossible to do alone—at least for any sustained amount of time. That value must resonate with others, for if it's only appreciated or accessible by the entrepreneur, it's one tiny notch above valueless. If, on the other hand, it is value that's recognized, prized, and shared, then its upside is enormous.

This is the first stage of a change catalyst's mission being transferred to others who will embrace it. When entrepreneurs inspire and instill in others the *capacity to create value themselves*, then they're on their way to catalyzing meaningful change. The ripple a change catalyst creates fans out into many ripples, which together form a wave. As the capacity to create and transfer value ripples out more, the wave's potential turns into a tsunami of change for the betterment of the world.

## GoodSearch Makes Value Viable for Masses

Ken Ramberg learned about the critical nature of first creating value and then transferring it in his first venture, JobTrak. Long before Monster, CareerBuilder, and other job listing and matching sites—even before prevalence of the Internet—JobTrak was serving millions of customers.

Today, it's easy to contemplate creating virtual communities unencumbered by geography. Back then, however, it was inconceivable for most people to imagine what JobTrak set out to do. But Ken never dwelled on hurdles that have blinded and discouraged others. Instead, he zeroed in on the value he could create, viewing the hurdles as a toll on the road to making his vision real.

Built tirelessly over 14 years, JobTrak connected college graduates with employers across a broad network that eventually included over 2,000 campuses. Before JobTrak, each student seeking employers was limited to the resources his or her college campus offered; recruiters seeking students were limited by the number of campuses they could get to one at a time. By merging the needs of college career centers, students, and recruiters regardless of geography, Ken and JobTrak gave all of them the chance to meet each other's needs better and create greater collective value than any one could summon alone.

In 2006, a few years after Monster bought JobTrak to springboard its own business off of Ken's entrepreneurial idea, Ken and his partner, J.J. Ramberg, founded GoodSearch. "I didn't plan to start another company after JobTrak," explained Ken, "but when I came up with the idea for GoodSearch, it was so compelling, I had to do it."

Recalling the genesis of this idea, Ken noted, "I read a study that said search engines were generating close to $6 billion in revenue. I kept thinking, 'What if even a fraction of that money could be directed toward good causes?' That's what I like so much about the Internet. We can have millions of people from all walks of life helping each other and serving more than one agenda."

On the surface, the concept is simple: the company provides a search engine that customers use to search the web as they would with any other search engine. There's no charge to users and the format of the search is much like Yahoo or Google, services familiar to those GoodSearch seeks to attract. But here's the subtle yet powerful difference. Every time someone searches using the GoodSearch engine, the company donates money to a charitable cause or nonprofit organization, either of the user's choice or one GoodSearch happily selects.

"With this service, you don't have to change your habits in any way and you don't have to buy anything," Ken pointed out. Remarkably, within the boundaries of people's established habits, Ken and J.J. have set up a powerful way to shift mindsets and extend value further than ever imagined. It's like JobTrak's value taken to the next level: people seeking out information, seeking out each other, and in the process generating exponential value for all.

Using Ken's experience with GoodSearch as an example, here's how the value transfer can work:

Ken and J.J. create GoodSearch, a for-profit search engine that both drives and is driven by people's desire to support causes and charities. Search engine users discover and use it. It creates so much value beyond fulfilling search needs that they tell their friends. They also tell people in the nonprofit organizations they support that GoodSearch provides an added source of donations for them. The bonus? It requires no more effort than just signing up.

From there, these friends and organizations spread the word about using GoodSearch. Other organizations, both for-profit and nonprofit, recognize the highly tangible merit of this model, so they formally team up with GoodSearch, expanding their own programs that help charitable causes, schools, and mission-driven organizations. This in turn broadens GoodSearch's exposure. Over time, other search engines and additional service organizations follow GoodSearch's lead (as they already are); they're finding ways to give away a portion of what they take in and help fuel other visions.

Suddenly, charitable giving touches every business's mindset and every customer's criteria for deciding with whom to shop. The spiraling value becomes incalculable, the cycle endless—from one to many, with value created, redefined, and expanded at every turn.

When Ken described the "ideal endpoint" for GoodSearch, he characterized three things that will ultimately create and transfer value. "First, I want GoodSearch to donate, year in and year out, a large amount of money to nonprofits. Second, as people use the site, I want them to see that they're helping good causes, and that doing so should and can be part of their daily routine. And third, I want to expose people to organizations and causes they were never in contact with before."

When all is said and done, these goals aren't about Ken, or J.J., or even GoodSearch. They address the good of everyone. GoodSearch strives to bring value to all people it touches. They in turn touch others with their own ideas and actions. Although the GoodSearch service may appear simple, its vision is complex and far-reaching because it's changing values, thinking, and even habits—with minimal effort on the part of those it benefits. Value created, value transferred.

## The 5ᵗʰ Change Element: Drive

It's impossible to overstate the enormity of what the entrepreneur undertakes. As you think about any one of the preceding four change elements, you can sense that this is no ordinary journey spurred on by common motivations. Go further to consider these change elements and the demands they require *in combination*, and you might just begin to imagine the magnitude of the drive behind an entrepreneurial undertaking and the change catalyst who starts it all. After all, the pursuit of any vision doesn't come with a handy road map. Even while applying the insights they generated after pausing to observe and analyze, entrepreneurs are constantly redefining the path.

Now imagine what it takes to convince others to come along with you on odysseys like those taken by Caren and Phillip Merrick, or by Ken and J.J. Ramberg. Reflect on the quests undertaken by Stephen O'Connor and Muhammad Yunus to change cultures, classes, and systems. Next, contemplate the need to act as a cheerleader, projecting hope and providing momentum when the path gets rocky. Consider the sacrifice needed to produce any results at all—let alone to generate enough value to compel others to change their habits, values, thinking, and actions.

It's difficult to hold all of these images in your head at once, let alone conceive of what could continue to propel a change catalyst forward with no promise of outcome, timing, or reward. But attempting to do so brings you closer to understanding the exceptional drive entrepreneurs possess—and why it's perhaps the most important element distinguishing the entrepreneurial change catalyst.

"Others would have looked at the things that happened to us along the way and given up," said Ken Ramberg describing the journey he and his team took over 15 years to create JobTrak. "Most would have looked at the obvious obstacles and considered them too difficult to overcome, too costly, and just thrown in the towel. We just couldn't and didn't."

This comment could have come from any true entrepreneur describing an entrepreneurial dream that changed the world in a positive way.

## Again, They Believe They Have No Choice

Entrepreneurs can't and don't give up because they sincerely believe they have no choice—the factor discussed in Chapter 2 that's at the heart of their motivation. It represents more than a willingness to work hard; it goes beyond tenacity and stubbornness. In essence, it's a visceral sense that the world needs a particular solution and the entrepreneur is the only logical one to catalyze it.

As the entrepreneur sees it, the world *must* change, therefore any hurdles to be jumped are necessary and their inconveniences irrelevant. When others stop because these hurdles seem too high or illogical, entrepreneurs press on. "They carry a vision of what could be but not necessarily an exact answer, and the best have a strong drive to operationalize the idea, too," explained Jed Emerson, co-founder of Blended Value and author of *Enterprising Nonprofits: A Toolkit for Social Entrepreneurs.*

Jed's story (see *Drive and Reflection Lead to Unending Paths of Value*) provides an excellent example of how the "no choice" factor drives these catalysts for change.

## Drive and Reflection Lead to Unending Paths of Value

Jed Emerson began his working life with the Presbyterian Church, but he quickly knew he wanted to, as he said, "take (his) learning outside the box."

In his work with the church at large, he rapidly moved beyond traditional duties to being instrumental in creating a consulting service for individual churches to help them understand what they were doing and how they could do it better. The value he gave allowed others to increase their own value contributions. This early work awakened in Jed what was to become a pattern of constant reflection—taking a deliberate pause and persistently asking this question: "This is good, but how can I create more value?"

In short order, the consulting service work led Jed to go out on his own and co-found Larkin Street, an organization striving to put a dent in poverty in the San Francisco Bay area. He challenged himself to deliver on what he had taught others.

By most people's yardsticks, Larkin Street went far above what most others were doing to combat poverty. But Jed's question persisted. "This is good, but how can I create more value?" He woke up one day and, amid all the good he was doing, concluded that he wasn't helping eliminate poverty as much as he was perpetuating the poverty industry. To most of his peers in that industry, it must have come across like an astounding, even preposterous, conclusion. But as Jed said, "It was a system in which we perpetually raised money and sold the cause with no link to whether or not what we did made a difference. We were good at it, but what good was it really doing?"

Most recently, under a newly founded organization called Blended Value, he's trying to crack the code on the many forms of value created by social ventures and is developing ways to measure and track them. Jed's journey won't end there. He carries a vision of *what could be* and has a strong, unfettered drive to see that vision materialize.

In many ways, it seems he has no choice but to follow his vision wherever it takes him. As he plants the seeds of value in his own way, he's expanding the aspen stand far beyond where he started.

First, helping the Presbyterian Church evolved into helping individual churches do better at doing good for others, which turned into more directly serving the needs of the poor at Larkin Street, which led to a determination to find a different and better way to approach poverty and the systems in place for fighting it, and so on. Such has been Jed's pattern. Every step in his journey reflects a pause to ask and answer once again—each time more fully—his core question. And with each pause, Jed creates value, he helps others do the same, and then he drives himself and his vision forward another step, and on to another pause. His pattern is to hone the vision, infuse others with it or use it to fuel other people's visions, create more value, pause, and repeat.

As Jed's experiences show, the entrepreneurial path to value need not take place solely within an organization of one's own creation. Nor does it have to happen within a single organization, or even in one at all. Jed's focus has been to make others stronger in their efforts to realize their own dreams, rather than to build and maintain a kingdom of his own. It's one of many ways that entrepreneurship can blossom, all of them pollinated by the drive to make a vision of how things could be better real. Form and control are secondary.

"Entrepreneurs do things without regard for the hurdles," acknowledged Jed. But bullheaded and unwavering as they may seem at times, entrepreneurs are not blind or reckless in their pursuits. Although they have what might seem to be an unbridled drive to catalyze change, for the best entrepreneurs—the ones who succeed in creating lasting change—the journey isn't fed by ego or greed. In every way, it's about making the world better—whether they do it directly or indirectly and whether they benefit materially or not.

## Combining the Five Change Elements

When viewed in combination, these five change elements further define the change catalyst. Sure, some innovators may display one or more of these characteristics from time to time. But few possess all of them, which is why fewer true entrepreneurs exist than the number labeled as entrepreneurs.

It's important to note that the presence of these elements doesn't automatically make an entrepreneur successful. Many other traits factor in. For example, the entrepreneur's ability to be comfortable outside the norm is important, yet others share this trait. Being somewhat risk averse is another supporting trait, but it's not exclusive to entrepreneurs either. Others might view the world similarly, seeing unique patterns and opportunities, but the majority fail to act on their views to the same degree entrepreneurs do. Their quest to create *something more*—something boldly new and better—also helps entrepreneurs stand out from the pack. But again, they aren't unique in this respect.

It's what entrepreneurs do with these traits *in combination* that enables them to find the balance they need and to maintain the perspective that serves humanity.

Just as strongly as these five elements combined affect how an idea comes to fruition, *not* being consciously aware of them can be one's undoing—a point that's made in our hypothetical cautionary tale (see *A Cautionary Tale About the Change Catalyst*).

## A Cautionary Tale About the Change Catalyst

There once was a technology visionary whom many, including the visionary himself, called an entrepreneur. (I have a particular one in mind, but I could easily substitute his face or name for countless others whose stories could be told in the same shocking way.)

At a glance, it was easy to assume this label to be accurately applied. After all, he was brilliant in his ability to see patterns in technology and commerce. He conceived of and even patented ideas for products that turned out to be more far-reaching than perhaps even he imagined they would be. Initially he attracted others to him—investors, business partners, even clients. He generated value, too. A number of clients bought his advice as a consultant, although they didn't go as far as buying his products. Still, he was off to a promising and not atypical start.

This young visionary clicked through one after another of the five elements of a change catalyst, or so it appeared. His ideas seemed boundless and so far ahead of others that it felt awkward to question his authenticity or his inherent ability to manifest his vision. But things aren't always as they appear. And the entrepreneurial path is long and bumpy.

In discussing entrepreneurs and their change-making capacity, Dan Pink made a great observation that foreshadows how this story ends. "Entrepreneurship isn't an act of genius so much as it's an act of being awake." As entrepreneurs become acutely conscious of the five change elements, these elements serve as a gauge not only for outsiders looking in but for the entrepreneurs themselves.

But our visionary didn't use the change catalyst elements this way, if he was even aware of them at all. Prophetically, his journey through them became the path to his demise. He was not, as Dan put it, awake to the role these elements played in his ability to change the world.

To be specific, while he was exceptional in seeing patterns in technology and commerce, he struggled to recognize patterns in relationships, teams, and organizations. True, he initially took action, securing patents and convincing others to join in, but only as long as it suited him. He exuded a laziness born of self-righteousness, expecting others to "get" his vision (and pay him for it). In the long run, he was unwilling to do the work necessary to mine the value in his vision, perhaps feeling above doing hard work himself. His limitations dealing with people undermined his ability to convert the seed of his idea into a thriving tree, let alone a full aspen stand. Consequently, in the absence of these abilities, he could catalyze no value. And when there's no value, any commitment attracted from others quickly wanes.

Over time, it became clear that his drive stemmed from his feelings of entitlement. His venture became all about him, not about improving the world around him. Today, his vision is on virtual life support because there's no engine, no fuel, no traveling companions, no map, and no way forward. This would-be entrepreneur stands alone with his big ideas.

**The 5 Elements of the Entrepreneurial Change Catalyst**
Figure 2

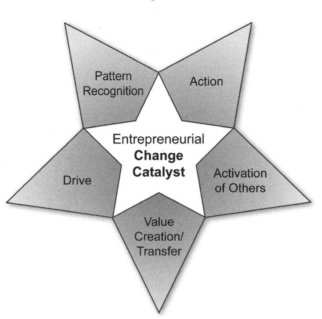

## *Ultimate Element: Making the World Rich with Value*

"*Meaning* is the new money," said Dan Pink, a catalyzing force in his own right with his books *A Whole New Mind* and *The Adventures of Johnny Bunko* (two brilliant books that turn our way of thinking about ourselves and the paths we walk on upside down). In that sense, we could conclude that entrepreneurs set out to make the world "rich" with the value they deliver. But how?

To answer this question, we must address two questions: how does the entrepreneur bring wealth to the world, and how do we define wealth itself?

At this point, the answer to the first should be self-evident, as the Founding Fathers might have stated it. It lies in their willingness to fulfill the role of change catalyst. As incredible as their ability to do so seems, they have no choice but to do so. And that fact helps us answer the second question, how should we define wealth?

The lack of choice is driven less by personal reasons and more by species obligations. Ultimately, true entrepreneurs—the ones who catalyze the greatest change—do what they do for the betterment of other people, not just themselves. Strong, reflective, and complex, entrepreneurs are calculated and balanced in what they do. Greed isn't their game. Certainly capital is necessary to fuel the dream, but money is not the output they seek. Rather than nurturing a penchant for short-term personal gain and glory, entrepreneurs have an orientation toward long-term social gain. This is wealth of a different kind altogether.

Describing entrepreneurs, Ashoka founder, Bill Drayton, said, "Some people simply define themselves in bigger ways than others." When entrepreneurs look out into the world, what they see and what they set out to seize can't be described by a single measure or currency. In that context, Bill's comment isn't just an observation about entrepreneurs, it's a lesson in our quest to understand them.

We too need to view them as producing a bigger impact than is often attributed to them. It may be hard to get your mind around the concept that this impact is intended for the betterment of humankind and not just personal gain. But it's hard to deny that the impact of entrepreneurs is one rich with value. That kind of wealth, as venture capitalist Harry Weller would tell you, isn't so narrow that it can be measured by dollars and cents alone.

"The entrepreneur," said Harry, "is the person who is willing to sail far enough into the ocean that they can't see land." It's a telling perspective for someone who invests money in entrepreneurial ventures for a living and expects to see a return in dollars as well.

True enough, Harry is a partner at the oldest and arguably most successful venture capital firm in the U.S., New Enterprise Associates (NEA). Since its founding in 1978, NEA has invested more than $6 billion in hundreds of entrepreneurs, at all stages of growth and in countless industries. It has also provided for those who entrust their money with NEA many times more that amount in return on their investments. That's the obvious job of the venture capitalist: to make money on money. But just as with successful entrepreneurship, there is more to successful and lasting venture capital than meets the eye.

Harry may ultimately invest other people's money in promising new ventures, but his real job is to determine which entrepreneurs are likely to meet with the greatest success. So when he describes the best entrepreneurs and doesn't even mention money, you know that the extraordinary returns he and his partners garner for their investors must be rooted in *something more* than an entrepreneur's ability to make money.

In the end, the answers to the question of how entrepreneurs make the world rich with value must be bundled back together as one. In successful entrepreneurship, the meaning of wealth is the same as the meaning that drives the entrepreneur to do what he does.

In his time, Harry has known many successful entrepreneurs and met many more who simply didn't make the grade. As he commented, "While it may help to have the courage, knowledge, or creativity to leave a safe harbor, what happens after you let go and chase your dream can't be determined by you alone. When you are way out there beyond sight of land, you have to be able to maintain context and keep a handle on *what matters*."

Once the entrepreneurial undertaking has been catalyzed, what matters most is much more than the person who first set sail. It's the impact that the entrepreneur has made on the many who joined the journey.

When you pause for a moment, I think you'll see it.

## Recommended Resources

### *Visual Explanations* – Edward Tufte

You don't "read" Tufte so much as you "allow your eyes to feast" on his work. If there were ever a book on how to paint a picture for someone else and fill it with information communicated clearly *without words*, this would be it. This book will make you take in the world differently and paint your own view of that world more powerfully.

### *Deep Survival* – Laurence Gonzales

I was humbled when Laurence suggested that *A Deliberate Pause* might do for entrepreneurs what his book did for survivalists. He, too, looked across a wide swath of stories and people in search of patterns that defined their capacity to go further and do more than most. I'll leave you to pass your own judgment on *A Deliberate Pause*, but Gonzales cuts through rumor and assumptions about who lives, who dies, and why under extreme conditions in a masterful, entertaining way.

### *Einstein's Dreams* – Alan Lightman

Want to see your own patterns—or at least be challenged to look at them differently? Consider *Einstein's Dreams* your nightly homework. A friend once suggested that each night I read one of what Lightman has imagined to be Einstein's dreams during the nights leading up to stating his theory of relativity. By doing so, I found myself thinking and dreaming from a new vantage point. Try it yourself—read only one tiny page (or so) a night. How can it hurt?

### *The Edge of the Sea* – Rachel Carson

A new mindset can be applied just about anywhere, but what it reveals can be especially rich when applied to the most obvious and least likely of places—the seaside. Although you may know Rachel Carson for her breakthrough book *Silent Spring*, she mostly wrote about her work as a marine biologist and observer of the sea. The result is this wonderfully poetic book written for the lay person. In it, Carson shows us the fantastic, inspiring world of adaptation and survival at the sea's edge.

# A Deliberate Pause
## The "May Be" Parable

An aging farmer had a horse that he relied on for working his farm. One day the horse ran away. When the farmer's neighbors heard of this, they came to offer their sympathies. "Such bad luck," they said to him. "May be," responded the farmer.

A few days later the horse returned bringing three other beautiful and strong wild horses with him. Again the farmer's neighbors gathered around, this time enthusiastically exclaiming, "What good luck!" Again, the farmer responded, "May be."

The farmer had a mischievous son and a few days after the horses returned, the son tried to ride one of the wild ones. He was quickly thrown to the ground and broke his leg. "What bad luck," the neighbors all commented, hanging and shaking their heads upon hearing the news. "May be," the farmer replied.

The very next week, a group of soldiers came through the village. The country was at war and the army needed young recruits. Seeing the farmer's son with his leg broken, they passed him by. "Such good luck," his neighbors told him. "May be," replied the farmer again.

# Part II:
## *Entrepreneurship*

# Contributors to Chapter 4

**Carl Safina**
> Founder, Blue Ocean Institute
> Author, *Song for the Blue Ocean, Voyage of the Turtle,* and *Eye of the Albatross*

**Peter Senge**
> Author, *The Fifth Discipline* and co-author, *The Necessary Revolution, Presence*
> Named Strategist of the Century by the *Journal of Business Strategy* (1999)
> Senior Lecturer, MIT

**Mike Devine**
> CFO, Secure Software
> Former Partner, Arthur Andersen and Deloitte Touche

**Mike Sutton**
> Founder, Marine Stewardship Council (MSC)
> Director, Monterey Bay Aquarium's Center for the Future of the Oceans
> Co-founder, Packard Venture Capital Fund

**Martin Goebel**
> Founder, President, Sustainable Northwest
> Co-founder, Conservation International
> Advisor, Walton Family Foundation

**Baiju Shah**
> President, CEO, Bioenterprise
> Former Consultant, McKinsey & Company

**Ann Webster**
> Instructor in Medicine, Harvard Medical School
> Staff Psychologist, Massachusetts General Hospital

**Robert Egger**
> Founder, DC Central Kitchen, Campus Kitchens, and more
> Author, *Begging for Change*
> Co-founder, the Nonprofit Congress

**Peter Seligmann**
> Co-founder, Chairman, CEO, Conservation International
> Winner, Order of the Golden Ark
> Former President, The Nature Conservancy

**Bijoy Goswami** (See Chapter 2)

# Chapter 4: The Entrepreneurial Ecosystem— From One to Many

*"The concept of the ecosystem is a very good framework. It speaks to thinking systematically. If you want to solve the big problems, you must think and act this way."*

- Carl Safina
Founder, Blue Ocean Institute
Author, *Song for the Blue Ocean*

In his 2005 book, *Presence*, Peter Senge wrote this: "When people in leadership positions begin to serve a vision infused with a larger purpose, their work shifts naturally from producing results to encouraging the growth of people who produce results."[10] Perhaps best known for his book *The Fifth Discipline*, Peter's groundbreaking work in learning organizations and the power of community shows that no idea is fulfilled through the efforts of one person. Peter would probably say that the lessons learned in Chapter 3 about the entrepreneur's need for others don't apply only to entrepreneurs. They are universal.

Emphasizing the importance of that theme in successful entrepreneurship, Peter told me, "What ultimately makes an entrepreneur unique is the ability to create new sources of value. It isn't just the energy and passion of the individual that makes creation possible. It's the ability of the individual to create the energy and space, the *environment*, that allows new value to be brought into existence by many."

In the entrepreneurial venture, the *environment* Peter referred to is best viewed as an *ecosystem*, a unique grouping of people and resources and an interdependent dynamic that surrounds each successful entrepreneur. In turn, each entrepreneurial ecosystem exists within a larger entrepreneurial universe, creating a similar dynamic among ventures that, within any one ecosystem, occurs among individuals. His point is extremely important. While it may first appear that an ecosystem supports the needs of the entrepreneur who catalyzed it, in reality, each member supports the needs and aspirations of each other. In fact, perhaps an ecosystem's most distinguishing feature is the essential interdependence of its community members—for survival, evolution, and enhancement.

The cultivation of such an ecosystem around the vision is a much greater challenge for the entrepreneur than catalyzing the entrepreneurial dream. It is, in fact, a point of distinction for true entrepreneurs because it requires that the entrepreneur evolve from acting solo to allowing others to share in the sculpting and stewardship of the vision. From one to many.

## A Universe Bigger Than One

The entrepreneurial universe is made up of a thousand points of knowledge and skills, resources and visions, people and dreams. Everyone who brings value to or derives value from entrepreneurship can be considered part of this universe. It's an extremely big pond that holds all the resources feeding many different entrepreneurial visions.

But on a day-to-day basis, that larger universe is far less relevant to the individual entrepreneur or entrepreneurial vision than the specific ecosystem that must come to exist around both the person and the dream. Let's use this pond-as-universe analogy to paint the picture more clearly.

### Pebbles in a Pond

Imagine the entrepreneur as someone who stands on the shore of the pond. When he reaches down to pick up a pebble and throw it into the pond, he is catalyzing something—an act that, by intention, must grow larger. When this pebble, no matter how small, hits the surface of the pond, it does more than make a splash at the point of impact.

It causes a ripple effect. From that central catalyzing point, a series of concentric circles extend outwardly over the pond.

In the entrepreneurial universe, a Ripple Effect forms around the catalyst in a similar way as the ripple effect in nature. That is, resources and people extending out from the entrepreneur's vision form the entrepreneurial ecosystem. They feed it, shape it, expand on it, and make its potential real. In effect, the vision's ability to survive, succeed, and sustain *depends* on its ecosystem forming and gaining strengths, allowing the vision to stretch far beyond the one who initiated it.

For every true entrepreneur and lasting vision represented by the pebble, a defined ecosystem exists. Because many entrepreneurs are launching their own pebbles into the pond, the entrepreneurial universe is made up of many, many ecosystems—all seeking to attract resources from a common pool.

## Power and Purpose Beyond the Ripple Effect

The image of ripples in a pond provides a simple way to understand the entrepreneurial ecosystem, but it runs the risk of going back to an image of all things in entrepreneurship being about the entrepreneur. (That's one risk; the other is missing an even more important concept, the Aspen Effect, detailed in Chapters 3 and 6.) But below the surface of any pond, teeming life forms can be easily missed when focusing only on the surface. Fish, plants, algae, insects, objects, and more all serve a function. And the most distinguishing feature of an ecosystem isn't any one of these things, just as it isn't the pebble or the person throwing it. It's the *interdependence* of its community members on one another—for survival, evolution, and enhancement. While it may appear that an ecosystem forms or functions to support the needs of one, in reality each member supports the needs and aspirations of the others.

"There comes a point in all entrepreneurial ventures when the entrepreneur needs help," said Mike Devine, an advisor to entrepreneurs, a builder of entrepreneurial communities, and an officer in entrepreneurial ventures, including Secure Software where he's CFO. Other people and resources are drawn to the entrepreneur from the larger entrepreneurial universe. But it's more than gathering those people and resources that makes entrepreneurship work. They're morphed into a successful ecosystem in which all the components thrive collectively in ways they could not alone.

## One Ecosystem Advances Another by Intention

Like ecosystems in the natural world, the entrepreneurial ecosystem weaves an intricate and interdependent web that evolves from the first actions and visions of the catalyst.

To give you a better sense of the ecosystem concept, consider the Marine Stewardship Council (MSC) founded by Mike Sutton. MSC was an ambitious undertaking, even as a concept, because this ecosystem's intent was to preserve and advance another ecosystem.

In his work at World Wildlife Fund before founding MSC, Mike was one of many acutely aware that the world's natural fisheries were being depleted at an alarming rate. He also knew that traditional approaches to protecting the oceans (advocacy, legislation, and education) weren't creating a large enough result quickly enough to reverse a potentially catastrophic trend. More people needed to be given the incentive to care, including fishermen, wholesalers, retailers—in short, anyone engaged in bringing fish out of the water and onto the dinner table. But for all of *those* people to care, consumers would have to care, too. They would have to demand that their seafood be harvested and delivered in sustainable ways. After all, it was their dinner table and their health.

Producers, consumers, and conservationists—three related but distinct groups—would have to work together and meet each others' needs. As Mike described it, "The MSC was formed to create market incentives, to harness the power of consumer choice, and to do both in the direction of marine conservation."

Along with those who backed his idea from the start, Mike wanted to change the way people generally thought about seafood—not just its production and consumption, but its existence as a precious and threatened natural resource. Mike and those aligned with him hold a vision of the world's oceans teeming with life, with seafood supplies safeguarded for this and future generations.

The MSC vision was born of the entrepreneurial mindset and, as Peter Senge might recognize it, a conscious effort to create a learning community—an ecosystem—right from the start. Mike's MSC vision recognized the necessity of a mutually supportive and beneficial ecosystem. By building toward that framework from inception, the fishermen, conservationists, wholesalers, retailers, consumers, and other contributors worked with and learned from each other. Today, they're building a collective solution that allows everyone to get what they want, not *in spite of* but *because of* each other.

A great vision involves delivering greater value than ever.

## The Idea is Bigger Than One Person

If you visit the MSC website,[11] it's nearly impossible to find mention of Mike, MSC's entrepreneurial founder. But if you spoke with him, you'd understand why he chooses to be low-key. As he said, "An important principle of entrepreneurship is recognizing that the true measure of success occurs if value persists long after the entrepreneur is gone."

"Entrepreneurship cannot be a universe of one person," noted the founder of Sustainable Northwest, Martin Goebel. "As an entrepreneur, you create opportunities. You attract the best, including yourself, and then do the best you can do to create value. But you have to learn to steer from behind, not just in front. This requires making room for others—a critical awakening to realizing entrepreneurial success. For ultimately, it's entrepreneur*ship* that matters most—more than the entrepreneur."

### Life Science Ventures Evolve into an Ecosystem

Baiju Shah, president and CEO of Bioenterprise, built his organization on the principle that entrepreneur*ship* matters most. Partnering with such elite educational and research institutions as Case Western Reserve University and the Cleveland Clinic, Bioenterprise aids the creation of ventures in life sciences and their evolution into entrepreneurial ecosystems.

Historically, entrepreneurship in the life sciences has presented special challenges. Founders of life science ventures are, not surprisingly, often scientists or information technology experts who have unique skills and insights in their own fields but lack other skills to bring their innovative ideas to a larger audience.

"One of the biggest hurdles they encounter," Baiju pointed out, "is their difficulty in seeing their own limits as entrepreneurs or as operators. They conclude, 'I made the better mousetrap so I am the best leader for the venture that will bring that mousetrap to the world.'"

Not always true, especially when these visionaries tend to be limited by backgrounds in academic or research institutions that don't lend themselves to building ventures or cultivating collective visions. "Their surrounding society and cultures train them in ways that don't anticipate the step of delivering a dream to the world," Baiju explained. Although these founders hold an important piece of the life science puzzle, most lack knowledge of or access to key components that make their discoveries marketable. Attempting to put them out into the world can be confusing, even foreign to them.

"Yet many are either unwilling or unaware that they must let go of their singular grip on the vision and the venture. They must add talents and resources different from their own, share the responsibility for the dream and delivery, and do what's necessary to make the venture work," continued Baiju.

Bioenterprise shows would-be entrepreneurs how to allow ecosystems to form and flourish around them. In fact, it helps entrepreneurs build their own ecosystems by bringing together the powers of *existing* ecosystems capable of filling necessary roles in the entrepreneur's vision.

Case Western and the Cleveland Clinic, as two examples, have patients who benefit from—even test out—life science innovations. As well, they do their own research, which often supplements, extends, or completes the discoveries of the life science entrepreneur. These partners have access to funds too, something that newly minted entrepreneurs struggle to come by. Their reputations as established, respected institutions can support a new life science venture's ability to advance.

Baiju's Bioenterprise team, whose members have deep experience, networks, and access to partners in strategy, management, financing, and team-building areas, extend the capacities of entrepreneurs even further. When Bioenterprise agrees to partner with them, reality hits swiftly and honestly. According to Baiju, "Bioenterprise insists on the founders allowing management to be added to the team if it's determined that they lack that capability. They insist that the scientific guys who want to stay anchored to the academic institution play advisory roles only." They push these entrepreneurs in the direction of what they know works and away from the *me*-centered attitudes that snuff out many start-ups. Push and pull, back and forth—part of a natural dynamic of an ecosystem that supports huge numbers of contributors and beneficiaries.

In learning the necessities of the entrepreneurial ecosystem, ironically they get a lesson that's central to the world from which their visionary ideas emerged—nature and life sciences.

**The Entrepreneurial Universe**
Figure 3

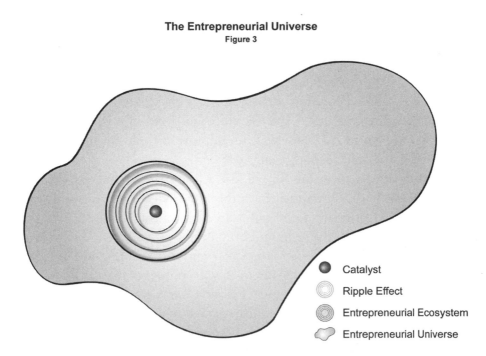

- ● Catalyst
- ◎ Ripple Effect
- ◉ Entrepreneurial Ecosystem
- ☁ Entrepreneurial Universe

## *Powerful Ripple Effect Leads to Ecosystem*

Both MSC and Bioenterprise are strong, distinctive examples of the ecosystems that must come to surround successful entrepreneurs. They include an array of people, talents, resources, ideas, efforts, and energy without which the vision could not survive. They are also powerful examples of the role that individual ecosystems play in a larger universe.

Indeed, each ecosystem is powerful enough to have a Ripple Effect of its own. The more conscious that Ripple Effect is, the more vibrant and valuable it is and, as a natural extension, the more its influence expands across the entrepreneurial universe and influences other ecosystems.

Sometimes the impact forces other ecosystems to be consumed or marginalized in some way. Other times the forces of individual ecosystems naturally merge and feed each other. In the best cases, ecosystems like MSC and Bioenterprise proactively set out to harness the power of other ecosystems.

### Pursuing Deliberate Ripples

People like Peter Senge, Mike Devine, Mike Sutton, Martin Goebel, and Baiju Shah understand the Ripple Effect and see opportunities to harness and direct it. More than that, they make a conscious effort to influence it further toward developing *community* (discussed in Chapter 6)—an added factor that can improve the odds of success and the creation of value exponentially.

But being aware of the Ripple Effect in pursuit of one ecosystem isn't enough. It's important to act on this knowledge. Learning to do so becomes part of the necessary evolution of the entrepreneur.

Not surprisingly, the technique employed by the best entrepreneurs to understand this and other concepts—and then adapt and leverage them—is using a deliberate pause. Only in moments that break from their frenetic pace can entrepreneurs clear their minds to see more patterns and create more Ripple Effects. Taking a deliberate pause (as you'll see in the story *The Ultimate Motivation for Taking a Pause* and later in Robert Egger's experience) allows them to continue creating what took them down the entrepreneurial path in the first place.

## The Ultimate Motivation for Taking a Pause

Ann Webster, a Ph.D. psychologist at Massachusetts General and instructor in medicine at Harvard University, helps people learn to take a deliberate pause as a matter of course.

No, she doesn't work with entrepreneurs (though some of her patients could be entrepreneurs). And she isn't building organizations or ecosystems (though her environment certainly contains both). But her work highly relates to this discussion, and it's therefore worth pausing here to consider her world.

Ann's patients are dying of terminal diseases. They've been told that their time for making choices has an expiration date. That gives them great motivation to learn the value of a pause. However, their motivation to pause differs from the entrepreneur's because they don't discover their own patterns; their oncologists or pathologists see them first.

Spurred on by this news, they turn to Ann's program that teaches mind-body techniques to help patients make emotional, physical, and spiritual gains by learning how to cope. But more than teaching them coping skills, "The goal is to quiet and calm the noise in the mind," said Ann. "When they do that, they see more clearly. Then they can go on to make meaningful changes."

Clearly, circumstances aren't the same for terminally ill patients as they are for entrepreneurs by any stretch, but here's what's similar: Like Ann's patients, entrepreneurs feel an urgency to change things in their world (and *the* world) before it's too late. If they can't "calm the noise in the mind" and do so repeatedly as a matter of course, then their world becomes complex and cloudy. Patterns and a sense of what matters most become obscured. Instead of empowering them, dealing with more and more "ripples" overwhelms them and leaves them unequipped to change anything in meaningful ways.

## *Multiple Ecosystems Brought to Life*

Robert Egger lives in a universe of many dimensions, each with its own ecosystem.

You might first think of him as one dimensional, but *which* dimension would depend on where you encountered him. For example, if you turned on TV and saw him on *The Oprah Winfrey Show,* he'd come across as a national personality. If you knew he was receiving one of her Angel Awards for his community work, he could appear to be a do-gooder basking in 15 minutes of fame. If you were homeless on the streets of Southeast Washington, DC, you'd likely encounter him as a nameless volunteer delivering food. If you'd frequented the Georgetown club scene in DC in the 1980s, you'd have pegged him as the manager of one of the hottest music clubs of the time—a wheeler-dealer and friend of the stars.

If you saw his book *Begging for Change,* you'd identify him as an author. If you follow nonprofit news, you'd know him as the co-founder of Nonprofit Congress, a movement that empowers individuals and nonprofits to act collectively for positive change. And if you walked the floors of the DC Central Kitchen, you'd easily assume he's a prep cook.

Clearly, Robert lives across many ecosystems, some he created and others he encouraged. All of them benefited from his entrepreneurial mindset. He brings such value, in fact, that it's impossible to calculate it within the boundaries of any one of these dimensions.

It's also impossible to gain a distinct impression of who Robert is and what he contributes. And when you spend time studying how he operates, you'll see his brilliance and his clear sense of how to harness the power of entrepreneurship.

### Started with Observing Patterns of Epidemic Waste

It all began in Casablanca, sort of. Growing up, Robert dreamed of owning his own "Rick's," the fictional über-club lorded over by Humphrey Bogart's classic character in the 1942 movie *Casablanca.* That youthful dream led him to run several clubs in the Washington, DC area. From there, he observed patterns outside the spotlight that changed his vision and the lives of countless people.

As a club manager, Robert saw the enormous amount of food thrown out at the end of each evening. It was not a phenomenon of his venue alone as this epidemic waste plagued his hotel and restaurant friends as well. In Robert's eyes, this status quo situation was interlaced with a worse one. As a volunteer for his church's program to feed the homeless, he saw the ineffective ways most organizations addressed the hunger challenge—by buying new, often expensive food, preparing it program by program, and then distributing it to those lining up at designated sites night after night. They'd show up, get fed, and return to their homeless lives, their hunger treated with a Band-Aid and its root causes unaddressed. Repeatedly.

When Robert connected that practice with the food waste phenomenon, something deep within him pushed to find a better way. The creation of DC Central Kitchen proved to be that way; his dream of "Rick's" would have to wait.

Robert's idea sparked the first venture of its kind that became the model for countless similar programs across the country. The model is simple: DC Central Kitchen volunteers gather unused food that would otherwise be discarded and bring it to a central location. The Kitchen's team prepares it into meals, then distributes these meals to locations where hungry people come to be fed. The concept achieved its goals: better use of food and much improved food distribution.

### Helped "Customers" Remove Their Own Barriers

But more was cooking in Robert's mind. What about those people being fed? Couldn't he address more than their hunger?

To really change things as they needed to be changed, Robert's dream had to include teaching these "customers" to remove the barriers to realizing their own dreams. They needed a hand. So Robert teamed up with organizations providing various resources and support needed by many of the Kitchen's patrons. "They already do this kind of work," was Robert's thinking. "I can't do it better, but I can make them be more effective." So through the Kitchen, he brought services to those who needed help rather than their having to find the organizations on their own.

More than that, he offered his customers jobs, training, purpose, and a chance to be a part of shaping the Kitchen itself. Such actions don't fall under the common categories of charity or employment. They are part of the mindset that recognizes that many people, many needs, and many dreams populate an ecosystem.

The Kitchen became a place to address hunger, homelessness, substance abuse, healthcare, job training, and education in an interconnected way. Everyone contributes to the vision and the value the Kitchen creates. Everyone benefits. Everyone shapes the future. Robert is but one member of a larger dynamic he sparked.

It seems the old adage is true: Great things always seem to happen in the kitchen.

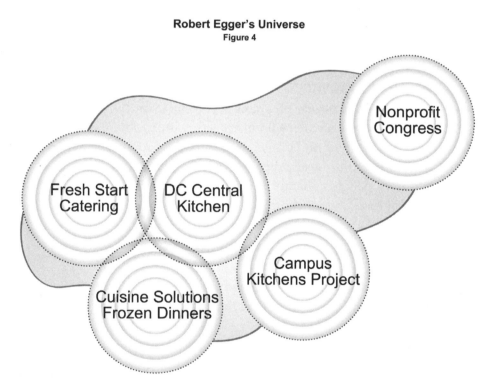

**Robert Egger's Universe**
Figure 4

### Intertwined Visions and Ventures

By any measure, the DC Central Kitchen has become a huge success. But as Robert said, "The Kitchen became a vehicle to a larger vision and a bigger opportunity to create value. It's not about the Kitchen." DC

Central created a change in thinking—not just for himself, but for those the Kitchen serves and other organizations helping the Kitchen's patrons who previously were unable to change their own circumstances. The result? Out of one (idea/person/venture) have come many (successes/dreams/forms of value), an example of one ecosystem spawning and overlapping with others. Fresh Start Catering and Campus Kitchens are just two examples of Robert's ongoing Ripple Effect.

## Fresh Start Catering

Robert's actions prove the perpetual evolution that can and should take place from idea to entrepreneur to venture to ecosystem to overlapping ecosystems. Also perpetual is the value derived. Yet every ecosystem, no matter how innovative it is, encounters constraints. One of DC Central Kitchen's was that it was a nonprofit. All nonprofits, even successful ones such as DC Central Kitchen, rely on capital to survive, just as for-profit ventures do. But traditional sources of nonprofit capital come with strings—for example, donors often limit how funds can be spent. In addition, funds from one source are rarely enough to meet total capital needs, so nonprofits are often forced to seek multiple sources for their funds, thereby answering to more than one master. Most nonprofits accept and live with this reality (and can suffer from it, too).

But where others saw an unchangeable situation, Robert saw patterns, needs, and opportunities for change. In response to his vision being compromised by traditional sources of nonprofit funding—grants, government funds, foundations, and the like—he founded Fresh Start Catering, a for-profit venture that both followed the vision of the Kitchen and fed its capital needs. The food the Kitchen produced was such high quality that it could meet any hunger, from homeless to corporate.

Fresh Start became Robert's way to expand his customer base to include not only those who needed a hand but those who had money in hand and could pay for his services. Pursuing this new venture gave Robert a separate but overlapping ecosystem and a capital source *he* could control. It gave his team at DC Central Kitchen more people to serve and more goals to aspire to. And it breathed life into an entirely new idea, venture, and ecosystem.

## Campus Kitchens

Even with its self-generated income source in Fresh Start, the Kitchen faced other limitations. One of them was having enough capacity to serve all those in need. Capacity—having space and equipment in which to prepare, cook, and deliver food—is particularly challenging for a venture that isn't primarily profit oriented. But to an open mind practiced in reflecting and asking why, new ideas constantly arise. For Robert, a solution became Campus Kitchens.

As those at DC Central Kitchen contemplated how to expand affordably, someone noticed that certain colleges and even high schools had huge kitchen facilities that went unused for large blocks of time. (Robert doesn't identify himself or any one person as the source of this idea, not because he couldn't figure it out, not out of humility, but because in the dynamic of his ecosystems, it doesn't matter. Every contributor was feeding a larger shared vision.)

What began as a way to creatively leverage this capacity evolved into an experiential platform for educating future generations about social missions. And what started in an effort to solve one ecosystem's challenges served to expand the overall vision, something larger than any one ecosystem. More than that, a complementary vision for a new venture was born.

Here's how it happened:

> The kitchens on college and high school campuses have excess capacity. Going otherwise unused, they offer it to Robert and his team for less than it would cost to buy or build capacity while making more of the facility than if it sat dormant. Campus Kitchens uses that capacity to further its DC Central model, but does so in a new community. Then they leverage up the value. Students from the schools that have incorporated Campus Kitchens go to work for the organization. They live and breathe and contribute to it. As a learning lab,

Campus Kitchens provides a "purpose check" for these young people seeking training and meaningful work. In so doing, this entrepreneurial nonprofit has sewn a new hotbed of ideas and planted them in the minds of future generations. Taking credit for developing those ideas isn't the point. Clearly, it took many to help the entrepreneur create an ecosystem in the first place. It will, no doubt, expand into other yet-to-be-imagined ecosystems.

## Blueprint for How Ecosystems Work

Robert's story—and many others—could be used as a blueprint for how entrepreneurial ecosystems ripple outward from the catalyst. They reflect how entrepreneurship itself works, whatever its final form turns out to be.

Certainly a bit of Robert exists in every part of the world he catalyzed. Rather than worrying about labels or polishing his own ego, Robert works quietly on his next idea. All the while, the capable people he has drawn to him enhance the many ecosystems that make up *his* universe. He sees, he seeds, he seeks out, and he connects others to his dreams. Then he offers plenty of room for them to grow and dream alongside him. When you visit any one of the organizations Robert has catalyzed, individuals greet you with a passion conveying that *they* created and own this world. They did and they do.

Bigger than a single idea, bigger than one venture, DC Central Kitchen has had a huge Ripple Effect in scope and ownership. It's part of a community of ecosystems in a larger entrepreneurial universe. These ecosystems feed and foster each other, even as they further their individual visions. The Ripple Effect never stops, nor should it, for that's the powerful idea behind entrepreneurship—*a perpetual opportunity to improve and advance humankind.*

Clearly, Robert continues to "get" the flow of entrepreneurship. The awareness of this powerful force and how to harness and direct it deliberately, proactively, filters into his continuing ventures. In 2008, he launched an initiative to sell frozen meals created by five of the DC area's best chefs and prepared by DC Central's team. He also invested in the Cadillac of portable kitchens to put tasty offerings on wheels, taking them to a whole new customer base of corporate lunchtime patrons. Both new formats provide nutritious, convenient meals that can't be found in the busy home or at the corner hot dog stand. They add value by saving time and money for a whole new set of customers while providing something good for the body and the mind. Through these ecosystems, Robert also spreads his entrepreneurial vision to a whole new audience.

Recently, Robert and his team put together a book of DC Central recipes and success stories of its team members. Like the mobile kitchen and the frozen meals, this book raises awareness and money for existing ventures. The ideas go on and on. Will one or more of these become stand-alone ventures? If it makes sense, yes, but that isn't the point. The point is to spread the vision and value as far as they will go, no matter the vehicle used.

Just as the successful catalyst goes beyond causing a ripple to form an ecosystem, the best entrepreneurs—while cultivating ecosystems that extend their dreams—realize that their efforts also perpetuate the well-being of the entrepreneurial universe itself, as Robert's example shows. Because each ecosystem draws its resources from this larger "pond," having a healthy pond serves to expand the principle of entrepreneurship itself.

### From Peach Pits to a Garden of Eden

Years ago, I received a greeting card from someone who valued my work and wanted me to know it had helped her and others significantly. On the front of the card, a character danced across the scene from left to right, dropping peach pits as he went—here, there, everywhere— deliberately but seemingly without concern for whether they landed in nice neat rows. When I opened the card, the character was gone and a multitude of peach trees filled the scene. What an imaginative way to convey the importance of planting seeds! It's as if to say planting those tiny peach pits doesn't seem like much at the time, but from these pits grow orchards of fruitful peach trees.

Entrepreneurs plant those tiny peach pits, too. And when their actions ripple outward, trees of every kind can grow. Some entrepreneurs are great gardeners; some are good at finding good gardeners or new fields to garden. Regardless, if you plant enough "peach pits" and teach others to do the same, you could well be blessed with a Garden of Eden.

The entrepreneur seeds a vision, then its method of delivery undergoes constant evolution and refinement, passing through many hands. To sustain that vision, the individuals who get drawn into its ecosystem become contributors. However, they must want to evolve the vision and have the skills to do so. Before long, the entrepreneurial *spirit* for the venture continues because an *identity* is established and *values* are spread—from one to many.

"The entrepreneur attracts others who share the same values and methods. The organization then begins to challenge itself the way the entrepreneur has been challenged in earlier stages. That is to say, there is a great part of the entrepreneur in what becomes the collective result. But the success of the venture, the value it creates, the form that value takes, and even the venture itself is no longer dependent on the entrepreneur. It is about developing a ball and then allowing it to roll by forces other than your own," confirmed Conservation International co-founder, chairman, and CEO, Peter Seligmann.

As Peter pointed out, there isn't one method of instilling the entrepreneurial spirit in others. And the ability to do so doesn't come from a single source. It's about *community* and its creation. Community can take a variety of formats (five of those formats are described in Chapter 6). Regardless of form, communities share common and powerful characteristics. They are grounded in beliefs that attract people with similar beliefs, values, and goals, but allow for variation around the common themes and within them. Everyone plays a different role, as you'll read about in the next chapter. Maximizing what each person offers requires honoring each role and giving each room to thrive.

## Lasting Impact Comes from Loosening the Grip

When a vision is first catalyzed into action, the entrepreneur often has "no choice" but to take complete control. Over time, though, others choose to join the enterprise, supporting what's new and unfamiliar. The problem? Too many would-be entrepreneurs believe that sustaining the entrepreneurial dream requires sustaining individual power and control over the dream.

That's not true, as this chapter has pointed out. The more successful the venture, the more the entrepreneur must loosen his or her grip. I like the way Carl Safina, author of *Song for the Blue Ocean* and founder of the Blue Ocean Institute, put it when he said, "People who seek immortality are on slippery ground. If those feelings occur to you as you pursue your dream, I think you need to look more deeply."

Remember, the attraction of entrepreneurship lies in the assumption that its ideas will not only be realized, but that they will have continuing value. Clearly, it takes more than one person to achieve continuing value with a lasting impact. From one to many—as nature designed it!

## Recommended Resources

### *The Fifth Discipline* – Peter Senge

It's hard to believe that, for decades, people wrote about organizations and management yet never talked about the *organization* itself—its people and their interactions or how it thrives through collective learning. Peter made this concept famous to the point of being commonly—and thankfully—accepted.

### *The Human Fabric* – Bijoy Goswami

Think about *The Tipping Point.* I mean really think about what this phrase Malcolm Gladwell popularized means, how it reflects centuries of similar thought, and how it applies to you. That's the approach Bijoy took in researching and writing *The Human Fabric,* and that's what his book enables you to do—find out what kind of person you are and how your essence connects you to others. Once you try on Bijoy's framework for understanding oneself, you'll be hooked.

### *Getting to Yes* – William Fisher, Robert Ury

Why does this classic book appear as a recommended resource? Because it reflects what makes a community come to an understanding of clarity of purpose, common ground, and compromise. People have to work together. This book provides one excellent tool for understanding *why* we should "get to yes" and, more important, *how.*

# Contributors to Chapter 5

**Joel Peterson**
    Founder, Peterson Partners
    Adjunct Professor, Stanford University's Graduate School of Business
    Former CEO, Trammell Crow Company

**Carter Cast** (See Chapter 1)

**Rick Toren**
    Founder, Chairman, CodeRyte
    Founder, Promedco

**Andy Kapit**
    CEO, CodeRyte
    Founder, April Family of Companies

**Lyles Carr**
    Senior Vice President, McCormick Group

**P.V. Boccasam** (See Chapter 3)

**Guy Kawasaki** (See Chapter 2)

**Harry Weller** (See Chapter 3)

**Rafe Esquith**
    Author, *There Are No Shortcuts* and *Teach Like Your Hair's on Fire*
    Winner, National Medal of Arts (2004)
    Teacher, Hobart Elementary School

**Muhammad Yunus** (See Chapter 1)

**Robin Chase** (See Chapter 1)

**Esther Dyson**
    Founder, Edventure Holdings
    Author, *Release 2.0*
    Editor at Large, CNET Networks; *The New York Times* bi-monthly columnist

**Jim Shaffer**
    Author, *The Leadership Solution*
    Founder, Jim Shaffer Group
    Former Partner, Towers, Perrin

**Ed Feeney** (See Chapter 3)

**Geoff Smart** (See Chapter 2)

**Scott Frederick**
    Partner, Co-founder Valhalla Partners
    Former Partner, FBR Technology Partners and Dean & Company

**Carl Safina** (See Chapter 4)

**Martin Goebel** (See Chapter 4)

# Chapter 5: Completing the Entrepreneurial Ecosystem—Other Roles

*"In entrepreneurial ventures, the most effective value creators are often those who don't control all the inputs but are given the room to create within the entrepreneurial venture and vision."*

- Joel Peterson
Adjunct Professor
Stanford Graduate School of Business
Former CEO, Trammel Crow Company

Too many people walking the entrepreneurial path think the only respectable or important role is being *the entrepreneur.* As a result, they often confuse the breadth of that role *and* they undervalue the other roles that must be played to create successful entrepreneurship.

This stems in part from confusion about what an entrepreneur really is, something we cleared up in Part I. It sounds fun and even powerful to be the solo cowboy who steals the scene, but we know that's not how the West was really won.

Confusion about the role of entrepreneur, however, may not even be the most significant error in understanding to correct. A lack of appreciation for the *larger picture*—that is, the *other* roles and their interdependent functions in the vibrant ecosystems in which entrepreneurs operate—is equally at fault, if not more so.

But what would happen if those aspiring to the entrepreneurial path became fully aware of other roles and their importance? They just might wisely and willingly give up the notion that they need to be *the one* and allow themselves to be more powerful in the process.

Indeed, in the real world (not a mythological one), the evidence is clear: not everyone *should* or *can* be the change catalyst in an entrepreneurial venture. If everyone tried, lots of fires would get sparked but the resulting energy would be as trivial as a single match flaring briefly and then fizzling.

While every entrepreneurial venture is unique, certain roles remain constant across ventures and contribute immeasurably to the impact of the kind of successful entrepreneurship we so admire. These roles don't always take the same form. They are also sometimes roles not undertaken in a one-role-to-one person fashion but instead *shared* by more than one person. And they can be both formal and informal, occurring within the venture or even outside it. But regardless of form, their functions remain consistent as each successful venture draws together a combination of these roles from the entrepreneurial universe to create its own ecosystem.

Certainly, the entrepreneur's role as catalyst is important, but when it comes to creating successful entrepreneur*ship*, other roles must balance the catalyst's responsibilities. You'll get a feel for those roles—and the value and balance they provide—in this chapter. You'll also come to understand why each role needs and enhances the other, not in a hierarchical way, but in an interdependent way, as one expects to find in a true ecosystem in nature. The roles described here, though not exhaustive, represent the most encompassing ones—those found in all successful entrepreneurial ventures.

What are the most common roles that populate the entrepreneurial universe and its ecosystems? Activators. Team specialists. Advisors. And (this may surprise you) customers!

**Key Roles in the Entrepreneurial Ecosystem**
Figure 5

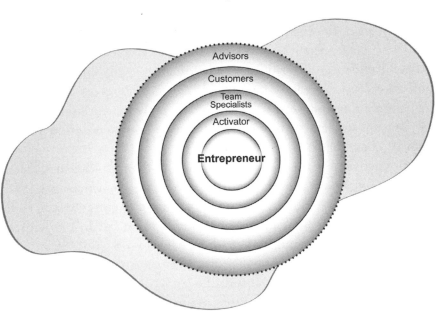

## *The Role of Entrepreneurial Activator*

In an entrepreneurial ecosystem, the activator role balances the catalyst enabling the venture to move forward—beyond theory and vision to reality and tangible value. The success of all entrepreneurial ventures stands on two pillars: perspective and discipline. Entrepreneurs bring the perspective; activators translate it into discipline.

Activators often closely resemble the entrepreneur in mindset, dedication, and drive (a key reason that so many of them remain confused and aspire to something they are not). But they differ from entrepreneurs in their unique capacity for fleshing out ideas and giving them substance. Entrepreneurs rarely have the capacity or patience to connect their ideas to others in meaningful ways, leading to far too many fires fizzling out. However, wise entrepreneurs find strong activators, and then learn to work with them to define and materialize the entrepreneurial vision.

In many cases, the activator's skills resemble that of growth managers, those talented individuals found in companies who clearly see what a vision requires operationally. They capably build and direct day-to-day details of their organizations. They know how to orchestrate the draftsman, the engineer, and the construction manager in concert with the entrepreneur's visionary architect. Typically, they possess a sound understanding and appreciation for which skills are needed and an exceptional ability to marshal the right resources. In this way, activators bridge between the ideas of the entrepreneur and the skills of the team specialists who provide the disciplined action to make the venture come together.

But activators bring more to the venture than typically associated with the implementation and growth roles of a good manager. They possess the same fluidity and flexibility that the entrepreneur does. That means they don't require components to be fixed or structured as they set up the organization. Others who do play more specialized roles need someone to lay out the path, set the ground rules, manage multiple changes, and even absorb the sometimes frenetic personality of the entrepreneur. The activator becomes their foil. In reverse, the activator becomes the entrepreneur's bridge to the operational aspects of the venture.

As the story *Entrepreneurs See Patterns; Activators Sort the Details of Those Patterns* explains, Carter Cast represents how an entrepreneur's dream can come true in the tangible world through the passion and talent of the right activator.

### Entrepreneurs See Patterns; Activators Sort the Details of Those Patterns

Carter Cast, co-founder and president of walmart.com, could easily be considered an entrepreneur, yet he plays the role of an activator to perfection.

He has created numerous ventures both within existing organizations such as Frito Lay and Pepsi and as co-founder of several standalone ventures, including Blue Nile, the first online exchange for diamonds.

Blue Nile showed off Carter's exceptional ability in an activator's role. Blue Nile was conceived as a way to make buying jewelry less complicated. Before, average consumers were at a disadvantage for understanding how the industry worked and therefore often hesitated purchasing anything.

Here's how Carter Cast described the dynamic reflected in his activator's role at Blue Nile: "Entrepreneurs live in the idea world. They see more; they try more; they filter more. They see patterns better than the rest of us. But they often need help shaping their ideas. Our antennae [as activators] are different from theirs. Entrepreneurs see a pattern; we see and sort the details of that pattern, making the idea come to life in a physical form. We legitimize it by looking at the factors, like the market, that allow it to become reality.

"Rather than letting entrepreneurs simply take an idea and search blindly for a need, I can walk it through the thinking that connects it to the people who have that need. I look for the process for how things can be capitalized on. Many entrepreneurs need people with my skill set. Perhaps I could be the person who comes up with the idea, but the role of activator and builder is something I enjoy and would like to think I'm pretty good at."

Even though Carter gets credit for helping create Blue Nile, its original idea preceded Carter's involvement. He was brought in because he could not only understand a yet-unrealized concept but because he also knew how to make this concept real. "When I arrived the first day at the company's 'headquarters'," Carter recalled, "I entered a largely empty room with various things scattered here and there. In the center of the room sat an upside-down trash can with a phone on it." He was told that was his desk, his wastebasket, and his office area all in one.

Carter played a critical role in evolving Blue Nile from that upside-down trash can into the largest online retailer of certified diamonds and jewelry—larger than the next three biggest online ventures of its kind combined. That activator role is a necessary part of every successful entrepreneurial vision.

The activator role takes many forms. Sometimes it's a hand off from entrepreneur to activator. In such instances the entrepreneur, aware of his or her limitations, steps aside to take on the role of advisor and visionary. On other occasions it is a role shared by several people who support the entrepreneur. A rare few entrepreneurs possess the activator capacity and assume both roles themselves. Yet even if they are capable of executing both roles well initially, eventually the entrepreneur and activator roles expand with the success of the venture and become too big for any one person to carry both. That's why it's often the case that, when entrepreneurs play an activator role, either they are deluding themselves or begrudgingly taking it on temporarily until an activator comes along. The wise (even if initially resistant) entrepreneur warms to the necessity and benefit of attracting a strong activator. That combination works best when it evolves from one person/separate roles into a partnership fueled by a shared passion and vision.

## Andy's "Activator" Complements Rick's "Entrepreneur"

A great example of this partnership can be found at CodeRyte, a software venture that streamlines the coding process for tracking medical data. Rick Toren, CodeRyte's founder and chairman, caught the entrepreneurial bug at an early age and has never been cured. In the last few decades, Rick has founded a series of highly successful healthcare ventures, CodeRyte being the latest.

Rick created CodeRyte to correct a nagging problem he saw. In the complex worlds of medicine and insurance, codes for tracking procedures don't align easily or often. Consequently, claims don't get reimbursed, putting financial pressure on patients and healthcare providers alike. And when data for critical treatment or business decisions go undetected, even more damaging results can enter the picture. Seeing this pattern and envisioning a way to fix it was a bold, powerful start. Yet from the moment Rick recognized the problem and envisioned a solution, he realized he'd need Andy Kapit to manifest it.

Andy plays the activator role to Rick's ideas. Like Carter, Andy doesn't get hung up chasing a desire to be the entrepreneur. And like Carter, he's not just the guy Rick hands assignments to for dutiful implementation. No true activator is.

"It's naïve to think of doing a venture like CodeRyte alone," said Rick. "I learned long ago to look for a partner early in the process." But what does "partner" mean in this context? Instead of an employee or someone who contributes a missing asset or skill, the activator is able to complete every thought expressed in the entrepreneurial vision.

Andy described Rick and his entrepreneurial catalyst role this way: "Rick has an unbelievable ability to thin-slice, to break a concept down into its smallest components, and then stand back to see its relevance and make something of it." This describes the critical catalyst element of pattern recognition in spades. As Andy went on to say, "Rick is intellectually brave and honest. He has good ideas and is willing to take appropriate risks to see them realized. And he surrounds himself with good people to execute those ideas well." To that, Rick added, "I don't have the patience for the details that Andy does." While this statement primarily underscored Andy's ability to execute details, it revealed how their differences complement each other. In fact, Rick trusts Andy to challenge his thinking, expand on his ideas, and make them highly viable and valuable.

That all-important trust comes from both Andy and Rick being actively and fully engaged in their CodeRyte venture. The venture is *theirs*. As they constantly demonstrate, the activator role doesn't substitute for the entrepreneur's role, a role that doesn't vanish or diminish in value with the arrival of an activator. Both roles need each other, like every member of an orchestra needs the other members to perform a symphony. Removing any lingering belief that Andy sees himself taking over where Rick left off, Andy said, "I work hard to be sure that (Rick) remains emotionally charged and engaged. That's when his thin-slicing kicks in." Andy needs Rick just as much as Rick needs Andy.

Imagine having the capacity to grasp an entrepreneurial vision, withstand its ever-shifting and at times seismic changes, and translate that into a vibrant, highly successful business. That's what the entrepreneurial activator does.

The ability of a venture to draw resources from the entrepreneurial universe into an ecosystem and ultimately succeed depends greatly on the strength of this activator role. As Andy stated, "There is a point when ventures have to go beyond the will and drive of the entrepreneur.

As an entrepreneur, you have to find those people who complement and extend you.

"We don't want to lose execution for vision," he stated bluntly. "We can't be visionary if we don't execute."

What we see when we awaken to the existence and importance of the activator role is a pattern that repeats itself across the many roles necessary for success in entrepreneurship. The McCormick Group's Lyles Carr reflected on the evolution of leadership and the diversity of roles in entrepreneurial ventures—topics he knows well having placed many into growing ventures as an executive recruiter—by saying, "When an entrepreneurial idea is sustainable, it grows bigger than the entrepreneur and outlives the leader to become a cause. That cause goes further to sustain relevancy, which means it must change and change hands with time."

The activator allows that evolution of ideas and roles passing from one to another and supporting each other to form a pattern that will continue in its own right.

## The Role of Entrepreneurial Team Specialists

Many players contribute to the formation of an entrepreneurial ecosystem. Each specialized role carries weight that's as critical as the entrepreneur and activist roles. In entrepreneurship, one role cannot thrive without the others. As Joel Peterson said in this chapter's opening quotation, "In entrepreneurial ventures, the most effective value creators are often those who don't control all the inputs but are given the room to create within the entrepreneurial venture and vision." To this he added, "Others come in behind the entrepreneur's vision to build around the core ideas and principles. The functional members of the team play the role of coming back to flesh it all out."

Those functional members are the *team specialists* of entrepreneurship, the expert technicians like a marine biologist within the Marine Steward-ship Council or a prep cook at DC Central Kitchen. Narrower in scope than the entrepreneur or activator, their actions firmly anchor the venture. It's within these specialist roles that things get done and the vision material-izes. So while the entrepreneur *sees* a new reality and the activator *orches-trates* the venture toward it, team specialists *deliver* that new reality.

While the role of entrepreneur requires having the greatest

perspective, team specialists offset that by having the most discipline. As P.V. Boccasam talked about in Chapter 3, entrepreneurs envision a reality yet unseen by most. That means team specialists take on the unenviable tasks of linking that imagined reality to an actual outcome.

This role is among the most challenging because team specialists sit on the opposite end of the ecosystem's spectrum from the entrepreneur, providing balance while materializing the vision—a tough job indeed.

## Facing the Problem of Distractions

Because team specialists have to be disciplined in an environment that tends to be fluid and operate on the edge of the chaotic, they face many distractions that typically come in two forms—entrepreneur-created and self-created.

Entrepreneurs aren't just disruptive to the reality of those in the world *around* them; they are disruptive to the reality taking shape *within* the very ventures they create. So even as team specialists need the entrepreneur to create the dream and catalyze action, they also need the activator to give them room to step out of the visionary clouds and deliver. This makes the various roles in the entrepreneurial universe symbiotic, each role needing the other.

By definition, team specialists have to be focused. Yet in the entrepreneurial environment, they also have to remain open to new ideas and the continuing evolution of the vision. These elements can cause even the most disciplined team specialist to become distracted.

But it isn't only dealing with dozens of contrasting demands that can be a problem. The environment's fluidity becomes an aphrodisiac. Sometimes specialists enjoy the fluidity too much, even though it goes against the key functions they're meant to perform in the entrepreneurial venture—again testing them with a balancing act.

What makes these entrepreneurial team specialists unique? They are able to play their roles well while bringing balance to a team with a leader whose biggest problem (and asset) is not recognizing boundaries. Team specialists who don't acknowledge that their distinct value lies in the role of specialist (rather than aspiring to be the entrepreneur) end up failing themselves and the ecosystem. But the ones who get it right create the magic that's coveted by all.

## Guy Started Out as a Team Specialist

Guy Kawasaki has played a lot of roles over his career and no doubt will play many more. Today, he writes about his experiences in the entrepreneurial universe in magazines and in classic books such as *The Art of the Start* and *Rules for Revolutionaries*. He's able to guide others about entrepreneurship because of the myriad roles he has played along the way, including his first role as a team specialist.

Certainly one of the entrepreneurial jobs that shaped him most was his work at Apple Computer in the 1980s—the decade when the Macintosh was born and personal computing arose as a concept that would forever change the world.

"When I saw what a Macintosh could do, the clouds parted and the angels started singing," he recalled. "For four years I evangelized Macintosh to software and hardware developers, and I led the charge against world-wide domination by IBM." He came to be recognized as kind of a cult leader for Apple, in all the good ways, and had a hand in shaping where the Mac, Apple, and personal computing would go.

Remember, Guy did not invent the Mac. He did not found Apple. Yet none of that mattered. As a team specialist, he played a critical role on a winning team.

After leaving Apple, Guy proceeded to found a series of start-ups that built on his successes. For example, he was among the early and most recognizable entrants into the Internet space when he founded garage.com—a company that helped other visionaries get started and thrive. He co-founded a venture firm and accepted board positions in other ventures in addition to playing strong roles as a father and husband.

Every role matters. Every contribution has its time and place. And one person can evolve up and down the spectrum while moving into, out of, and across ventures. As he learned to deliver increasingly greater value with each evolution, Guy found a truer reflection of himself. And his every venture—and the entrepreneurial universe itself—are better for it.

## The Role of Entrepreneurial Customers

As stated in Chapter 3, the value created by an entrepreneurial venture must be delivered to and appreciated by others. That means if entrepreneurs and their teams only satisfy themselves, ensuring lasting change in the world becomes impossible. The idea, the product, the service, the cause ultimately need an audience. That audience may not "buy" something with currency of whatever form, but they "buy into" supporting and assigning value to what the entrepreneurial venture offers. Whatever form they may take or whatever value they derive, these *customers* are critical to the successful entrepreneurial ecosystem.

Why? Not only because they spend money but because they become converts to the vision. And not passive converts. Sometimes they become employees; other times they're inspired to pursue their own version of the entrepreneurial dream. And all of them spread the religion, attracting other customers and believers to the entrepreneurial venture.

In effect, customers make the entrepreneurial vision real because they validate, often define, and even enhance its value. Further, they serve as the extension of the entrepreneurial dream. Reflecting on what makes entrepreneurship work, venture capitalist Harry Weller emphasized, "Constituents have constituents. It's a chain of ecosystems." Winning ventures must acknowledge a myriad of connections inside and outside their venture. Perhaps "customers" is a misnomer because it implies they're viewed only as recipients of what the venture creates. But as *constituents* of the dream, they play the roles of connector and even evangelist to other prospective constituents.

Consider what Apple had become in the 1980s and 1990s. Few would argue that Apple customers were the envy of any catalyst seeking a loyal audience. They spoke evangelically about the products Apple provided and the culture those products fed. Even today, think of any iPod, iPhone, or Mac user you know. Or go to an Apple store and see the cult that has spread to customers by way of evangelists like Guy. Then you'll have a tangible sense of just how much customers mean to an entrepreneurial ecosystem bent on changing the world.

Yet what's provided to customers need not take the form of a product. And those customers need not hand over their wallets to prove they see the value in what the entrepreneurial vision means to them. For example, at first glance, the work of Rafe Esquith would seem the polar opposite example of Apple. But after seeing what he's accomplished, you could put any one of his students at Hobart Elementary in Los Angeles up against Apple customers when measuring loyalty, involvement, and lasting impact.

## Engaging His "Customers" in the Fullest Sense

In the mid-1980s, Rafe Esquith left the comfort of a cushy, enviable assignment as a teacher in Beverly Hills for a challenge no one wanted—even those already teaching at the L.A. school in the low income, immigrant dominated neighborhood to which he voluntarily transferred. In his 2003 book, *There Are No Shortcuts,* he described his new setting as "20 minutes but as much as 20 light years" from his old school.

The community feeding students into Hobart Elementary had one of the highest and most ethnically diverse immigrant populations in the country. Everyone faced language, economic, and even cultural barriers, often limiting the students attending the school as well as the school's ability to attract, motivate, and retain staff. What an understatement to call what Rafe voluntarily embraced a "challenge."

Rafe knew if he was going to reach these kids and offer them a springboard to productive life paths, he had to engage his "customers" in the fullest sense. Their minds, their hearts, their time inside and outside the classroom, and their belief in the possibility of their own futures was the currency he dealt in. And the product he was offering? The power to perceive and experience themselves as changemakers.

Like a Muhammad Yunus but using a different currency, Rafe gives power over to his customers, offering them Shakespeare, music, math, and other opportunities that most believe eight to ten year olds can't handle, perhaps shouldn't even be given. Rafe sees it differently. In his eyes, all his students need is permission and the chance to realize that anything is possible—even in their little slice of the world that many too often and too quickly write off.

In a world where they feel empowered as changemakers, Rafe's students set their own study goals. They manage and invest their own assets. No surprise to Rafe, they choose to invest extra time and energy—before school, after school, and on weekends and vacations—to gain a return higher than even Rafe could imagine. They produce plays, put on concerts, and see how far they can take their talents in a wide variety of ways. And when they come back years after they've left Rafe's classroom, they share their success stories, invest in others, and reinforce the message to Rafe's new "customers" that they too can be changemakers.

In every way, they facilitate their teacher's vision and repay the value he has created with unimaginable returns on his investment.

You never know just how far customers will take a vision that captivates them. Robin Chase, for one, has been delighted by where her customers have taken her Zipcar dream, bringing new meaning to the concept of ride sharing and public transportation.

Yes, loyal customers still religiously rent Zipcars for an hour here, an hour there. But their advocacy and support have spawned campaigns to change laws and policies where they live, stretching the vision far beyond the original draft. For example, Zipcar loyalists got local governments to set aside public parking spaces just for share cars. In this and other ways, customers are creating their own value, even controlling the direction and destiny of the entrepreneurial vision. Like Rafe's students, they don't think of themselves as customers or think of the vision as belonging to Robin. It's *their* vision, their undertaking, their definition of value, and their world to change. *That* is the power of entrepreneurship manifested. In a full-circle effect, Zipcar's customers have inspired Robin to create a new venture called Meadow Networks, focused on applying the latest in networking and technology to build more effective infrastructures within communities. A ripple becomes a cycle and humanity advances.

The value customers bring to the entrepreneurial ecosystem is beyond question.

## *The Role of Entrepreneurial Advisor*

Understanding *who* is behind successful entrepreneurship requires stepping away from common defaults—the stories, the myths, and the accepted views. Realizing that it takes "many, not just one" was the first step. But to fully appreciate the vibrancy of the entrepreneurial ecosystem, let's drop all mental boundaries around the *venture* and talk about the role of entrepreneurial advisor, a critical one in the successful ecosystem, but one often overlooked because it is assumed to be outside the venture. (As the role of customers demonstrates, not everyone within the ecosystem is directly or formally within the venture.)

Esther Dyson, founder of Edventure Holdings, is perhaps best known for her *Release 1.0* newsletter that tracks trends and leaders in technology. She watches the entrepreneurial universe within the technology sector, sees patterns that most don't, and guides participants according to what she believes works and doesn't work. Deeply knowledgeable yet objective, Esther cares about the success of technology ventures and the trend line for tech's evolution, maybe even more than many CEOs who count on her advice.

Esther feels passionate about the need for human progress. Listing her qualities, many of them sound entrepreneurial in nature, but she considers herself less of an entrepreneur and more of an *observer* of entrepreneurs. As it turns out, that benefits countless people who do call themselves entrepreneurs.

Beginning our discussion of advisors through Esther's example makes sense because her profile doesn't line up with common perceptions.

First, for most clients, she advises from a distance even though we tend to think of an advisor offering advice face to face. Yet her unique combination of perspective, knowledge, and objectivity adds value even when clients don't meet with her directly. Second, Esther doesn't spell out what to do (actions) when she offers advice. Rather, she encourages entrepreneurs to listen to themselves. Finally, by paying attention to the patterns across Esther's observations and advice, we see that she doesn't provide *the* answers, at least not in the sense of solving specific problems. More accurately, she encourages those who consider her advice to ask questions, reexamine activities, and come up with answers of their own. Doing that emphasizes the reflective, not the instructional, side of learning.

As with every other critical role in the entrepreneurial universe, advisors aren't substitutes for entrepreneurs. They only allow entrepreneurs to more fully realize and reveal their own humanity and human potential, which is exactly what entrepreneurs seek to do for the rest of us.

## Providing a Mirror for the Leader

While hailed as visionaries possessing unique perspectives, entrepreneurs are often far *less* capable of turning the skill around on *themselves* and seeing in new ways than they are applying that skill to the rest of the world. "The biggest need and role provided by others around the entrepreneur is to be a mirror for the leader," observed leadership expert Jim Shaffer, author of *The Leadership Solution*. "Often, the day leaders become leaders is the last day they hear the truth. So, consistent with that reality, entrepreneurs need to have someone coach and guide them in places where they can't see clearly or objectively." This is exactly where advisors can be invaluable.

In a sense, what advisors do for entrepreneurs is what entrepreneurs do for humankind—they offer tough, unvarnished, wise distance. Specifically, they encourage entrepreneurs to return to their unique gift once more, to pause and reflect, and then to act entrepreneurially as they expand the entrepreneurial undertakings in which they're engaged.

When advisors guide entrepreneurs, they not only encourage them to step back and gain (or regain) perspective. They also engage them in the process of questioning—the critical practice of regularly asking why. Why are certain activities not working? Why is *this* the best way to do things? Why isn't there a better way to see this situation more clearly? Why must value be limited to what exists today?

These are the kinds of questions entrepreneurs initially ask to break free of the status quo, but they need to be reminded—even encouraged—to *continue* asking them as they pursue their dreams. Having a trusted, objective advisor who fills that role can be invaluable.

## Are Outside Advisors Always Necessary?

The concept of objectivity raises important points about advisors and should cause us to ask questions like "why must advisors come from outside the venture?" The simple answer is "they don't have to."

Entrepreneurs are wise to surround themselves with smart activators, team specialists, and others *inside* the venture. They can count on them to bring new ideas, challenge the entrepreneur's own view, and teach as much as they learn. But it's important to understand the limits on the value those working close by day after day can bring.

Sometimes you need a specialist from the outside who brings a perspective or skill you don't have inside the venture, such as a lawyer, financial or marketing expert, information technology expert, and countless others. Although these skills can be vital to a venture's ultimate success, you can't always justify having them full time in house. Uniquely, outside advisors can serve to bolster the venture precisely when they're needed.

Being outside the venture affords another critical advantage—the chance to access an objective peer network. Being an entrepreneur is a tough and, at times, lonely role. As the person who catalyzed it all, the entrepreneur is naturally viewed as the one with all the answers, the head cheerleader, and the person who can absorb all the frustrations, worries, and conflicts that arise. Feeling pressure from others expecting the catalyst to be all-knowing can be all-consuming. Ed Feeney, an applied behavioral science expert, described the magnitude of the burden this way: "Beyond the underlying constants, as an entrepreneur you have to ask and know what was before this point, what is now, and what will be after." That's a lot of responsibility to shoulder. And it can be hard to find an outlet, a buffer, or a sounding board from people entrenched in the venture itself.

Frequently, entrepreneurs need an empathetic peer to help them shake off feelings of being all alone or being consumed by others. After all, only an entrepreneur who's also immersed in the venture can know what that pressure feels like. Finding others capable of seeing through an entrepreneurial lens and doing so objectively can be a breath of fresh air.

### Wise Entrepreneurs Engage With Advisors

As important as advisors clearly are, oddly, many would-be entrepreneurs don't seek them. Sometimes it's a result of guarding their ideas too closely and keeping their own counsel. Other times entrepreneurs don't know where to begin to find advisors or fear they won't find the right ones.

But true entrepreneurs get engaged. They consciously, actively, and perpetually seek out advice—in many forms and from many sources. They open up and share the truth with their advisors, seeking it in return. They know that, unless they throw their ideas out and listen to honest, objective feedback, they may be fooling themselves and failing their visions. And just as they know that it takes many *within* the venture to succeed, they recognize that it takes many more, even beyond the chalk edges of the venture, to make an ecosystem complete and effective.

## Learning to Rely on Key Advisors—At Least One

Geoff Smart, founder of ghSMART, played an instrumental role in the research and theory behind *Top Grading*, a highly acclaimed and widely used hiring manual based on the premise that to become an 'A' Level organization, you have to hire 'A' Level players. He furthered that work and insight with the 2008 release of *Who: The A Method for Hiring*, a book he co-authored with Randy Street. Geoff's advice has guided thousands of leading executives, nearly half of whom he's identified as entrepreneurs. "In countless assessments of successful executives that I have done, zero made it to the top without at least one key advisor," he has concluded from his work.

That pattern is validated everywhere you look in the entrepreneurial universe. And it takes a variety of forms, several of which appear more often than others.

Peer groups are perhaps the most pervasive and easily found source of advisors for entrepreneurs. There are local, regional, national, and even virtual groups that have formed over the last decade and a half in particular, giving entrepreneurs a place to find each other and find advice at many levels as never before. TIE (The Indus Entrepreneurs—self-described as "successful entrepreneurs and professionals with roots in the Indus region" around the Indian Ocean) is one such group. Today it comprises 53 chapters in 12 countries and has more than 12,000 members. Those members include entrepreneurs, investors, law firms, and technology and management professionals. Think of the countless interactions such a large group of peers generates!

Whether they participate in peer groups or not, an increasing number of entrepreneurs are choosing to form boards of advisors. Different from boards of directors, advisory boards tend to be more informal and less focused on the dubious (but all too frequent) "3 Cs" (cash, connections, and cache) used to choose members of many boards of directors.

Instead, entrepreneurs ask those who have perspectives that differ from their own to become part of a regular series of discussions—some one-on-one, some group—to reflect on how the entrepreneur and the venture are growing. These boards can include representatives from partner organizations, leaders from unrelated businesses, past or even current customers, or any other perspective that offers diverse and balancing viewpoints.

Hiring executive coaches is another increasingly common route entrepreneurs are taking. It was once borderline taboo for entrepreneurs to acknowledge they needed help; some viewed having a coach as an acknowledgment of weakness. But someone who knows you intimately, understands your venture, and can provide guidance to the highs and lows of transformational growth can be critical to your evolution as an entrepreneur. For many, coaches fit that bill.

Regardless of the form an advisor takes, it may take just *one* to help an entrepreneur see the venture more clearly and move it forward.

### Four Lessons About the Roles Played

In this chapter, we've discussed roles beyond the entrepreneur's role that are vital to creating a vibrant ecosystem. In the process, we've not only learned about the nature of these roles, we've also learned valuable lessons about how these roles interact—lessons that need to be underscored.

The first lesson is that *all the roles in an ecosystem need to share a common anchor.* Recall that entrepreneurs are able to recognize patterns in great part because they've lived in a particular environment for a long time, enough to know it intimately. They've breathed the space in which they see certain patterns develop; what happens in that space matters to them. In short, they know the world their efforts address, and they care deeply about making it better.

The same is true for those who join the entrepreneur in key roles. More than simply working at the entrepreneur's *company* to do a *job*, activators, team specialists, and others become *invested* in a world they hope to change. It's *their* venture as much as it is the entrepreneur's. They are (or quickly become) members of a community, a concept explored more fully in Chapter 6.

Activators and others who team with entrepreneurs follow in their footsteps to the extent that they recognize the same patterns and want to bring their knowledge and skills to bear on those patterns. They see opportunities and are able to apply their skills effectively because they know the space in which they are cultivating a collective vision. They then leverage that knowledge to find solutions that make the vision work and, by so doing, make their world better. This common anchor, this intimacy with their world, and this communal connection provide two things all entrepreneurial ventures need: the motivation to change things and the specific knowledge as to how.

A second more subtle lesson is this: *While each venture consists of many distinct and equally important roles, those who fill them won't always take on the same role in every venture.* The role and the person are not one in the same. It isn't productive or even accurate to label someone as an entrepreneur or a team specialist for all time. As Guy Kawasaki and Carter Cast showed, the roles in the entrepreneurial universe exist along a fluid spectrum. The evangelist in one ecosystem may become the entrepreneur in another; the activator in today's venture could evolve to be the entrepreneur in tomorrow's.

If you consider the lists of contributors at the start of each chapter, you will see a pattern emerging that reinforces this lesson. Nearly every one of them has played different roles in the entrepreneurial universe. If you examine the full listing of contributors in the Contributors appendix at the end of the book, you will see the pattern repeated many times over. I invite you to enter the lives of these contributors and discover that many play different roles in different ventures at the same time. The key is to play the *right* role at the *right* time and maximize the value that's contributed to human progress.

The third universal lesson reveals that *each role enables and depends on the other roles within the entrepreneurial ecosystem.* As an example, we talked about the activator playing the bridge, foil, and buffer between the entrepreneur and the team specialists. The activator identifies the people and pieces that evolve the vision from idea to ecosystem, making the puzzle complete and functioning. Similarly, *each* role extends from, supports, and adds to the others. The entrepreneur's vision is defined by the activator who counts on specialists to manifest that vision and make it tangible to the customers who validate its worth and share their own passion about it. This symbiotic chain causes the entrepreneur to see new forms of value never before imagined, thereby reshaping the vision and the venture to add value *ad infinitum.*

The fourth lesson brings us full circle. Over the last five chapters we've described an evolution that occurs in entrepreneurship—the evolution from one to many, the growth of an ecosystem comprised of many roles, and more. What cannot be overlooked is that none of these things can occur if the entrepreneur fails to evolve into a leader. *Although it's easy to assume, an "entrepreneur" and "leader" are not the same* (something we will explore in depth when we discuss the four fundamentals of successful and sustainable entrepreneurship in Chapter 9). Being perceptive enough to see patterns and opportunities to advance the world provides a great start. But as Scott Frederick of Valhalla Partners said, "Intelligence is a lot like four-wheel drive in a day-to-day car; it just allows you to get stuck in more remote places."

More often than not, those who kick off entrepreneurial ventures struggle with recognizing the need for others. Even if they do, they tend to treat them as *employees* rather than partners in a mutually shared quest. The need for other roles may be clear, but embracing them fully isn't automatic or easy. "People get focused on single issues, single sectors, or narrow views," explained Carl Safina, author of *Song for the Blue Ocean.* "Somehow we get ourselves bound up in our own problems or dreams and aren't willing to help others unless they address our needs first. This thinking gets us nowhere fast. Thinking systemically—in terms of an ecosystem—works because it forces us to get down to the fundamentals, to examine how things are interconnected, to share. To solve the big problems, we must think and act this way."

## The Test of the Leader

It's always a delicate balance learning how and when to seek out others, and then to know how best to integrate them. Jim Shaffer called this *the test of the leader.* "The true leader has to embrace that it isn't all about them," said Jim. "They have to be willing to hear the truth. They have to be willing to discern the truth, too, when to listen and not. They have to be willing to act on it. They have to know when to step in and when to step aside. That takes a very stable moral compass and ego in addition to knowledge and expertise." And it requires a willingness to seek out and integrate others in something more than one person's dream and one person's role in making that dream real.

"To be truly entrepreneurial, the solutions are dynamic," reflected Martin Goebel. "Many have to work together. And entrepreneurs do more than catalyze ideas. They have to create the environment for dynamic solutions so it's capable of moving and continuing on its own. Sure, a lot of people want control. But in the context of moving large objects, you can't be a control freak. Commonality and collective ego is key."

Those who take on these roles—activator, team specialists, customers, and advisors—come to a point of integration anchored around the entrepreneur's initial vision and purpose. But ultimately, they all shape that vision in ways that make it their own. By the time a vision is realized, it looks nothing like what the entrepreneur first thought it would. (Any true entrepreneur will tell you that while flashing a smile.) The fingerprints of every role are equally visible on the final product, ultimately making all roles relative to their collaboration as part of a vibrant ecosystem.

## *Recommended Resources*

### *The E Myth Revisited* – Michael Gerber

This book does a great job of showing how people might think they're entrepreneurs—or think that entrepreneurship provides a ticket to freedom and riches—but clearly shows that it's just not that simple. While focusing on how to successfully run and expand a small business, Gerber makes it clear that however you define "entrepreneur" just assuming the moniker isn't enough to make someone an entrepreneur and that even if you truly are, being one doesn't lead to instant success and happiness.

### *The Great Game of Business* – Jack Stack

When Jack Stack suggested the idea of "open book management"— that is, sharing the finances of your business with your employees to show them their impact on the bottom line, positive or negative— people declared him crazy. As the expression goes, he *was* crazy—like a fox. This wonderful book shows how building a business together really works.

### *What Should I Do With My Life?* – Po Bronson

Everybody has a role, a place in the world, a passion, and a dream of seeing all these gel. Don't read this book looking for an answer to the question its title poses—at least not a direct, specific one. Instead, read it to get a sense of the diversity of the human endeavor and why people do what they do and dream what they dream. It's mind opening. Suddenly, the only important role becomes the one that is right for you.

# Contributors to Chapter 6

**Robin Chase** (See Chapter 1)

**Sandy Robertson**
> Founder, Robertson, Stephens & Company and Francisco Partners
> Lifetime Achievement Award in Entrepreneurship, Haas School of Business
> Director, salesforce.com and Schwab Fund for Charitable Giving

**Guy Kawasaki** (See Chapter 2)

**Craig Johnson**
> Founder, Venture Law Group
> Co-founder, Garage Technology Ventures
> Former Partner, Wilson Sonsini

**Ching Ho Fung**
> Co-founder, Performix
> Board of Directors, BlackBoard and Parature

**Michael Chasen**
> Co-founder, President, CEO, BlackBoard
> *SmartCEO* magazine CEO of the Year, 2006
> Ernst & Young Entrepreneur of the Year, 2000

**Duke Chung**
> Co-founder, CEO, President, Parature
> Contributing Author, *Inside the Minds: Software Leadership Strategies*
> *Fast Company* magazine's Fast 50, 2006

**Casey Golden**
> Founder, Small Act Network
> Contributing Author, *Do Your Giving While You Are Living*
> Co-founder, Parature

**Najlah Feanny Hicks**
> Co-founder, President, The Heart Gallery of New Jersey
> Contributor to *America 24/7* and *An American Journey*
> Editorial and Corporate Photographer

**John Zitzner**
> Founder, E City Cleveland, the Entrepreneurship Preparatory School
> Founder, Former CEO, President, The Bradley Company

**Steve Mariotti** (See Chapter 2)

**Brad Whitehead** (See Chapter 2)

**Ray Leach**
  CEO, JumpStart
  Founder, Former President, Capella Capital
  Co-founder, Publishing Solutions
**Baiju Shah** (See Chapter 4)
**Mario Morino** (See Chapter 3)
**Bill Drayton** (See Chapter 3)
**David Green**
  Founder, The Eye Fund and Project Impact
  Ashoka Fellow, MacArthur Fellow

# Chapter 6: The Necessary Power
# of Community

*"It's a wide and shallow stream, one which we get across by all individuals buying and throwing in their own rocks until there are many paths across."*

- Robin Chase
Co-founder, Zipcar and GoLoco
*Time's* 100 World's Most Influential People, 2009

Entrepreneurs are often seen as the ultimate outsiders, individuals who belong only to themselves. By this point, we know better. To make an entrepreneurial vision real takes others—many others—that go far beyond the entrepreneur. In that sense, entrepreneurs *need* others the way members of an ecosystem need one another to survive. But entrepreneurs who achieve lasting success evolve beyond need. They instinctively want to reach others, change lives, and make the world better—for many, not just for themselves.

Such entrepreneurs go beyond the creation of *ecosystems* to influence, change, and even create *communities*.

## Distinguishing Communities from Ecosystems

Viewed from the surface, ecosystems and communities can at first appear much the same. Below the surface, however, lie important differences.

An ecosystem is necessary for survival; a community goes beyond necessity. The links within an ecosystem—for example, the purpose each part serves, the ways in which its members support one another, and its collective purpose for existing—are more basic and obvious than in a community. Within a community and across its interrelated components exists a richer texture. The reasons for community, the purposes it fulfills, and how its members intertwine are complex. A community isn't concerned solely with the survival or fulfillment of one objective; its reasons for being don't depend on one idea or single measure of value. Rather, its members come together for something more, not out of need alone but by choice.

## Communities and Ecosystems Seen Through the Aspen and Ripple Effects

Comparing the Aspen Effect (Chapter 3) to the Ripple Effect (Chapter 4) helps make the distinction between a community and the ecosystem even stronger. Let's first consider the aspen tree itself to provide a helpful analogy.

Aspens innately and purposely spread out a root system beneath the meadow floor to form a thriving ecosystem. The more area the aspen stand covers, or the more "sprouts" or trees that are pushed to the surface, the more the aspen stand gets the nutrients—sun, water, soil, and air—necessary for survival.

At that level, the level of survival, we are witnessing the Ripple Effect of an aspen as it grows—that is, the natural force that causes a ripple to spread across the surface of the water from the point where a thrown stone enters the pond. To a large extent, the occurrence of a ripple is inevitable, an expected reaction to its catalyst. Left on its own without further influence or deliberate action, that ripple expands outward, but its growth is largely random and inevitably limited.

In the same way that a community is much more than an ecosystem, the Aspen Effect is much more than the natural force of a ripple.

As an aspen stand matures, its reasons for being multiply. To be specific, as the number of trees growing out of the common root system increases, the stand is able to provide its members more than the nutrients of basic survival. It also provides shelter from the wind, its expansive root system holds the soil firmly and protects it from erosion, and its canopy of quaking leaves offers visual cover and protection from the sun. As it turns out, these elements benefit more than the trees or their basic survival. Birds, animals, even other plants embrace them and become part of the community. These symbiotic members of the community return the favor in their own way, providing the trees with additional benefits as each makes the aspen stand its home. Clearly, one reason for existence grows into many reasons, and choices layer upon choices until the original ecosystem becomes part of a larger, more complex community (the Aspen Effect, not just the aspen stand).

While the Ripple Effect in entrepreneurship may begin with a conscious choice, it can peter out if it fails to become something more than the original event and person that catalyzed it. Sure, an ecosystem may stem from that first catalyzing moment, but to last and thrive takes more and more energy, contributors, and reasons for being. It needs the Aspen Effect, which reflects more thoughtful, layered, and purposeful actions.

Taking it further, the Aspen Effect represents repeated, deliberate choices to come together, stay together, and form *something more* than an ecosystem that minimally survives. As an example, in the dynamic of the Zipcar community that Robin Chase catalyzed, she is now one small part of it. As she said, "We choose to be associated with each other and, together, we will pursue more."

In a community, "choice" trumps "necessity."

## The Fluid Dynamic Between Catalyst and Community

To reshape and transform a community into something better, an unusual and fluid cycle of interaction between the entrepreneur and the community takes place.

First, the entrepreneur must be willing to break *from* the community. Notice the critical word choice here: Rather than breaking *with* the community, which implies a sense of never returning, entrepreneurs break *from* the community temporarily. They unplug for a length of time, often to take a deliberate pause. This separation helps them think apart from those entrenched in the community, allowing them to see patterns and opportunities that others do not. During such periods, they act on behalf of the community but *in contrast to* it—and even *in defiance of* it. They go it alone for a time because they believe they have no choice; it's the only way to advance the community with which they feel connected.

Eventually, inevitably, consciously, these entrepreneurs seek a path to *rejoin* and *advance* their communities. They want others to follow their thinking toward something better. They want to share the value they envision with others; indeed, they understand what others need to do to create, expand, and perpetuate value. This rejoining must occur for the resulting entrepreneurship to be effective and long lasting.

In this go-away-come-back fashion, entrepreneurs *remain part of* their communities as they seek to create something new and better—to initiate a transformation. Were they not willing to break from it for a while with the intent of rejoining it, their ideas would be no more valuable than a candle lit in the rain, its flame not able to endure.

## Exposure to Entrepreneurial Communities

It's one thing to know that community is a powerful tool in successful entrepreneurship; it's quite another to know how to create community or what it should look like.

This isn't easily addressed because entrepreneurial communities, as any community, reflect the purpose, circumstances, and people who create them. Their formation and format are as individual as the visions and visionaries that shape them. The good news is that entrepreneurial communities don't require taking on an exact format to have the potentially powerful effect they do. In that sense, there's no one format that needs to be adopted to unlock their secrets. Instead, what's required is a heightened awareness of various formats that entrepreneurial communities can take to make entrepreneurship thrive.

To give you a sense for how communities emerge, the nature of the power they can have, and the various forms they can take, this chapter features five distinct entrepreneurial communities. As you read about each one, regard this as a concentrated exercise in *exposure* to what's possible—and the powerful influence community can have on human progress.

**Types of Entrepreneurial Communities**
Figure 6

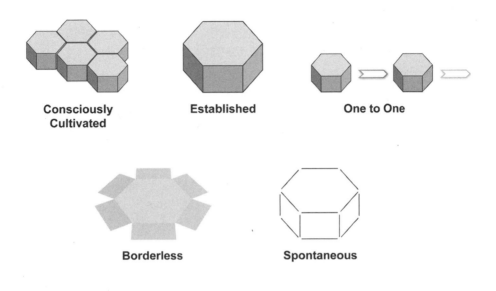

**Consciously Cultivated**

**Established**

**One to One**

**Borderless**

**Spontaneous**

## *The Established Community: Silicon Valley*

Perhaps the best-known example of an entrepreneurial community is Northern California's Silicon Valley. Exactly where and when the Silicon Valley community began and who started it is open to debate. One version holds that it began as a company—not just any company but the storied technology company Hewlett-Packard (HP).

Legend has it that in 1939, Bill Hewlett and Dave Packard pooled $538 and formed a partnership to develop technology. Others give credit to the unique classroom environment created by Stanford University professor Frederick Terman. Tired of seeing his highly qualified graduates leave the Bay Area for jobs elsewhere, Terman set up a program to encourage students to build their own dreams and companies in the area. (Hewlett and Packard just happened to be two of his star graduates.) In the end, Silicon Valley's starting point is much less relevant than *how* it evolved and what it has become.

Regardless of its actual origin, Silicon Valley got its name in the late 1950s and early 1960s when a number of start-up companies began to produce silicon wafers, the key ingredient in semiconductors, or chips.

141

Hewlett-Packard was among them. The success of semiconductor innovation in this area led to a wave of related start-up companies producing instruments, electronics, and computers. One idea sparked many. Team members from one team moved to other teams or spawned teams and ventures of their own. Before long, a whole series of innovative companies occupied a tight geographic region near the San Francisco Bay.

That's the short version of how Silicon Valley came to be. But that popular version ignores the amazing fact that Silicon Valley came to fruition in a time when the idea of an entrepreneurial community was virtually unknown. Certainly entrepreneurs existed in many locales before this era, but rarely had a large group of them gathered in one place. A whole community built on a shared entrepreneurial mindset had yet to be formed.

## Entrepreneurship Embraced as an Integral Part of Life

Today, from the community's way of teaching to the laws that guide it, Silicon Valley naturally embraces entrepreneurship as an integral part of life. This entrepreneurial aura prevails not only in high tech, life sciences, and more recently green tech ventures for which Silicon Valley has become famous; its influence is felt across the community at large. Because of this, entrepreneurial successes are not only pervasive, they also return immense value to the region and far beyond, and repeatedly deliver on the promise of entrepreneurship.

What's most important yet is declaring what Silicon Valley has come to represent: *a community in which entrepreneurship is ingrained, and where entrepreneurial successes consistently flourish.*

Silicon Valley evolved from a collection of ventures into a community because of the mindset that spread beyond those ventures into a broader "pond." As each venture grew, not surprisingly it required certain resources—employees, capital, real estate, various professional services, and more—all the things that helped form and feed each venture's ecosystem. One could argue that any one venture forming in this region individually held great promise, enough to attract the required resources. But in fact multiple ventures formed in the same area around the same time, and what followed ushered in a whole new meaning to entrepreneurial community.

Collectively, these ventures represented staying power for all the resources needed to support them. Their growing numbers offered assurance that these or similar "ventures" would be around for the long haul. In this kind of community emerges a "feeling" that no entrepreneurial venture stands completely alone against the odds of succeeding. When everyone around embraces this entrepreneurial thinking, greater achievement seems possible and risk becomes relative to the grander opportunities being pursued. In such an environment, those who play critical roles in any venture's success sense this dynamic. When they do, the risk of supporting it becomes relatively small.

So as Silicon Valley's ventures grew in number, more and more innovative thinkers and believers caught on to the vision of the early tech entrepreneurs around them. Because of this dynamic, entrepreneurial thinking quickly spread to areas typically not associated with it, including law, banking, accounting, and education.

Iconic venture capitalist, investment banker, and entrepreneurial thinker Sandy Robertson is a good example of this dynamic. In the early 1970s, a young Sandy came to the San Francisco Bay Area from the Midwest to source new clients for his employer at the time, Smith Barney. In Silicon Valley, he witnessed something he'd never seen before—elements far removed from the airline companies and other large corporations that made up the bread and butter of the Smith Barney clientele. Here were innovators building new ventures, even new industries, based on fresh ideas and offering the promise of the future.

### This Cutting-Edge Culture Called Sandy's Name

When he returned to Chicago, Sandy told his managers about the cutting-edge technologies he'd witnessed around him. The higher-ups at Smith Barney didn't (perhaps couldn't) see what Sandy saw. Instead, they perceived lots of risk and little reward in the tiny start-ups Sandy got excited about.

Still, this rapidly blossoming culture of Silicon Valley kept calling his name. Sandy found himself caught up in a wave of new thinking.

Everywhere he turned in Silicon Valley, that thinking reinforced itself. Strong and compelling, it enticed him to leave his established firm and become part of this exciting community. And he did so by forming his own entrepreneurial investment bank.

At that time, few took notice of any investment bank that wasn't servicing Fortune 500 clients and wasn't located on Wall Street. To conceive of one that would serve pure start-up ventures—and do so even before those ventures could pay back—was considered insanity. Except to Sandy and a handful of others who followed his lead.

Sandy kicked off a new wave of investment banking with the formation of firms like Robertson, Coleman, Siebel & Weisel (which became Montgomery Securities) and Robertson Stephens & Company. Driven by a belief in forming intimate relationships with companies before they were viable and gaining deep knowledge of their emerging industries, Sandy and others earned the rebuke of established firms who called these upstarts "boutique" banks. But the two firms Sandy founded during that time, along with Hambrecht & Quist and Alex Brown & Sons, became known as the four horsemen. The nickname stuck, no doubt because of the now-legendary impact that changed the capital markets forever and helped develop such innovative leading companies as Dell, Pixar, and Sun Microsystems. Without the Sandy Robertsons of the Silicon Valley world, these companies might never have become more than bright ideas.

Sandy is one of many examples of the Ripple Effect becoming an Aspen Effect in nascent Silicon Valley, fueling a conscious drive to form an entrepreneurial community. While people like him were breaking new ground in investment banking, others such as Larry Sonsini and his partners did the same in law, establishing Wilson Sonsini as a firm exclusively focused on providing guidance to the Valley's young entrepreneurs. Where Sandy was creating a means to access capital for *growth*, the founders of Kleiner Perkins (still one of the world's preeminent venture capital firms) were developing sources of *seed capital* to get new ideas out into the sunlight. Soon a full and complete chain of resources critical to a venture's growth existed, not in ones and twos but in entire blocks, neighborhoods, and subsets of the larger entrepreneurial community. Their collective willingness to step out on a limb has continued to regularly generate the likes of Amazon, Google, TiVo, and more.

Over time, Silicon Valley's entrepreneurial mindset became so engrained, the feedback loop so strong, and the overlap of ecosystems around individual ventures so frequent that looking forward became much more important than looking back. "What would be, could be, or should be next?" became the driving mantra.

### Entrepreneurial Wave Picks Up Velocity

Silicon Valley offers a clear view of the importance community can play in tapping the power of entrepreneurship, with critical elements— including education, capital, legislation, human resources, and human will—aligning to help the entrepreneurial mindset flourish. Today, hands from many corners of the community continue to push the entrepreneurial wave forward with a breadth and velocity that has given staying power to entrepreneurship—again, one that no single venture could have provided.

In fact, the force of this wave gained power so quickly that eventually Silicon Valley residents had no reason *not* to support what was being created. Everyone benefited. And because of that, wide support for entrepreneurs kept spreading—evidence of the Aspen Effect. The results continue to speak for themselves.

The benefits of having an entrepreneurial mindset have extended beyond physical boundaries and crossed the boundaries of generations. Someone who's born into, or even dropped into, such a community can't help but be influenced by its omnipresent entrepreneurial mindset. Guy Kawasaki and Craig Johnson are great examples (see *Into the Community, Into the Mindset*).

### Into the Community, Into the Mindset

Although Guy Kawasaki was born in Honolulu, he went to school at Stanford, graduating in 1976. There was no Horatio Alger rags-to-riches influence or lemonade-stand exposure to entrepreneurship before he came to the Bay Area. Guy said, "I had a normal upbringing. My father was at different times fireman, real estate broker, and politician." But rather than walking a traditional path like his dad, Guy became one of the original employees at a little start-up firm called Apple Computer.

For an embryonic venture to suck in a seemingly regular guy, you have to consider the surrounding community that could even make this conceivable. You see, Guy didn't just join Apple; he became, as described earlier, its chief evangelist for the Mac. "If you liken Apple Computers to a country," Guy once said, "it would be like Israel, and I (was) in charge of the Mossad (The Israeli version of the CIA, the secret service, and special operations all rolled into one)."

The Silicon Valley environment permeated Guy's thinking and choices. To do his job at Apple effectively, he had to believe in the power and inevitability of the new world Apple was proposing—a world in which computers would go from the size of a lecture hall to one on every person's desk top (at the time, a concept those outside the Valley flatly dismissed). But in Silicon Valley, it was almost pedestrian to have such ideas. Plenty of evidence surrounded newcomers like Guy to believe such changes were not only possible but inevitable.

In the early 1990s after he left Apple, Guy founded garage.com to help other catalysts get started and spread the entrepreneurial culture further. Later he co-founded a venture capital firm to bring capital resources and start-up expertise directly to these ventures. Since then, he has become a prolific educator, evangelist, and author of more than eight books and a popular blog.[12] Guy's mission? To spread the wisdom he's derived from the entrepreneurial community in which he has lived for more than three decades.

An entrepreneurial community influences more than the common mindset; it has the power to influence outcomes, as the experience of one of Guy's partners shows.

Craig Johnson graduated from Stanford Law School in 1974 and joined Wilson Sonsini as one of its earliest attorneys. After helping build an innovative law practice to support this thriving entrepreneurial community, he left to start the Venture Law Group in 1993. Some people thought he was crazy to do so. Here was Craig, a top partner in the firm earning a dream income, contemplating walking away from it all. But to the people closest to him, Craig's moving on was a natural progression of his entrepreneurial mindset.

Breaking out allowed him to channel changes in the very community he'd actively supported for nearly 20 years. "I had two choices," Craig said about his decision to leave Wilson Sonsini. "I could pursue what I believed in, or spend the rest of my life regretting not pursuing it. I knew my model for Venture Law Group was important and right. I saw the flaws in the current structure, and took the chance to change that.

"They say entrepreneurs want to change the world, but that isn't exactly right. They want to take something they know and *do it better*. They see that they have no way to do it within an existing framework, so they're left with two choices: do nothing or change things."

The Venture Law Group far surpassed Craig's expectations. Since leaving it, he has gone on to found or co-found numerous other ventures, including Garage Technology Ventures with Guy. They joined forces because they could see the added benefits of working together—not out of survival echoing the Ripple Effect, but out of choice represented by the Aspen Effect.

Most people believe that 9 out of 10 ventures are destined to fail. Some highly relied-upon statistics about entrepreneurship bear out this belief. So it seems strange to hear Craig Johnson say he's experienced this 9-out-of-10 rule *in reverse*; that is, instead of 9-out-of-10 failures, he's had 9-out-of-10 successes. And he's seen many others achieve a similar pattern.

Craig explained this exceptional success rate by saying, "Maybe it's because of the filtering, asking, learning, and allowing myself to be coached." It's simpler than that. It's the community around him that taught him those skills.

Stumbling along the way is commonly expected among entrepreneurs, but as Craig noted, "Failure is less of a stigma in Silicon Valley" than in other places. It supports a cultural mindset that teaches perseverance and the value of seeking experienced help. Trial and error is accepted but it's also minimized by the breadth of exposure, the shared experience, the openness, the high standards for learning from mistakes, the depth of resources, and the countless other things that an established entrepreneurial community lends to anyone trying something new.

No question, it all comes back to the power of community.

## One-to-One Community Building: Ching Ho Fung

Examples of entrepreneurial communities like Silicon Valleys are too few and far between. If nothing else, that means that too few people become immersed or at least exposed to the entrepreneurial mindset.

Where entrepreneurial communities are rare and exposure to entrepreneurial ideas informal and individual, it helps to have a guide—someone dedicated to influencing others to think entrepreneurially. It may not seem like it at first, but the efforts of such people form communities and help pass on cultures; they just happen to do it one-to-one.

It makes sense that the best guides have experience manifesting dreams. It better enables them to advise and expose others to the entrepreneurial mindset. That personal experience also helps them realize their deep desires to pass on what they know to others and, in the process, instill in them an entrepreneurial mindset and capacity. That sharing element—creating community at the simplest individual level—often gets incorporated into their own definitions of success and value.

Ching Ho Fung exemplifies how one-to-one community building can powerfully enhance the entrepreneurial wave beyond a single venture and even a single relationship.

In the late 1980s, Ching Ho co-founded Performix, a software company that developed innovative approaches to evaluating performance efficiencies in large-scale computer systems. After a meteoric rise, Performix sold for tens of millions of dollars to Pure Software. Its original software products went on to fuel the value of this company and its eventual acquirer, software leader Rationale.

Declared by industry, media, and others as a success (based on common measures), Performix was actually only one point on the spectrum of success that Ching Ho envisioned. It's not to say that such success as defined by others wasn't fulfilling for Ching Ho. It's just that his vision had always been bigger than one venture or even one dream, forged and guided by him alone.

Performix was largely successful because Ching Ho created software that gave others the ability to spread value on their own—a critical role of the catalyst. But sharing that goal and way of thinking is where the real power of entrepreneurship reveals itself. With Performix successfully placed in the hands of others, Ching Ho wanted most to discover himself at a deeper level, leverage his abilities, and provide opportunities to help others achieve, too.

## BlackBoard Benefited from Ching Ho's Guidance

Ching Ho's first opportunity came when he met Michael Chasen and Matthew Pittinsky in 1997. These young men were armed with little experience and a big idea to take education online. That idea blossomed into BlackBoard, arguably the leading online education company today. Without question, Ching Ho played a key role both in bringing this opportunity to Michael and Matthew and teaching them how to seize it. True, the idea belonged to Michael and Matthew. But Ching Ho brought the experience, the culture, the mindset, and the guidance they needed to help that idea flourish.

While tutoring them in how to determine their needs and make decisions on their own, Ching Ho showed Michael and Matthew a complete view of entrepreneurship and its pieces—the tools, the time, the reinforcement, the camaraderie—he knew to be so vital. Yes, a community provides these naturally over time, but usually does so in pieces drawn from many areas. The one-to-one community requires a dedicated mentor willing to get involved directly.

Fortunately for Michael and Matthew, Ching Ho gave them his expertise and personal commitment in both a hands-on and hands-off way. For a time, they had an on-call CEO in Ching Ho who demanded no salary and expected to step aside when they outgrew the need for his guidance. He was tough and demanding yet equally encouraging. He challenged them to hone their own thinking. He showed them the way, and he willingly got out of their way when the time was right.

On a small scale, Ching Ho tapped into the Aspen Effect. First, he spread out his own success, allowing Michael and Matthew's achievements to be nurtured by his own. Second, he let success be defined by more than himself. Ching Ho may have guided them at times, but he let BlackBoard's founders chart their own course. And third, Ching Ho facilitated the growth of first an ecosystem and then a larger community around Michael and Matthew by introducing them to the experiences, views, and resources of others. This exposure helped BlackBoard's founders more effectively mitigate the trial-and-error route and thrive more quickly.

And in the process of providing them with core elements for community building, Ching Ho realized success on a whole new level for himself.

### One-to-One Repeated

Both Ching Ho's definition of success and his impact continue to expand. After working with Michael and Matthew, he went on to similar partnerships, including guiding Duke Chung, Casey Golden, and the customer support management software company they co-founded, Parature—now an industry leader.

Today, Duke still runs Parature, guiding it toward a bright future. He learned a great deal from Ching Ho, not the least of which was the value of community, something the entire Parature model is built on. It's no coincidence that Parature's software solution relies on the community of its customers and its customer constituents to provide solutions to one another and help the company evolve its products.

Perhaps taking a page from Ching Ho's own story, Casey has spread the aspen stand further, taking the lesson of community he used to design Parature's products and formed an entirely new venture to build and spread community itself. (You'll learn more about Casey's Small Act Network in Chapter 11.)

With each new entrepreneur he supports, Ching Ho broadens the overall understanding of entrepreneurial success. Rejecting a self-serving view of success, he offered this advice: "You can't just *ask* why.

You have to *answer* that question, and be honest with yourself about the answers. It's often the hardest part of being an entrepreneur. The answer, it turns out, isn't always within yourself or about yourself."

Ching Ho's one-to-one approach shows us yet another reason why community—no matter how large or small—is critical to the evolution of catalysts and the successful pursuit of their entrepreneurial dreams.

## Spontaneous Community: The Heart Gallery Project

Community in its many formats doesn't always happen out of conscious creation or purposeful exposure. Some communities aren't even geographically centralized or bordered. But regardless of form, when a community collectively sees the world differently and acts in a deliberate way, the powerful force of the entrepreneurial mindset can be seen. The example of the Heart Gallery projects that have expanded into 45 states displays this phenomenon beautifully.

The Heart Gallery project began in 2001 in Santa Fe, New Mexico. Or did it? Maybe it began before that in a family room in the New York Metro area over a cup of coffee. Perhaps it began 10 years before as the seed of an idea simultaneously conceived by several people who didn't even know each other. When it's spontaneous, community building often takes off because many have been looking around on their own. Then one person lights a match and sparks all the others like a string of Chinese firecrackers.

Far less important than knowing where community begins is understanding how entrepreneurial ideas take hold. Let's start with painting the proper picture that, after all, has much to do with describing the success of the Heart Gallery project.

### A Picture with Power

Diane Granito was working with the New Mexico Youth and Families Department (it handles foster care in that state) when a local photographer suggested that doing portraits of the kids could influence their adoptions out of foster care. At that moment, two presumably unrelated worlds collided to create greater value for both.

The goal was to photograph foster care children in a way

that brought out their personalities, showing them as wonderful human beings and not as "products" to be offered up for adoption. Traditionally, prospective adoptive parents got to know children in foster care by reviewing their paperwork and files—all the forms, facts, and figures about the forgotten kids. At best, a mug shot of the child might be stapled to the inside of his or her file folder. All that stood out for prospective parents were labels—"older, placed in 10 homes, disabled"—and details that conveyed nothing meaningful about the children themselves.

So Diane worked with local Santa Fe photographers and the Gerald Peters Gallery to set up a portrait exhibit of foster care kids. They placed special emphasis on children who are hardest to adopt because of all the "labels" in their files.

And magic happened. When families thinking of adopting saw beautiful photographs of these kids displayed in a gallery, their *souls* responded. They saw in these portraits the kind of *meaning* that sent them in search of a family addition in the first place.

Ten years before Diane set up the photo exhibit in Santa Fe, a similar idea had occurred to photographer Najlah Feanny Hicks in New Jersey. "I had tried contacting adoption services in New Jersey to offer my services as a professional photographer," Najlah recalled. "I knew the power of photography and I knew if I could just take even a few pictures, I could show these kids in a different light." But the agencies she contacted couldn't picture what Najlah saw, so she let the idea fade into the background. Until one Saturday morning, when Najlah read a small article in *Parade* magazine about Diane's Heart Gallery project. "I can do that, too!" Najlah said out loud to her husband. He responded, "Well, then do it."

## Catalyzing Something More

Najlah not only took her cues from Diane's experience, she catalyzed something bigger, instinctively knowing this idea needed the multiplier effect of community. She contacted some of the world's premier photographers she knew from her two decades as a photographer—top New York and international pros. Their work had graced the covers of magazines from *Newsweek*, *Time*, and *Forbes* to *Focus*, *People*, and

*MacLean's*. Although they traveled the globe constantly, Najlah knew they'd be captivated by her idea. So she cast her pebble into the pond and it rippled far and wide. Her idea appealed instantly to foster caregivers and administrators as well. "I knew that once people saw the professional images of these kids, they would be drawn to them," stated Najlah, determined to connect the power of photography with the power of humanity.

Perhaps underestimating this dual power at first, she described her thinking at the start by saying, "I thought that maybe we could photograph twenty or thirty kids. Then I contacted the New Jersey foster care system and they said, 'We have three hundred and twenty-eight kids we consider to be the hardest-to-adopt children. Can you photograph all of them?' So I said sure. What could I say—no? I mean, how do you determine that one child's life is more important than another child's life?"

From a simple initial ripple, the power created by community was about to take hold and grow into a strong, powerful wave.

## Tapping the Power of Existing Communities

Najlah contacted several more of her colleagues. Moved by the power of the idea, they turned to their own communities and contacted hundreds of others. Amazing things happened. Speaking in hindsight as if this should have been self-evident, Najlah said, "It took only about two weeks. I was getting emails from the Super Bowl, the Sudan, Nigeria, Hong Kong, people wanting to be part of this. I didn't know all of them, but many of them I had worked parallel to for years. When I asked them to participate, the answer was universally *yes*. 'Just tell me when and where and I'll be there,' they said."

She brought together about 150 photographers and major picture editors, then delivered the idea to a larger community yet for input. The expanded community, sharing similar values and perceiving the potential, wasn't just embracing Najlah's or Diane's or any one person's idea. They were feeding off of it, adding to it, owning it, and making it richer. Said Najlah, "It was a universal chord that struck us personally, too. Many of us realized that our own kids were just a step or two away from what these foster kids were going through. Some of us had been adopted or in foster care ourselves. And one guy's father had fostered over a hundred children in his lifetime." Miraculously, the professional photographers' community and its power and purpose overlapped with personal principles and experiences.

Within a few weeks, they had photographed hundreds of kids. The fuse had been lit. The idea was catalyzing others. Logistical walls were crumbling at the force of a new way of thinking. This message came roaring through: "Whatever *you* can do with this idea, do it!" It translated into an infectious feeling that gave people the freedom to do something similar. One photographer suggested all photographers tap into their press contacts and their marketing and PR savvy to get the word out *beyond* professional photographers. *People* magazine embraced the story, inviting readers to enter a new community in a four-page spread, and dozens of other media eventually followed. "They warned us we'd get inundated with requests and asked, 'Do you have a website?' We were all juggling this new project with our other jobs. Of course not! We hadn't even thought about a website, or fielding inquiries, or much else."

Yet, they responded by reaching out to their known communities for further ideas and help. "A guy from Sprint knew this designer at eMax Studio and put us in touch. Within a hundred hours, he'd built a website from scratch and had it up and running. The website opened just hours before the *People* magazine issue came out. In the first few months, we had well over thirteen million hits."

Power.

### Ripple Effect in Action for Greater Good

And so it went. As the idea to photograph foster kids rippled through this newly forming community and across many old ones, the collective delivered ideas, resources, and energy. Other Heart Galleries—at least eight—formed around the country. Like Najlah, others had heard about the Santa Fe story and mimicked it. But none had tapped the power of Najlah's large community of professional photographers, and their connections to media and broad geographic exposure. "In New Jersey, we became the first Heart Gallery to attract this high caliber of photographers and others with critical skill sets.

We drew publicity, which in turn drew more people." For example, they attracted the *New Jersey Star Ledger* newspaper and it profiled *every* child photographed, plus continued to profile children new to the system each week. Suddenly, the Heart Gallery project reached multitudes through stories in daily papers in addition to the publicity in *People* magazine—a far cry from the idea of a single gallery in New Jersey or New Mexico.

### The Power to Change History

After the New Jersey Heart Gallery's first exhibit in August, 2005, inquiries for housing foster children in New Jersey's Division of Youth and Family Services went up nearly 300 percent. The overwhelming majority of those were linked to the initial gallery show. Today, Najlah's group sets up regular traveling shows across the state. They formed a nonprofit organization and hired staff to move this concept forward. "For decades, we had *assumed* history—that things would stay the same. Now we've created the chance to *change* history, even for just one child," Najlah commented with pride and excitement.

And that's exactly what this Heart Galleries community continues to do as people reshape how value is defined and created. They're following the flow, nurturing the idea, and letting it grow like a stand of aspen in an increasingly larger meadow.

## *Consciously Cultivated Community: Cleveland*

So far, the three examples of community explored demonstrate how exposure to an entrepreneurial idea can expand to eventually become a community. But none of these reflects a primary goal of *converting* the community to an entrepreneurial one, nor do they consciously expect an increase in entrepreneurship to result. There are, however, examples of entire communities seeking to actively promote entrepreneurship—as a mindset, as an activity, and as a core driver of the community itself.

When does a community knowingly begin to promote entrepreneurship? Most often, it occurs when individual entrepreneurs who happen to share the same geographic area find success of their own doing. Their achievements encourage others to take notice, especially when there's an associated economic impact—new jobs created, new demand for supporting services, a growth impact on real estate, increased tax base, and so on. Certainly an entrepreneurial community can slowly evolve this way, but it's not the only way.

Increasingly, civic leaders who realize the benefits of entrepreneurship are unwilling to let nature gradually take its course. Instead, they deliberately *speed up* the entrepreneurship clock. Cleveland, Ohio, is an excellent example.

## A Tradition of Re-Creation and Newness

Over its lifetime, Cleveland has more than once been a thriving economic center. Founded around 1800, it was named after an investor in the company that first settled this new region within the Western Reserve. Its history reflects a continuous cycle of re-creation and newness. Built on the banks of Lake Erie and centrally situated between the East Coast and the Midwest, it started as an important market and trade center in the northern part of Ohio.

During the late 19th and early 20th centuries, Cleveland gained importance as an industrial hub after John D. Rockefeller located Standard Oil and Samuel Mather located his steel production in the city. Professional baseball and the formation of the American League in the city, the growth of Cleveland's role in politics, and its hosting two Republican National Conventions in the early 20th century helped Cleveland develop. Today, in the early 21st century, it's returning as an important economic and cultural hub after facing challenging times following World War II.

As Cleveland reinvents itself, this time it isn't doing so around a single advantage (such as geographical location) or key individuals (like Rockefeller and Mather). Rather, it's a collective and conscious effort among its fiercely loyal citizens who believe that Cleveland has the makings of a great entrepreneurial hub. Touting several exceptional universities and research labs, its prime geographic location, and a devoted community feeling, Cleveland is tossing out peach pits—in handfuls—to establish a thriving entrepreneurial community. John Zitzner's story (see *Entrepreneurial Mindset is the Real Asset*) and others that follow show what can happen.

## Entrepreneurial Mindset is the Real Asset

After selling his first venture, John Zitzner founded Bradley Company in Cleveland because, as he said, "I wanted to create an environment in which people made exceptions." In the 15 years that John ran Bradley before selling to Xerox in 1998, that's exactly what he did.

John believed he could use Bradley to teach companies how to do more for themselves, more efficiently, and at a lower cost than some outside firms were charging companies for similar services. He also decided that his employees and customers were as much a key to his success as he was to theirs. So he enlisted them to find better ways of working together as they invested in each other—forming a community, not just a venture. On the day he sold Bradley, its real asset had become the mindset and the community that John, his team members, and their customers had created.

Previously, John heard Steve Mariotti speak about his National Foundation for Teaching Entrepreneurship (NFTE). He immediately saw what Steve had achieved to help disadvantaged youth, teaching high school kids about the power of making exceptions. This NFTE concept gave John a vehicle for carrying his message to a hungry audience—students.

John started spreading entrepreneurial concepts through his own teaching programs that he began from scratch. His after-school programs grew into additional sessions and summer camps. Today, John is pursuing the creation of the Entrepreneurship Preparatory School under his E City Cleveland organization. He seeks to build a whole school based on applying the entrepreneurial mindset to all subjects and students.

John Zitzner's "seed" of learning is one of many planted in Cleveland soil. Early in his pursuit of a NFTE-like program for Cleveland, John connected with the Cleveland Foundation and senior fellow Brad Whitehead. Brad had spent two successful decades with McKinsey & Company before joining the Cleveland Foundation. During his time at McKinsey, Brad had focused on entrepreneurship and organizational growth, even establishing ventures of his own. At the Foundation, he focused on Northeast Ohio's economic transformation agenda "to proactively create a thrust of entrepreneurship and ignite a larger economic development agenda," he explained.

Drawing its funds from Cleveland citizens, Brad and the Cleveland Foundation have used a portion of their vast resources to provide education and infrastructure to would-be entrepreneurs in the Greater Cleveland area. He has created nonprofit organizations like the Civic Innovation Lab to offer mentorship and nominal seed funding for ideas that would lend a positive impact to the city.

The Foundation seeds initiatives that, in turn, spread entrepreneurship through the area. No boundaries exist dictating goals of profit, scale, or industry focus; they simply inspire and support people to see differently and seek something more.

As an example, one Civic Innovation Lab grantee *Back Talk* magazine connects teens online by engaging them in issues they care about. Another, TUBA Group, is an Internet-based services company that rents high-tech equipment to entrepreneurs. Cool Cleveland, another grantee, inspires the Northeastern Ohio community to participate in "cool" arts and events, and has established a network of over 30,000 people in doing so. City Wheels rents fuel-efficient automobiles at an hourly rate to keep the number of cars and fuel consumption down. And the Lab supports John Zitzner's efforts to create his chartered school (Grades 6 through 12) oriented toward entrepreneurship.

The more formats entrepreneurship takes—civic, educational, philanthropic, or commercial—the more entrepreneurial thinking becomes an accepted mindset. But once it takes a specific form, it often needs a boost and more specific support to thrive. Brad knows this intimately. He addressed contributing factors to failed ventures this way: "There are a ton of bad ideas needing to be filtered out. There are a ton of people who don't have the necessary resources and access to test their ideas (for good or bad) and make them happen. Many can't overcome the massive inertia (in the marketplace). It takes much longer than you think to make an idea come to life. People either run out of money, time, motivation, or support." Often that occurs because their access to guidance is either dispersed or unknown.

That's where a strong community plays its pivotal hand in spades. And that's why organizations like the Foundation support initiatives to serve entrepreneurial needs at various levels. One strong initiative is JumpStart, led by Ray Leach.

## Fast-Tracking Ventures

JumpStart aims to accelerate growth of early-stage ideas turning them more quickly into thriving companies. In the process, it establishes community around individual entrepreneurs and their ideas. Through its JumpStart Exchange, entrepreneurs exchange ideas at a series of networking events. JumpStart also provides investments from its own pool of resources to add financial support. Further, it lends specific, hands-on support of selected companies through its entrepreneur/executive-in-residence program.

Wherever JumpStart invests, it plants a mentor inside the venture it supports to provide guidance and expertise to its leaders as they work toward their milestones (like layering one-to-one community within the larger support communities of JumpStart and Cleveland). "You can have a good idea and work as hard as possible, but things *will* go wrong," noted Ray, who has first-hand experience as the founder of several ventures over the last two decades. "You have to learn to deal with the stumbles, and recover and progress. You must have the ability to attract the resources you need. And you have to have the siren factor, which is the ability to attract others to you," he added. The need for those skills becomes apparent—and the skills themselves become available faster—if the catalysts are surrounded by a strong entrepreneurial community.

## Mindset Influences Established Institutions

A conscious effort to establish an entrepreneurial community in Cleveland spreads far beyond these examples (recall Baiju Shah's Bioenterprise from Chapter 4 and Mario Morino in Chapter 3 as two strong contributors to Cleveland's entrepreneurial efforts). One approach hands off to the next.

In this dynamic, entrepreneurship doesn't just take the form of creating new ventures; it influences the thinking and actions of established institutions throughout the Northeast Ohio region. Baiju's efforts, for example, rely heavily on his partnerships with the Cleveland Clinic, Case Western Reserve University, and several large healthcare systems.

In an environment like this, even when freshly planted, entrepreneurship permeates what already exists. Cleveland seems to recognize that to create a true entrepreneurial community and spread the mindset requires broader connection to, education of, and support by the community at large. The exact long-term outcome is yet to be determined, but the undertaking is conscious, deliberate, and wise.

## Borderless Community: Ashoka

Before concluding with a fifth example of community, let's pause to consider a feature of community that can actually constrict entrepreneurial thinking: borders.

Borders are more than geographic or physical; they can be cultural, social, and mental as well. To understand this, let's examine the typical pattern of entrepreneurship in the U.S. beyond the examples of community already discussed.

In the U.S., we like to think we have the "entrepreneurship thing" down pat, that we excel at it. Many assume America was built on successful entrepreneurship, that it's a natural and a national asset from coastline to coastline and border to border. Why, then, do we not find more thriving, expansive entrepreneurial communities in America?

True enough, some stand-out locations nurture a blossoming culture of entrepreneurship, for example the San Francisco Bay Area, Boston, Austin, TX, Seattle, and more recently Washington, DC, and Raleigh-Durham, NC. In these communities, supporting entrepreneurship has become a mantra. Entrepreneurs formally and informally interact, share ideas, and foster entrepreneurial success. And because these communities are entrepreneurial, access to support infrastructure including capital, professional services, and educational resources becomes relatively easy. As a result, more entrepreneurs emerge and thrive.

However, although we sometimes see it the other way around, these locations represent *exceptions* to the general rule across this vast land.

Even if the U.S. fosters more occurrences of entrepreneurial ventures than other countries, entrepreneurship anywhere is far from immune to the natural forces of society. And even in the U.S., pockets like Silicon Valleys exist too rarely. It, too, isn't immune from the arguably more powerful social demographic and geographic region that surrounds it in California. Indeed, there's a greater human tendency toward defending the boundaries of the status quo than cultivating an entrepreneurial mindset or community.

In discussing limits placed on our ability to tap the power of entrepreneurship, Ashoka founder Bill Drayton pointed out, "It's not the genetic code or some birth disposition that limits us. We are limiting the entrepreneurial potential at whatever level by the structures and habits we have put in place and continue to do so." These make up the true borders constraining entrepreneurship.

## Entrepreneurship Without Borders

Although they're far from being the only factors, geography and physical proximity strongly reinforce community. Therefore, it can be easy to assume that community needs proximity to succeed. However, the change catalysts Ashoka supports don't have the option of physical proximity. Its changemakers (as Bill calls them) are spread far and wide across the entire span of the globe. And yet despite this, Bill Drayton firmly believes that it is community that holds the key to success in tapping the power of entrepreneurship.

Ashoka does many things for its changemakers. In fact, a key part of the Ashoka model is what the organization has become widely known for—bringing capital to these entrepreneurs through its social venture fund. Ashoka's rigid screening of would-be entrepreneurs and their ideas—and its willingness to provide advice and expertise post-investment—also contribute to the success of these nascent entrepreneurs. Still, along the way, Bill and his team recognized something they now argue is far more valuable to these entrepreneurs and more instrumental in their ability to thrive. Community.

Ashoka believes that, more than funding or exposure to business skills, entrepreneurs need access to others who have struggled with the same challenges they're struggling with. It isn't so much answers they seek from one other, but the chance to share common context and environment in which they can arrive at their own answers. They support each other, borrow ideas from each other, and at times overlap their efforts and reinforce one another's visions.

## Ashoka Fellow Brings Sight, Hearing to the Poor

David Green is a great example of the regenerative power of this community. A serial venture founder, his earliest venture was a mission in India that brought sight to the sightless or severely vision impaired among India's poorest citizens. For his Eye Fund, David benefited in part from Ashoka's investment in his project. But he also gained access to other Ashoka changemakers, learning from their experiences and adding to his own model.

Several years after being backed by Ashoka, David came to work for the Ashoka organization for a time. There, he could directly share his own experiences and help Ashoka enhance its community of changemakers. Recently David returned to the world of changemakers, founding a new venture called Project Impact. His newest effort aims to bring affordable hearing to people in developed countries, enabling them to receive fast, inexpensive, and state-of-the-art care even in rural areas.

Over the years, David joined, took from, gave to, and rejoined the Ashoka community. Expressing his strong beliefs and the power of this borderless community, he said, "Reality is highly malleable. It's the entrepreneur's job to shape it for a better good. It's possible to do that yourself, but it's never as lasting" as when you do it for and with others.

When a truly supportive community is formed around entrepreneurship, a power surge occurs, creating a safe space in which to try out ideas. Within this space, the community pushes back against the societal tide—the status quo—that generally finds discomfort with entrepreneurship. It proves that boundaries *can* be overcome.

## Necessary Community Results Regardless of Format

What do we learn from Ashoka? That the concept of community is critical and its format is basically irrelevant.

Bill and his Ashoka team have perfected the idea that, while physical proximity may have its advantages, community is so powerful that it can and must be cultivated among entrepreneurs no matter where they reside. Doing so makes them stronger and increases their odds of success. It can even go a long way to combating engrained societal factors that support the status quo and work against the entrepreneurial viewpoint.

Consequently, a big part of Ashoka's purpose and Bill's personal crusade is to counteract societal limitations while providing empowerment and encouragement. His distinct approach takes the form of a borderless community. And every day, Ashoka proves just how powerful a force community can be by the unique hurdles its more than 1,800 official changemakers (Ashoka Fellows) overcome.

In many ways, their efforts stand in stark contrast to the undertakings of other entrepreneurs. You see, Ashoka focuses its efforts on entrepreneurs who measure the value of their ideas in terms other than profit—that is, those who seek to address social issues and alter the systems underpinning them. In a way, they are "border fighters."

More than most, these entrepreneurs face steep challenges to fulfilling their ideals. They must fight the most entrenched ideas and patterns in society, often taking on the biggest, best-resourced opponents: governments. Such entrepreneurs often can't easily quantify the value they seek or produce. And in building community around their own visions, they don't have the advantage of tempting early converts to their views with the promise of economic gain. Typically (often perpetually) they lack resources, thus rarely getting a leg up as many of their for-profit counterparts eventually do.

## Community Provides Essential Boost

Spread across more than 60 countries, many of the ventures begun by Ashoka Fellows lie in the most economically depressed and disadvantaged regions of the world. Fighting systems that favor the few (or in some cases fighting the *absence* of systems) makes the challenges Bill's legion of changemakers face all the more difficult. Community gives them an important boost, adding a salve to their challenges.

Long before most, Bill realized that to tap into the power of entrepreneurship, one could not wait for the process of building community to organically run its course. That's why Ashoka proactively provides ways for its Fellows to exchange ideas and skill sets, to interact, and to establish an ongoing connection virtually. As they support, promote, and facilitate environments worldwide, they find that much of the power community brings to bear on an entrepreneur's chances of success need not be based on territory, that many important elements can be generated in the absence of a single home base. The facts plainly support the model and the idea that community plays a critical role in entrepreneurial success.

This borderless community works, which is perhaps why *U.S. News & World Report* named Bill Drayton one of America's 25 Best Leaders in 2005.

## *Entrepreneurship Involves Community – No Choice*

Ultimately, the "no choice" conclusion that entrepreneurs reach isn't about betterment of self; it's about betterment of humanity, of our species. If it weren't, how could individual entrepreneurs share the vision with others and pass on the responsibility? When the effort centers on others in the first place, that maturation process comes more easily. And more quickly and naturally, it enables the catalyst to enlist and gradually embrace others.

In contrast, when the entrepreneur's efforts relate only to self-reward and self-fulfillment, the ego has a difficult time letting go. That's why those who understand entrepreneurship best know that, without community, the entrepreneurial path can be both hard as well as short.

## Recommended Resources

### *Planetwalker* – John Francis

Here's a guy who traversed the country as a walker and a bicyclist for two years. Doesn't sound unique, does it? Well, consider this. As John explored new places and lived his life all that time among strangers, he did so without saying a single word. So even though his story appears to be a journey of one, it becomes a remarkable story of community and how he couldn't have done it alone.

### *Adrift* – Steven Callahan

Sometimes the greatest appreciation of community comes from not having it when you most need it. Imagine being alone and adrift in the middle of the Atlantic in a failing life raft for 72 days. That sounds like an extreme way to find out about community, but that's exactly what happened to Steven Callahan. His journey—both internally and across the ocean—reveals a lot about what a person can do alone, yet at the same time, reveals so much about just how much we need others.

### *It's Not About the Bike* – Lance Armstrong (with Sally Quinn)

We evolve individually, by choice or by force. We also rely greatly on others, even as we appear to be focused completely on ourselves. But we rarely take the time to examine either journey—the one of self or the one interlaced with others—or to realize the overlapping nature of these paths. That kind of search makes Lance Armstrong's story a powerful one. Sally Quinn helps him tell it in an honest, unvarnished way. Like Francis and Callahan, Armstrong reveals the power of community in the most personal of journeys.

# A Deliberate Pause
## The Stone Soup Parable

A group of hungry and weary travelers arrives in a small village. They go about knocking on door after door in the village seeking a small handout of food and perhaps a place to rest. At every stop, they are repeatedly told there is no food to be shared and no shelter to be had.

After they have visited every home, they return to the central square where they loudly reminisce about the fabulous stone soup they used to make and lament that they lack a pot to make it in. Soon, a villager, curious about this stone soup the travelers are raving about, emerges from one of the shuttered houses and offers up a pot.

The travelers take the pot down to a stream, fill it with water, and bring it back, placing it over a roaring fire in the middle of the square. Then they set about to find the perfect stone for their soup. The villagers all are peering out doors and windows, wondering at the excitement of the travelers and curious about their ability to make a delectable soup from a mere stone.

As the soup heats to a boil, the travelers begin to talk about how their last pot of soup was made all the more wonderful by a bit of salt. Soon, one of the villagers arrives bearing salt where previously no provisions had existed. Before long, the travelers speak about how the last time they made the soup, carrots added such amazing flavor. With a growing enthusiasm, the curious villagers bring forth carrots. Soon potatoes, beef, beans, and more emerge from the homes of the villagers, each adding an ingredient to the boiling pot of stone soup.

In short order, the town comes together to create a feast, bringing out big tables, bread, wine, and more. When the soup is finally served, everyone agrees that it's the finest soup they have ever had. The villagers even argue over who will have the honor of housing the visitors for the night.

All this joy, all this reward, and all because of a single stone. Or so the story goes.

# Part III:
## *Perspective and Discipline*

# Contributors to Chapter 7

**Allen Grossman** (See Chapter 1)
**Doug Epstein**
 Co-founder, President, Evolve Sports
 Founder, Washington, DC Office, Former Managing Director, Katalyst Capital
 Former Consultant, Dean & Company
**Mike McCaffery** (See Chapter 2)
**Robin Chase** (See Chapter 1)
**Kevin Burns**
 Founder, Sage Software
 Co-founder, Partner, Lazard Technology Partners
**Maria Gomez**
 Founder, Mary's Center
 Recipient, *Washington Post* Award for Excellence in Nonprofit Management
**Rick Toren** (See Chapter 5)
**Andy Kapit** (See Chapter 5)
**Kristi Hedges**
 Co-founder, Principal, Shea Hedges Group
**Craig Burris**
 Founder, Publisher, *SmartCEO* magazine
**Lyles Carr** (See Chapter 5)
**Ken Getz**
 Founder, Center for Information and Study on Clinical Research Participation
 Author, *Informed Consent* and *The Gift of Participation*
 Former Consultant, Arthur D. Little and Corporate Decisions

# Chapter 7: The Evolution
# from Dream to Reality

*"The filter ability of the entrepreneur is critical, that ability to diminish and crowd out the noise. An entrepreneur should be open. An entrepreneur should be disciplined. But the skill is in the filter."*

- Allen Grossman
Professor of Management Practices
Harvard Business School
Former CEO, Outward Bound

Surfing is amazing to behold. A person standing balanced on a small platform of polyurethane, foam, and fiberglass trying to hold on to a force of nature. More mind-blowing yet, bodysurfing is the art of riding a wave with nothing more than your body—no surfboard, no body board, just you and the wave. It's more about taming nature than holding on to it.

If you've ever seen an upper torso and head poking out of the middle of a huge wave as it rolls toward shore, you've probably reached one of two conclusions: "No way in hell" or "I've got to do that." Most people conclude the former. And of those who try bodysurfing, most quickly abandon it for something easier.

Because bodysurfing isn't a natural activity, most people don't have an innate inclination to do it. They work hard to *avoid* waves, not tame them. And those who jump in among the swells typically want a form of protection—a board, a boat, a life preserver—that aids them psychologically or physically or both.

Frankly, most of us would rather stick with what we know. On occasions when we do venture beyond our knowledge base, we want (perhaps even expect) a clear, unambiguous set of instructions to follow. Therein lies an important lesson of entrepreneurship. Let me explain by carrying the bodysurfing analogy further.

## Defying the Will of the Ocean

When I was about 10 years old, I begged my father to teach me how to bodysurf. I'd seen him emerging from the middle of waves, held for what seemed like minutes in suspended animation. I saw him defying the will of the ocean to roll him over and pound him into the sand.

I wanted that excitement, too! Having already decided to do it, in my view, all I needed was for him to tell me the secret. "How hard could it be," I wondered, feeling a little cocky. "Just tell me the *rules*, Dad."

I can imagine someone like Doug Epstein thinking the same thing. Before blazing his own entrepreneurial path as co-founder of Evolve Sports, Doug spent many years as a venture capitalist evaluating and investing in entrepreneurs. He knew these people called entrepreneurs better than most. After all, in his investor capacity, his job was to pick out the best among them.

When Doug and his partners made investments in entrepreneurs, they were no doubt drawn by the entrepreneur's unique view of the world—a *perspective* that separated them from others who sought capital from them. But to venture capitalists in general, perspective is what's assumed to be present in the entrepreneur before they're ever even invited to the table to play.

When evaluating entrepreneurs, Doug and his partners looked for an additional component beyond perspective. They pushed entrepreneurs for a plan. "How will you go about delivering this vision of yours?" they would ask. They wanted a clear articulation of the path, the milestones, and the outcomes. They wanted dates, and dollars, and signs of discipline.

Similarly, when I asked Dad to teach me how to bodysurf, I wanted a formula, but for a slightly different reason than Doug's request for a plan. I'd actually tried bodysurfing on my own. Rather than a spectacular ride on top of the wave, my early attempts ended with a mouth full of inhaled seawater and a tumbling ride *below* the water. Once I'd coughed and sputtered out sand and sea, I staggered to the beach, tail between my legs, and plumbed my dad for exact instructions. There have to be rules—a set of instructions to follow, I'd insisted. How could doing this *not* be precise, straightforward, and logical? "Dad, just tell me what I have to do," was my daily summer plea. But every time I asked, he gave me a tip or two, and then said flat out, "Son, you have to get in there and get the feel."

As an investor, when Doug asked entrepreneurs for a plan, he knew this one thing that ironically seemed to fly in the face of his request: In entrepreneurial ventures, things rarely go according to plan. (Clearly, Doug understood that better than I did in my quest to learn how to bodysurf.) But in reality, this request wasn't ironic; it was deliberate and calculated.

When experienced investors look at the logistical details of an entrepreneur's plan, they're not looking for a strict formula the way I did on the beach. While they may ask for a business plan and predictions about how a venture will grow, they're really after a reality check on the entrepreneur himself or herself. They know the organizational details of entrepreneurship are fluid and, at times, unpredictable. Therefore, what becomes most important is assessing if the *entrepreneur* recognizes and can *manage* that fluidity. That's a very different kind of discipline.

"We want to see if the entrepreneur has a sense of reality," said Mike McCaffery, former president of Robertson, Stephens & Company. While Doug began as an investor in entrepreneurs and then walked the entrepreneurial path himself, Mike has stayed on his original course. For more than three decades, he has forged a well-worn trail investing in entrepreneurs. In that time, his experience has reinforced that what matters most is assessing the way the entrepreneur thinks about the challenges of delivering the vision, less so the accuracy of the plan for implementing it.

"I want to feel that the entrepreneurs I invest in have a sense of the tasks and the risks ahead," Mike said. "I'm looking for signs of that element of 'getting it'—that is, being able to describe the business and the vision in a simple, clear, straightforward way that shows me they are confident, clear-headed decision makers who can handle the pressures.

"What I want to know," Mike summarized, "is what the entrepreneur will do in a volatile world," even one of their own making. Mike isn't asking the entrepreneur for a precise *how-to* recipe. Instead, he's gauging how the entrepreneur will likely respond every time the plan falls short of reality.

Two critical messages come through from what Mike and Doug know.

First, though we clearly honor the unique perspective of the entrepreneur—that distinctive capacity for questioning and envisioning how things could be better—it means nothing without having the discipline to implement it. Ultimately, perspective and discipline are the pillars that, together, hold up the storied power of entrepreneurship. Within the balance between them lies the capacity to change the world.

Second, while it *is* a critically important element, discipline is *not* the formulaic and unyielding adherence to a plan it's often assumed to be. Its distinction is revealed to each entrepreneur, over time, in a quest for the right balance.

## Constant Search for Appropriate Mix

Bodysurfers tend to be minimalists. Knowledge, experience, and skill are the arrows in their quiver. That doesn't sound too detailed or plan oriented. But here's the reality of bodysurfing. Every wave presents new conditions and opportunities, all of which must be approached with a moment-specific combination of perspective and discipline.

So it is with entrepreneurship. As much as we *want* to know how to do it, it bears repeating that entrepreneurship isn't a "how to" undertaking but a constant search and adjustment to an appropriate mix of perspective and discipline. That said, gaining the capacity to first appreciate and then achieve a balanced mix is far from easy, even for those who know entrepreneurship well.

"What surprised me most about becoming an entrepreneur," Doug Epstein told me, "is just how many countless things you've got to deal with to be successful." From Doug's past role as an investor, we recognize he has a comprehensive view on the topic—one that offers him the ability to be harsh and unsympathetic, yet fully cognizant of the trials and tribulations entrepreneurs face. But dealing with entrepreneurship on the front lines is altogether different than supporting or observing it, as Doug found out establishing his own venture.

His vision for Evolve Sports was to take "unique" athletes and combine them with "unique" events and sponsors for a "unique" outcome. As Doug and his partners like to say, they want to "maximize the opportunities inherent in the soul-stirring world of emerging sports." For a taste of what they do, consider their flagship sporting venue, the Maverick Surf Contest.

Enthusiasts affectionately refer to the Maverick Surf Contest as "the wave beyond." I like the broader analogy of that phrase, but here's what it means to them. Mavericks constantly look out for the "perfect storm" opportunity—literally. Watching the surf along with meteorological and geological data, Maverick Surf Contest organizers anticipate the rare moments when a huge opportunity appears: "Giant wave faces. Swirling boils. Explosive speeds. Huge peaks." This is exactly what the Mavericks are waiting for. And when it all comes together, they put out the word. Once all would-be contestants are notified, they have only 24 hours to get prepared and arrive at the designated location along Northern California's coastline where they'll face towering waves up to 50 feet tall.

For Doug, bringing attention to extreme (or emerging) sports and their athletes has proven to be innovative and extraordinary. But "extraordinary" doesn't equate to "easy." In line with his investor experience, Doug and his partners began with a plan—one that's shifted countless times in minor and sometimes major ways. "Having the perspective to see it all into the future was important," said Doug, looking back, "but it still requires having the willingness to roll up your sleeves, try it, and see what *really* works." It takes discipline, not just perspective.

### "You've Got to Get the Feel"

It's different on the front lines. The level of demand placed on entrepreneurs and their teams can't be precisely described or calculated until it's experienced directly. Yet it didn't take long for Doug to appreciate the distinction after stepping into the entrepreneur's shoes. Balancing the discipline of accomplishing tasks with the perspective to evaluate the effectiveness, even the correctness, of the effort is difficult yet crucial. It requires a certain *sense* that's rooted deeply in the entrepreneur and cultivated over time. As my dad told me, "You have to get in there and *get the feel* to really understand bodysurfing." In the short time since Doug began walking down the entrepreneurial path, he's learned a lot and we can, too, by listening to his reflections about his experience.

"It's hard enough to see what's possible, and then plan and execute on top of that," Doug confessed. "Planning plays an important role, an evolving one. Execution and details are critical. But making both (the execution and the details) flexible and efficient to the point of being second nature takes time. The variety of people, communities, businesses, and ideas that have to be integrated to make it work is towering." At least as towering as the waves his Mavericks face. "An extreme level of patience is required. And there's great difficulty *taking the time* to keep an evolving perspective alive. Yet doing so has to be a priority."

Entrepreneurs find out, as Doug did with Evolve Sports and as I did in reflecting on my bodysurfing experience, that no formula for entrepreneurship exists. Hearing this, however, can sound contradictory to the need for balancing discipline with perspective. It's not. Discipline isn't about rigidity. Entrepreneurs and their teams figure out what works and then show discipline in getting things done.

"If I can't think about how to get from here to there," said Robin Chase, "I have to throw out that version of how I think the vision will turn out, or how I'll get to that end." She's not saying *not* to plan or develop clear, time-specific tactics. She's simply advising not to be wedded to the tactics, especially when the signs indicate certain logistics aren't working or signal that a better way exists. That's a different kind of discipline than is commonly assumed. Founder of Sage Software and venture capitalist, Kevin Burns, put it succinctly when he said, "The plan is everything; the plan is nothing. A plan is about balance and refinement, not a crystal ball."

I know it feels frustrating *not* to get a precise answer. I felt it on the beach at age 10. And even with the wisdom of time, I still feel it when things don't come as quickly as I think or wish they would. For many, not having a formula is unacceptable—so much so that they might force-fit precision, only to later acknowledge that jamming a square peg into a round hole left them bruised, battered, and no better off. Like bodysurfing, successful entrepreneurship just doesn't work that way. It's not how true progress comes about.

Regarding the challenge of balancing everything, Maria Gomez, founder of family support nonprofit Mary's Center, said, "At an early age, we're taught to follow recipes and feel afraid or irritated about moving forward without having them." But an entrepreneurial mind doesn't follow a straight line, and neither does successful entrepreneurship. Concluded Maria, "If I'd written a strict formula to follow when I started this journey, I would have been dead on arrival."

## Acutely Aware of Both Perspective and Discipline

The following tale about a man's search for happiness has been told countless ways over time. It makes a critical point about perspective and provides a great mental bookmark.

I am partial to the version Paulo Coelho used in his internationally best-selling book *The Alchemist*.[13] He tells it far better than I do, but the upshot is this: A father sends his boy into the world to learn the meaning of happiness from the wisest man in the world. Many people want to know the wise man's secrets, so when the boy arrives, he finds that circumstances and the will of the wise sage require him to wait before he can get his answer. While he is waiting, the wise man suggests that the boy explore the grounds and take in all the amazing splendors of the surrounding palace and estate. The wise man asks only that while he does this, the boy do him a favor and carry with him a teaspoon filled with precious oil without spilling it.

The boy wanders through the marvelous palace, all the while being careful not to spill the oil. So careful is he that when he returns and is asked by the wise man what he saw in his tour of the grounds, the boy recalls nothing. He focused only on not spilling the oil.

Told to travel around the estate a second time and not miss the splendors of life gathered in the wise man's palace, the boy does so, this time returning wide-eyed at what he has seen. But on his second trip, he has spilled the oil. The wise man leaves him with one piece of advice as to the secret of happiness: "See all the wonders of the world but never forget the oil on the spoon." The crucial lesson? Happiness and fulfillment result from a balance of perspective and discipline—a principle that also applies to successful entrepreneurship.

## *Growth and Evolution*

It's reasonable to compare the desired balance between perspective and discipline to a dance between two partners, especially when the lead keeps changing and the goal is to appear as if no one leader exists.

For a sense of this dance, think back to Rick Toren and Andy Kapit at CodeRyte in Chapter 5 and their catalyst-activator partnership. Rick constantly asks questions, pulling apart what exists (at least in his mind) to see if a better way or stronger value exists. That's *perspective*. Andy, on the other hand, has his own way of filtering facts and events. He listens to Rick's ideas with an open mind while ever-consciously translating them into a mechanism for delivery that will make them real. That's *discipline*.

Their responsibilities continually move back and forth. Rick "thin slices" today's reality to see if a better reality is in the offing while Andy provides an environment tolerant to Rick's need and gift. Then Andy plays a hand bringing discipline to the environment and putting stakes in the corner of the tent, anchoring what Rick might otherwise forever shift around, while looking for the perfect site to camp. One leads, then the other. Even when two sets of footprints gloriously merge into one, it's never a permanently straight line, a hierarchy, or even a set direction, yet it's always a progression toward something better.

Entrepreneurs know (or quickly find out) that the real story of entrepreneurship takes place in the *middle* between the beginning (the catalyzing idea) and the end (fulfillment of the vision). The middle of the story—where perspective and discipline seek balance—isn't simply about a directive to grow, grow, grow. Unfortunately, most often that's exactly what's assumed, and worse, expected.

### Emphasizing Evolution Over Growth

Although they're often related, growth and evolution are not the same. The language of growth tends to be aggressive. Grow or die. Get faster, better, cheaper, bigger. Dominate. Win. It reflects a mindset measured purely by the numbers—revenue, profits, employees, margins, and market share. There isn't anything wrong with growth except when it occurs out of context or becomes *the* goal. Said another way, growth becomes problematic when it becomes growth for growth's sake.

Intuitively, we know that growth in the sense of a perpetual move forward and upward isn't realistic, in large part because it isn't natural. Nature allows for ebbs and flows, migrations, mutations, adaptations, even extinctions. And although this evolution involves moving sideways or even backwards at times, within the greater scheme, it works. Bent on long-term survival, on advancement and improvement, nature emphasizes *evolution* over *growth*.

Successful entrepreneurs also emphasize *evolution* over *growth*.

This lesson, in fact, is symbiotic to the need of constantly striking a balance between perspective and discipline. That said, if you look at the goals and actions of most organizations, it appears that we human beings expect to suppress and control the natural cycles of evolution (or at least the portions that aren't characterized by constant growth). We lock into a plan and narrow our view to take in only the numbers, which we fully expect to increase. And when the numbers don't rise as anticipated, we turn our efforts to ensuring they will.

But more important is what's *behind* those numbers in the first place. What do they actually represent? What do they reveal about the viability of the vision, not just the status of the venture? And, perhaps most important, do the numbers indicate we're actually headed where we really want to go?

When we can't clearly answer these questions, we become confused about the role of growth within the larger context of evolution. What is appropriate?

## Putting Growth into Context

"People tend to view entrepreneurial ventures like scaling a mountain," said Kristi Hedges, co-founder of public relations firm Shea Hedges Group. "There's a hard climb to the top, and then a downhill coast with lots of options and benefits. In reality, most entrepreneurial journeys are a constant series of hills."

If you're a hiker, you know that some hills are easy to traverse; some feel like you're climbing the Rockies; some climbs are familiar, allowing you to draw on past experience and skill; and some are full of obstacles you never imagined.

Even though it's characterized by a desire to advance, entrepreneurship is never a story of constant growth, of climbing mountains in only one way. You just have to be open to different definitions of what it means to advance. Let me share an example from my life.

In the summer of 2005, I was lucky enough to join a small group of just-turned-another-decade guys in the French Pyrenees. We went there to mountain bike in these wise and magnificent mountains while attempting to physically defy our ages. Some of us were experienced mountain cyclists; others at least knew how to ride a bike; all of us were unknowingly headed into some of the most diverse terrain we'd ever encountered, either on bike or foot.

To add to the challenging atmosphere, Lance Armstrong would be riding his last (at the time at least) Tour de France that same week. The Tour was to take him right through the heart of our chosen destination, an area where traditionally the race gets decided. Lance was racing for his record-breaking seventh straight Tour victory. Between Armstrong's quest and our individual desires to test ourselves, outdo each other, and emulate Lance, the testosterone levels were overwhelmingly high.

On the first day, our guide for the week, James, sat us down for a quick orientation. He went through the standard fare—the locations we'd visit, the provisions we'd take, the ways we'd operate each day, and the fun and challenges ahead. Then, without changing pace or specifically calling us to attention, James provided us with one simple thought by which the value in our trip would be realized or lost. "Remember, boys," James said, "speed is your enemy; momentum is your friend."

Here's how I apply his advice, past, present, and future: When you're hurling your bike and yourself down a mountainside without a clear trail, you must juggle two equally critical goals so you can have fun and emerge uninjured—you must progress down the mountain and manage the obstacles simultaneously. You have to keep moving forward with enough momentum to clear whatever boulders, logs, or other surprises you encounter. If your pace is right, you can even go around obstacles or adjust your route. But often, you don't have that choice. You must go over whatever lies in front of you. In fact, responding to these obstacles has a lot to do with why you throw yourself down the mountainside on a bike in the first place.

But if you ride too fast, you can't anticipate the trail ahead enough to know how to respond to the obstacles. That's when you're likely to crash. And even if you fly down that mountain unscathed, you may well have missed the point of the journey. You may declare victory, but it will be harder to retain the experience and its memories if your speed is too fast.

That's also true when applied to entrepreneurship and growth. Of course you want to progress, but you can't expect to move forward in one direction or at one pace or in a straight line. Successful entrepreneurship adapts to the terrain and the opportunity to advance the vision, which set up the journey in the first place. Craig Burris, founder of *SmartCEO* magazine, summarized this point well when he said, "Success is about momentum. In business, successes might not happen as quickly as in a sport, but they happen—at the individual, team, and organizational level. There are times when forces align and you can ride the momentum. There are other times when you have to tend to it and drive it back in a positive direction. Not tracking momentum is a big factor for why people get surprised and fail."

Lyles Carr, senior vice president and executive recruiter for the McCormick Group, emphasized the venture's evolution by saying, "Entrepreneurial ventures and their environments are like all other living things—they are either in a process of growing or one of decay. But the ability to grow and survive is really found in the ability to morph and mutate, to adapt to be better. Entrepreneurs are a catalyst for the kind of evolution that feeds growth." The example of Ken Getz (see *The Evolution of Ken Getz*) underscores this point beautifully.

### The Evolution of Ken Getz

Somewhere along the way of what appeared to be a typical corporate career, Ken Getz had a vision. Although he'd always wanted to "travel the entrepreneurial path and take [his] own lead," initially he went to work for someone else because he hadn't yet found a need or opportunity he felt passionate about. You might say he hadn't found his calling yet.

A great deal of the learning that seeded what became his vision occurred in his role as a consultant at two large management consulting firms. There, his focus was in healthcare, specifically drug development. Most of those he worked with, clients and partners alike, considered this market to be highly mature. But Ken saw different patterns in the same data, which translated into real opportunities. Most important, Ken was constantly assessing ways to better serve patients—those who often got lost in the weeds of corporate goals and industry practices. He knew changes were needed, and believed he could be—even *had* to be—the catalyst to make them.

In his work, Ken could see that pharmaceutical companies were regularly introducing new drugs that patients needed sooner than they could be developed and approved. He knew drug trials that took place before formal FDA approval played a critical role in many patients' treatment plans. But getting accurate, complete data on those drug trials in a timely manner was incredibly difficult for patients and their doctors. Not only was there no clearinghouse for such information but, worse, most of the information came from the drug companies, and thus lacked objectivity. In this environment, patients were being "underserved," which is a clinical term masking the fact that many were suffering and dying, perhaps unnecessarily. Something had to be done.

At the time Ken chose to pursue the need for change he saw, he had what most considered a great job with good money. He'd even enjoyed a recent promotion. He and his wife had two young children and had just bought a house. Despite all this, Ken confessed, "I felt I needed to create something more, to pursue what I saw and believed in. I had this irrationally high confidence level that leaving the safety of what I had was right. So I opened the window and jumped."

Ken began his journey by first setting up a software company to create a means for gathering, analyzing, and sharing information. Its mission was to find a better way to monitor, research, and report on the world of clinical trials and drug development. In the late 1990s, because software companies and healthcare were two hot sectors, capital to fund start-ups in these areas was readily available. In every way, his plan seemed right.

But a funny thing happened on the way to growing his software company. Ken also started a newsletter that provided information and a way to connect those interested in clinical trials as a community that hadn't previously existed. It unexpectedly became a point for pausing to reconsider and refine the vision of why the software company and newsletter had even come into existence. Ken described the first signs of this need for a deliberate pause by saying, "I had raised capital to grow the software company, which was the logical area for growth. But the newsletter intrigued me as well as an increasing number of readers. They passionately became devoted to it and the information gap it was filling."

Now, the financial markets interpreted his newsletter as "a nice PR sideline to the software company" and indicated that growing the software company was the logical, sane, and business-savvy activity to focus on. Consequently, Ken was pushed to choose between defining his own brand of success and accepting the formula "the marketplace" deemed the right choice.

Yet Ken believed that providing an objective source of knowledge was paramount in serving the needs of patients and their doctors. Even if not measured in dollars, achieving that value was most important because of its immeasurable positive impact. The newsletter took him closer to that view. As a result, he decided that adjusting his course to pursue the publishing business was the best way to reach his audience and advance his evolving vision. For Ken, a *growth* decision took a back seat to *evolving* his entrepreneurial vision over the long haul.

Based on Ken's determination to follow his vision and his willingness to adapt the plan to do so, his company, CenterWatch, quickly became a successful business that attracted suitors to acquire it. Ken didn't care much about the financial reward. Instead, he saw the opportunity to be acquired as the logical way to "increase the value and the benefits" to the audience he was serving and reach more people in need at the same time. "It never felt like selling out," said Ken. "Instead, it allowed me to grow and gain stability. It eliminated a lot of concern, even as it added to the corporate burden. For its time, it was the right trade." But was he selling out? Was it all a rationalized cover for growing and getting bigger, perhaps for ego or wealth's sake? Ken's actions that followed dismiss such notions.

If wealth or notoriety were his goal, he wouldn't have left Thomson, the large publishing company that acquired CenterWatch, to start a nonprofit. Ken knew it was another step in his journey rather than the end point. He said, "I felt I could only achieve success as I saw it when I was able to express myself in a way truest to my ideas and ideals. [When we sold the company], we had credibility, reputation, respect, and resources to truly express our vision. That had taken me to Thomson. But ultimately, personally, it was more about the credibility, reputation, and respect than the resources we gained or the successful sale. I kept a core set of values and principles always. Ultimately, Thomson did not share my larger vision. I knew only by [leaving Thomson and establishing the nonprofit as the logical next step] could I be close enough to fulfill the real needs of the market and do so with credibility.

"In the end, leaving Thomson and CenterWatch behind created more value for patients and families."

CenterWatch still plays a role in Thomson's vision, and in the larger vision of better informing patients while pressing drug manufacturers to higher levels of quality and integrity. Today, as the founder and leader of the Center for Information and Study on Clinical Research Participation, Ken is pursuing other ways to create value within a broader vision that he sparked and many others are shaping. In effect, he's catalyzed multiple versions of how to fulfill his vision. To that end, Ken also serves as chairman of the Tufts Center for the Study of Drug Development and sits on the board of directors of Harvard Medical School's Osher Institute. As Ken stated, "The value creation feeds many aspects of the same big vision." And it continues to evolve.

Ken's example shows that evolution, not growth, underlies sustainable entrepreneurship. Once you embrace the evolutionary nature of entrepreneurship, you can leverage it to continually expand value and, through that process, sustain it. In a sense, you come full circle and realize that what got you started keeps you moving forward. In the process, you understand that pursuing change is a quest rather than a race and that momentum is more important than speed.

**Lessons On The Way From Dream to Reality**
Figure 7

## *Challenges of Moving from Dream to Reality*

In the fall of 2008, I heard Tom Friedman (author of *The World Is Flat*) speak about his new book, *Hot, Flat, and Crowded: Why We Need a Green Revolution—and How It Can Renew America*. Listening to his talk proved to be a wonderful but sobering experience. Here's why.

Friedman has a gift for sponging up unbelievable amounts of disparate data and synthesizing it into new visions—patterns if you like—of what it means, or could mean, to all of us. His talk focused on problems that many (including Friedman) believe will require innovative thinking and bold new initiatives (read: *entrepreneurial* thinking). Listening to his words, I heard both the call for perspective and discipline, and the acknowledgment that forward progress occurs in an evolutionary way. I also heard the wise recognition that these things don't come easily or without a price, even when they are necessary and their long-term payoff great.

That night, Friedman outlined several megatrends he believed were pushing society to the brink of change. These included concerns about global conflicts over energy and natural resource supply and demand, climate change, and biodiversity loss. Clearly, not minor issues but then again, Friedman isn't known for focusing on incidentals. Nor is Friedman naïve. As he considers these threats, he worries that our society is in dire straits and questions the ability of our current systems to deal with these challenges. (For example, he described the U.S. government as "the pilots in the cockpit fighting over the flight plan when someone ought to be looking for an escape hatch to get us to the next moon shot.")

Still, Friedman feels optimistic. He also sees opportunities that just so happen to overlap with the solutions to the problems the world currently faces. For instance, he advocated for a Green Revolution, one in which innovative technologies can address our energy needs and environmental crises at once. In his view, this revolution would provide a vibrant future economy for the world and especially for its innovative leaders.

For me, it wasn't only the parallels to this book's discussions that make Friedman's observations captivating; it was his choice of words, specifically using *revolution* not evolution. He referred not to small change but seismic change, not to small stakes but the fate of the species. Yet one becomes a stepping-stone to the other, for without revolution, evolution isn't possible. Yes, revolution is a big step—on par with one entrepreneur undertaking a vision to transform the world into something more, something better.

We know that evolution requires many people, many ideas, and many steps—like a revolution layered upon itself countless times over. I'm not saying this to undervalue the concept of revolution or its challenges, far from it. Rather, it demonstrates the complexity of continually balancing perspective and discipline—well beyond one moment, venture, person, or time.

When Friedman asked the question, "Have you ever seen a revolution where no one got hurt?" it caused me to pause and reflect on the reality that there simply isn't an easy way *through* entrepreneurial change—whether it's one version of change or the hundreds of ripples of subsequent change catalyzed from the first. And yet, there's no choice to avoid such change either. As he concluded, "If you don't change, you die. That's the rule."

## Recommended Resources

### *The Starfish and the Spider* – Ori Brafman and Rod Beckstrom

Do you think the centralized, top-down order of organizations and communities in which a single person leads is the only format for lasting impact? Think again. If you can't make your vision something that, like the starfish, can lose a "leg" and still function successfully, you have to question your ability to influence lasting change in the world. This book offers an insightful, entertaining comparison between centralized organizations and decentralized communities, with surprising revelations about where and with whom power truly lies.

### *Touching the Void* – Joe Simpson

There is something both similar and completely unique to the stories mountain climbers like Joe Simpson tell, especially when those stories find them in trouble. Similar among them is an individual-against-the-odds theme that reveals times when he's tested to his very soul. Every time, he asks himself "what matters?" and "why?" Yet no two stories, no two sets of answers to those questions, and no two people are alike.

When you read this nonfiction adventure book, you won't believe what Joe willed himself to do. You'll be asking yourself (as he did) "what is fundamentally important here?" and "how do I get there?" Important questions—but ones I hope you won't have to ask, as Joe did, while on a remote Andean mountain on the verge of death.

### *The Source* – James Michener

To my way of thinking, *The Source* could have been called *Look Deeper, See More*. This book is like sifting through layer upon layer to find a common thread. I call it history written backwards as Michener's characters dig through a mound in the Middle East, both sifting through artifacts and assuming their contemporaneous characters—as if they'd lived in the period associated with each artifact. By the end, it feels as though we humans over time aren't so different and really want the same advantages and advancements.

# Contributors to Chapter 8

**Melinna Giannini**
 Founder, President, CEO, ABC Coding Solutions (formerly Alternative Link)
**Irv Grousbeck** (See Chapter 2)
**Richard Tait** (See Chapter 1)
**Bill Drayton** (See Chapter 3)
**Dave Jilk**
 CEO, Xaffire
 Co-founder, Former CEO, Wideforce Systems and Feld Technologies
**Anil Gupta**
 Research Director, Dingman Center for Entrepreneurship, University of Maryland
 Author, *The Quest for Global Dominance*
 Professor of Strategy and Organization, University of Maryland
**Oran Hesterman**
 Program Director, W.K. Kellogg Foundation
 Professor, Michigan State University
**Mike Morris**
 President and Founder, OceanOptics
**Edie Fraser** (See Chapter 1)
**Jeffrey Hollender** (See Chapter 1)
**P.V. Boccasam** (See Chapter 3)
**Will Finnerty**
 Founder, The Finnerty Group
 Professor of Entrepreneurship, Georgetown University
**Arjun Rishi**
 Founder, CEO, Enterprise Bleu
 Co-founder, Former CEO, Vastera
**Laurence Gonzales** (See Chapter 2)
**Dan Pink** (See Chapter 1)
**Steve Mariotti** (See Chapter 2)
**Julie Kantor**
 National Vice President, Entrepreneurship in America, NFTE
 Author, *I Said Yes*
 Youth Entrepreneurship Program Leader, The Aspen Institute
**Bill Shore** (See Chapter 3)

# Chapter 8: The Entrepreneur's Filter of Perspective

*"Once my filter was clear I was more like a flute where the air could blow through me rather than the specific music or sheet. Once I had a clear filter, it was easy to see the right details and the opportunity. I did not start with the specifics, but with the very large vision and the proper filter that produced the specifics."*

> - Melinna Giannini
> Founder, President, CEO
> abc Coding Solutions

We noted in Chapter 3 that entrepreneurship *begins* with perspective, but that the catalytic point of an entrepreneur's capacity to see differently doesn't end there. The dance between perspective and discipline goes on and on. Yet where does this perspective come from in the first place, and how does it evolve beyond recognizing those first glimmering patterns of opportunity?

It turns out that both the origin and evolution of entrepreneurial perspective share common anchors. This chapter explores how these anchors have come to define an entrepreneurial filter used by entrepreneurs and their teams to evolve the vision itself.

### The Nature of the Entrepreneurial Filter

What exactly is the entrepreneurial filter?

Director of Stanford Business School's Center for Entrepreneurial Studies, Irv Grousbeck, called it a compass. Cranium co-founder

Richard Tait described it as an entrepreneur's unique antennae. Ashoka founder, Bill Drayton, regarded it as an internal gyroscope.

Regardless of the term chosen, those who know entrepreneurship well refer to a means by which entrepreneurs (and those who join them) mitigate the "noise" around them to hone in on the essentials and realize powerful change. They may use different terms, but all of them recognize this filter's presence and importance in guiding the entrepreneurial dream forward.

Let's use Irv's image of a compass to describe the entrepreneurial filter in more detail. A compass provides a more tangible direction than a vague idea of where you want to travel. At the same time, a compass isn't as rigid as a map, with the exact route and obstacles along it laid out with precision. Reading a compass isn't like reading a map, either. Map reading is a science; using a compass is a practiced art and a feel. It requires processing multiple points of information, not only what the compass needle indicates but also what you see in the landscape around you and perceive with your senses beyond sight. Using a compass requires judgment, assessing what's relevant—and what's not—while keeping in mind the point of traveling in the first place. It's neither an easy nor impossible skill to come by and it draws heavily on intuition and a toolbox of other skills.

The best entrepreneurs possess this filter or compass. Relying on it and constantly refining it makes all the difference in their ability to walk a road less traveled.

### How the Filter Comes to Be

People may label it differently, but the entrepreneurial filter comes to be in similar ways. Knowledge, connection to self, and continual practice all play critical roles, as any entrepreneur will tell you.

The entrepreneurial filter may come more naturally to some than others, but it works best when it's deeply rooted in what one knows and believes and then directed at what's deemed most important. This judgment develops in part because, as Bill Drayton put it, "Entrepreneurs possess a deep knowledge of their areas of interest. Without that knowledge, they are incapable of effecting change."

"But those with such a filter also demonstrate a self-guiding capacity and a knowledge of *self.* It's not just intellectual capacity or a good idea that allows them to succeed. Knowing themselves and their areas of focus is an iterative process that continues over time."

Achieving balance within this iterative process takes practice. Serial venture founder and Xaffire CEO, Dave Jilk, used a quirky analogy to explain it. "Knowing *when* it's right and *what's* right in the entrepreneurial venture is like sexing a chicken," said Dave, discussing the art of determining a chicken's gender. "You can't really describe to people how to sex a young chicken. Instead, you have to show them hundreds of examples and eventually they just get it. It's a patterned gut feel."

The same is true of radiologists and how they learn to read x-rays. The more they do it, the more refined their skills become. Similarly, successful entrepreneurship is all about practiced judgment, and depends on the circumstances and needs of each venture. As University of Maryland entrepreneurship professor, Dr. Anil Gupta, said, "Entrepreneurship requires that entrepreneurs proactively sift through their information and assess their ability to build the elements that align with their convictions."

As time goes on, the continual process of sifting, filtering, and judging in thousands of different circumstances becomes automatic—a sixth sense develops and, with it, an ability to know and seemingly attract what's needed at the right time. W.K. Kellogg Foundation program director, Oran Hesterman, whose team finds, funds, and supports entrepreneurs oriented toward social advancements, mused, "There is a kind of synchronicity that feeds our creativity if we learn how to hear it, see it, feel it, taste it, and trust it."

Naturally getting to that place collectively described by Bill, Dave, Anil, and Oran takes practice. But it's worthwhile and it makes the process work. Completing this thought, OceanOptics founder and president, Mike Morris, added, "If you know your guiding principles, the details are easy and if you *really* know them, you don't need to go back to continually consult some business plan document. If it's well conceived you *know* it, and as you use it, the principles guide everything."

## *The Right Stuff*

No matter where you look in the entrepreneurial universe, you'll see this uncanny ability to use the filter at work. To Irv, it's the "key for sorting out what [entrepreneurs] need, at what stage, and from whom. There will be those you attract to your venture and those you won't; resources you critically need and those you can do without; opportunities that make all the difference and those that add distraction. As an entrepreneur, you have such a broad influence that you've got to have an orientation before you begin."

This sixth sense for knowing what it takes to make the vision real becomes so deeply rooted and personal that it guides the entrepreneur's every action and thought. It determines not just what is right for the venture but also what is *right*. In that sense, the filter ties back closely to the original choice entrepreneurs conclude they must make that propels them down this path in the first place. They begin their odyssey because they believe the world is waiting for them and that humanity will be better off for what they are doing. After they embark, their entrepreneurial filter becomes the agent by which they stay the course. In that sense, this filter doesn't only have a brain; it has a *soul*.

"In this kind of career more than anywhere," noted Irv, "you need to have a strong *moral* compass—to do what's right, to treat others fairly, and so on—because your whole organization and beyond will take its cue from you." More than guiding a single person, this compass or filter guides the entrepreneurial venture in its entirety. It may begin with the catalyst, but it's passed on to others, and to the surrounding ecosystem and communities. In the most successful cases, it becomes imbedded in the environment itself.

## *Origins of a Filter and the Three Triggers*

While a formula can't dictate how an entrepreneur develops a filter any more than a single person can dictate how entrepreneurship succeeds, three common factors typically form a *framework* around which the entrepreneurial filter develops. The presence of these factors—called *triggers* because they most often trigger the original entrepreneurial perspective as well as a continuing need to return to it—portend a greater probability of success over entrepreneurs and ventures that don't include these triggers. They are exposure, actualization, and calling.

These three triggers don't always occur in the same order. Some entrepreneurial journeys begin with only one of these triggers; others continue on for a time before all three triggers are "pulled." But consistently, the most successful and sustainable journeys happen once all three have been tripped—in part because each makes a significant contribution to how an entrepreneur's filter develops.

Actually, if you think about it, any choice you make (and the related odds of that choice leading to a successful outcome) would logically depend on three things. First, to do anything, you have to know the option is available—exposure—as well as have a clear sense of what it means to pursue that option. Second, once you decide to pursue something, to do it well, you must know yourself and what you're capable of—actualization. Third, whatever you set out to do, you need a strong sense of direction—a calling—and a means for returning to course. Let's briefly examine each one.

### First Trigger—Exposure

The role and meaning of this first trigger is simple: Without being exposed to an entrepreneurial way of viewing the world, it's downright hard to be an entrepreneur or even to know that one has the option to think differently. Recall author of *Risk to Riches: Women's Entrepreneurship in America* Edie Fraser's comment in the Introduction: "We are not taught in this country to constantly stop and evaluate where we are, to be willing to shift strategically, to change." In short, most often we simply aren't exposed to the entrepreneurial mindset and the importance of viewing the world differently. In this way, most of us flat-out lack the first and perhaps most crucial trigger encouraging and facilitating an entrepreneurial approach to life.

Truth be told, most of our world is oriented toward an opposing goal. Most of what we take in from childhood forward emphasizes learning and accepting prevailing methodology. Such thinking becomes the backbone of societies and conformity. The intention isn't all bad, but it's certainly limiting.

Entrepreneurial thinking differs from prevailing norms in that it assumes many ways exist to do things, and that proactively exploring and pursuing alternatives is the right and best thing to do. It isn't reckless as much as it's freeing. It's based on the assumption that we must advance and are capable of doing so. Recklessness comes (or is avoided) by how that freedom is used.

At the most basic level, exposure is about *awareness*. That is, to consider walking the entrepreneurial path, you have to be aware of other ways of looking at the world beyond the views society trains us to follow. More than that, the exposure trigger advocates an awareness that such thinking is available to anyone, not just an elite (or unrestrained) few.

Seventh Generation founder, Jeffrey Hollender, uses words that bear repeating to describe the possibilities brought forth by exposure. He said, "We are such creatures of habit and of pattern that so much of today is what we already lived yesterday. Yet so much of the possibility in the world lives outside that pattern." To those who are aware that other ways exist, that speaks of duty as much as possibility.

As a potential entrepreneur, getting enough perspective on yourself helps (or hurts) you in seeing that your existing patterns are powerful drivers, ones that enhance (or obscure) the recognition that you have so much more possibility, choice, and ability to do things better. If you aren't aware of your own filter, you can too easily choose *not* to change or even recognize what's possible. In a word, exposure is the training ground for forming an entrepreneurial mindset and freeing your brain and, dare we say, freeing society to the possibility of something better.

Why is exposure rare enough to be identified as a unique trigger to an atypical path? *Because most people aren't exposed to examples of entrepreneurial thinking in their lives.* They're not taught to look for different views or diverse ways, and rarely encouraged to embrace them if they do see them.

P.V. Boccasam, CEO of Approva, offered a telling insight about the give and take between society and the entrepreneurial thinker by stating, "Everyone is born an entrepreneur. But the education system, families, and colleagues kill it along the way." By his accounting (echoed by many others), an entrepreneurial mindset isn't the result of a unique genetic strain, the born-with-it theory. It's available to all people to whatever degree they become aware of it and choose to embrace it.

P.V.'s comments referred to being part of a society as a potentially powerful force *against* entrepreneurial thinking. Rarely are children raised to cut against the grain of society's norms. As Georgetown Business School Professor Will Finnerty observed, "If you are raised in an environment in which you have to be self-sufficient or are invited to think independently, you are and you do." That kind of upbringing exists, but it's far from dominant in today's society.

In fact, more often than not, society and entrepreneurs find themselves in conflict with one another, with entrepreneurs directly challenging the norms. They aren't merely aware that alternative ways of looking at the world exist; they seek them out. Doing so adds to their empowerment. "The whole idea [of the entrepreneurial mindset] is that you don't know anything but want to find out," mused P.V. "The source for the idea-generating machine is in everyone. For most of us, it just happens to get rusty or die." Entrepreneurs feel a need, even a right, to pursue ideas. They want to make the world better. Still, too often what they face are dismissals of their ideas as idealistic or "out there," rather than finding others equally eager to explore new ways. That reflects the natural mechanism of society—to reign in the outliers and set a norm. It's also a natural result of far too few of us being exposed or encouraged to use an entrepreneurial mindset.

Entrepreneurs clearly go against the flow in their quest to better humanity. Thankfully they do, but we'd be a far cry better off if more of us more often looked at things their way. The world is not a static place. Whatever we do or don't do, the world keeps moving forward, changing, advancing. Exposure to entrepreneurship lets you know you have a choice to either take what's handed to you or have a hand in changing the world. Entrepreneurs distinguish themselves because they embrace and work to steer and alter the "inevitable," rather than resigning to it. They are unwilling to let humanity operate on autopilot if they perceive that decay lies ahead or better can be had.

Exposure usually represents the first level at which the switch is flipped for those who walk the entrepreneurial path. It can happen at different points in life, in different ways, to different degrees, and be followed by different choices for action. Regardless, exposure to what's possible becomes a typical and logical starting point for pursuing what can be. The sooner would-be entrepreneurs are exposed—and the more often—matters a great deal.

Remember, entrepreneurship and the filter that guides it are practiced and refined over time. So the earlier and deeper the exposure, the more likely those exposed will leverage their entrepreneurial mindset. Referring to her unusual upbringing, Melinna Giannini, founder and CEO of healthcare innovator ABC Coding Solutions, reflected, "It doesn't hurt to have been exposed to this stuff from childhood on. You are more accustomed to it then. It feels less burdensome. And it puts you in a place where you have almost an innate recall for how to navigate the entrepreneurial path."

Why is this true? Because the odds of success go up the earlier and deeper the exposure, in part because the sooner exposure takes hold, the more likely the other two triggers will get tripped.

## No Other Way

Edie Fraser has never known any other way but to unendingly be on the lookout for *other* ways to do better and give more. It seems only logical, having grown up in the home of Lester Fraser.

Lester served as a lieutenant commander in the U.S. Navy during World War II and immediately afterwards went to work for Macy's in the late 1940s. Neither R.H. Macy nor the United States Navy were known for their flexibility or looseness. But despite these rigid environments, somewhere Les carried his own way of looking at the world.

In 1951, when setting out on your own was rare, Les and his wife, Muriel, started their own chain of women's clothing stores, which evolved into the successful enterprise known as Casual Corner. After running his own venture, Les dedicated thousands of hours voluntarily counseling small business owners in an organization known as SCORE. Most of the individuals he helped had never had the exposure he did, but to Les that didn't mean they lacked the capability. This was his way of "paying forward" the advantages that had opened up his own world.

When you think with an entrepreneurial mind as deeply and consistently as Les did, it can't help but rub off on everyone around you—not only those you formally counsel but those who live under your roof, too. That mindset colored his daughter Edie's upbringing in every way.

Looking over Edie's voluminous résumé, it's hard to find an entry that doesn't scream of thinking differently, of looking for a new and better way. Among countless other examples, she founded the Business Women's Network to empower women executives and encourage them to help each other reach for more. She established Diversity Best Practices as well to teach organizations large and small that there should be opportunities for everyone. She's written books on women's entrepreneurship and creative philanthropy, reaching an ever-broadening audience with a message of opportunity. In so doing, she's helping them see opportunity as a *right* as well as a *responsibility* to pass on to others. In a sense, Edie is on an exposure mission that shows no sign of stopping.

Following in her father's footsteps, Edie has also become deeply involved in SCORE and other organizations looking to spread the entrepreneurial mindset. In 2007, she had the privilege of being a part of honoring her father's 32 years as a SCORE volunteer counselor, helping to present him with the first annual Lester Fraser Entrepreneurship Award. Not surprisingly, the award was established as a recognition of successful entrepreneurship. More than that, it honors a legacy of exceptional volunteerism, civic leadership, and a mission of exposing others to seeing the world differently.

## Second Trigger—Actualization

While the exposure trigger reflects a looking *outward* point of view, actualization is about looking *inward*.

The second trigger of actualization has two separate but related aspects to it. The first is knowing oneself. Without question, entrepreneurship is a test of *oneself.* Not knowing who you are and what you have within to rely on is a setup for failure.

Like many who choose to walk the entrepreneurial path, Arjun Rishi, founder and CEO of Enterprise Bleu (a family of high-end personal service companies), recognized that, in a sense, an entrepreneur has to be willing to place a bet in order to have the opportunity to make a humanity-advancing change. "I learned that my best bet is on myself," said Arjun. Not only do successful entrepreneurs reach this same conclusion, but so do survivors, according to *Deep Survival* author, Laurence Gonzales. "All conscious survivors soon learn that experience, training, and equipment can betray you. The maddening thing for someone with a Western scientific turn of the mind," he wrote, "is that it's not what's in your pack that separates the quick from the dead. It's not even what's in your mind. Corny as it sounds, it's what's in your heart."[14]

No one other than a pure gambler places a bet on an unknown. And as stated earlier, entrepreneurs are far from gamblers. If anything, they trend toward the risk averse end of the spectrum, doing all they can to avoid failure. That's why the best entrepreneurs come to know themselves quickly. Most, in fact, know a great deal about who they are before they ever embark on an entrepreneurial journey.

The second aspect defining the actualization trigger is that those who create lasting success keep expanding on this awareness of self as they go. They learn at every turn what they are capable of and what they are not, what matters to them and what is secondary in importance. From this self-awareness they draw strength, confidence, clarity—all characteristics of actualization.

It isn't hard to imagine this awareness of self at the root of that spirit and confidence we associate with entrepreneurs or as the fountainhead from which a unique perspective springs. As Laurence would say, it's at the heart of things and comes from the heart.

Actualization—knowing or being connected with who you truly are—can often be scoffed at as too right-brained, even too sensitive or touchy-feely. But those who choose to ignore actualization risk failure and perhaps even invite peril. Support is mounting. In recent years, the world has warmed to the idea of embracing a better understanding of "who we are" and also to the role of the right side of our brain, often identified as the emotional and creative side. Dan Pink's eye-opening book *A Whole New Mind* wisely shows that "who we are" in fact isn't one side of our brain or the other, but the *whole* mind combined. Acknowledging our "other" side is important, but it's still part of a larger mix. Therefore, knowing "who we are" means knowing our *complete* self.

The truth is that many of us don't know ourselves (or avoid getting to know ourselves) because we've buried our right-brained side for fear of embarrassment or some such nonsense. As a result, most of us have settled for an *incomplete* look at who we are and what makes us tick—to our detriment. But increasingly the arguments for and the acceptability of knowing ourselves in the larger sense are growing. In a world in which, every day, both the number and scope of the challenges presented are expanding, we must be able to draw on either a structured, linear response (left-brained discipline) or a flexible, creative response mechanism (right-brained perspective) as the circumstances require. As if further motivation were needed, the added silver lining of fuller self-actualization is this: as we attempt to actualize, we may discover an entrepreneurial side that's been long buried. As Dan wrote, "The keys to the kingdom are changing hands. The future belongs to a very different kind of person with a very different kind of mind—creators and empathizers, pattern recognizers, and meaning makers."[15]

Logically, a decision to pursue *anything* begins with understanding what you're capable of. It's equally important to see the link from actualization to the first trigger, exposure, because this second trigger takes on more power in combination with a strong awareness of, and capacity for, an entrepreneurial mindset. Exposure to this mindset creates an invitation—even a tool—to get a clearer grip on your complete self. As the story *Compelling Quest Triggered by a Fateful Day* indicates, Steve Mariotti of the National Foundation for Teaching Entrepreneurship (NFTE) understands that well.

## Compelling Quest Triggered by a Fateful Day

NFTE is a unique organization for many reasons, including its role in helping a special group of people actualize. Two other reasons are its founder and the impetus for its founding. You see, founding NFTE became Steve Mariotti's response to being mugged and severely beaten by a group of young men while jogging in New York City in 1987. As he recovered from his injuries, rather than getting angry, he got curious. Why had these kids chosen to mug him in the first place? Why, after telling them that he carried no money in his sparse jogging attire, had they beaten him so severely? Did they think they had no other options?

These aren't the kinds of questions most of us are programmed to ask. But Steve thought differently and his questions led him to explore how he could help young people like those who attacked him. He decided to create an organization to help change the outlooks and options of these youth—something most would never dream of doing. Perhaps it all happened because Steve came to know himself better during his time in the hospital, uncovering questions and answers that had once been outside of his awareness.

Steve began his quest by teaching in a school comprised largely of students like those he'd encountered that fateful day. More than that, he began teaching them entrepreneurship, economics, and what it meant to conceive, start, and run one's own business. As he did, he realized that, for the first time ever, his students were being asked who they were, what they liked, and what they dreamed of doing or being. No one had ever before asked them these questions! No one had ever even told them they had the right to consider the answers!

In these classes, entrepreneurship as a subject became a vehicle for them to explore themselves while they learned about applying it to small business. As Steve fondly said, "More than starting a business, entrepreneurship is about freedom. At the core of that freedom are people asking who they are and exploring where they best fit in the world."

Julie Kantor was one of the first to join Steve in expanding NFTE beyond a few classrooms to the worldwide organization it has become. By the end of 2008, it had served more than 150,000 students, and trained and certified nearly 4,000 teachers in 45 states and 16 countries. Julie, who built NFTE's Washington, DC office, wrote a book about NFTE's impact called *I Said Yes*, cataloging many of the stories of transformation NFTE and these students made in their lives. The common theme of these stories is this: before these students could say yes, they had to learn that it was their right to succeed and to learn who they were.

Describing NFTE, she said, "What we do is not so much about teaching entrepreneurship with an expectation of creating or guaranteeing entrepreneurs. It's about exposure and awakening people to themselves and their potential, no matter how it plays out."

### Third Trigger—Calling

*Exposure* nurtures awareness of entrepreneurship and the entrepreneurial mindset as an alterative to the status quo. *Actualization* concerns knowing ourselves and determining how entrepreneurial thinking might advance "who we are." The third trigger, *calling*, refers to discovering the specific place or path we choose to take to fully leverage "who we are" while simultaneously making the world better for others.

Although the idea of entrepreneurship is exciting, you can't just one day wake up, decide to be an entrepreneur, turn to a listing of jobs for entrepreneurs, and then apply for one. The *possibility* of entrepreneurship must connect with the *capacity* for entrepreneurship, which must in turn connect with *something more*: a specific opportunity to act.

Calling shouldn't be confused with an epiphany either—a seemingly magical moment when *the* idea suddenly appears in your head from out of nowhere. Many assume that if one could only arrive at a good idea, all else would fall into place. But having a good idea doesn't imply a need exists; if you build it, people won't necessarily come. And a good idea doesn't arrive packaged with the ability to execute it or attract others to help. Certainly good ideas abound, but in reality few represent an opportunity for entrepreneurship. Calling—and the vision of and need for seismic change held within it—is transformational. It's a gradual awakening more than it's an unanchored moment of divine revelation.

In fact, the calling trigger turns on the hard-to-describe aspect of *connectedness*. To get at it, consider that most successful entrepreneurs pursue ventures in topic areas they know intimately. Also, recall that those familiar with entrepreneurship advise you to be close to every aspect of what you do and whom you serve to have any chance of convincing others to embrace your dream. These points speak loudly to the idea of connectedness and to ideas themselves being deeply rooted. Knowing how to pursue the entrepreneurial path doesn't happen like a lightning bolt striking you on the head and telling you where and how to be an entrepreneur. Calling is akin to *real* lightning—that is, the point at which many forces converge to create a spark.

Remember, lightning doesn't strike randomly as we tend to think. Instead, it's drawn *to* something when it strikes. Formed from many forces, it has both a source and a base. Similarly, an entrepreneurial vision gets anchored in the foundation of what the catalyst knows well—a certain topic, market, culture, or part of the world. This provides the grounding from which the strike is made.

Given that, this calling trigger has much to do with what entrepreneurs know about themselves and an entrepreneurial way of looking at things—both part and parcel of the person and the passion that led to the strike. It's that point when the *desire* to be an entrepreneur aligns with the *confidence* to act, further aligning with a *need* and *opportunity* to create value. That need drives a choice—and for many, it's the *only* choice.

In this way, the calling trigger typically draws on the other two triggers. So when you know yourself and when you know your subject area, market, or challenge intimately, you become well-positioned to discover the right path—and then to passionately and intelligently pursue it.

## Catalyzing a Solution for Many in the Face of Individual Failure

These days, Bill Shore is best known for his visionary role in fighting hunger in the U.S., played out in great part through his Share Our Strength organization, his many books, and the leadership he generously gives to countless others fighting his cause and pursuing callings of their own. That image is a long way from a presidential campaign suddenly being cut short, but it reveals how every journey happens in stages. And no journey bent on changing the world reaches completion in a single event.

Bill's story started in the late 1970s and early 1980s when he played leading roles in the senatorial and presidential campaigns of then rising star Gary Hart. At the time, Hart was known as the candidate of new ideas—young, bold, and visionary in the changes he sought. Observing Bill today, it isn't hard to see why he was attracted to Hart's candidacies.

With the help of Bill and other key players on his team, Hart won his 1980 bid for reelection to the Senate and in 1983, ran a to-the-wire losing race against Walter Mondale for the Democratic presidential ticket. He seemed unstoppable for the 1988 race for the White House—a race that ended in an instant. Dogged by rumors of poor choices in his personal life, on May 8, 1987, Hart dropped out of the presidential race before it had begun.

Pause for a moment and imagine the typical senior members of any campaign team. They bank everything on a single event, one that takes place on the first Tuesday of November every four years. If their candidate wins, the world is their oyster. If their candidate loses, they have a hard climb ahead to find, affiliate with, and support the next person they hope will win. But if their candidate falls from grace in a highly publicized way as Gary Hart did, their political futures are likely over or, at best, severely stunted.

However, it's impossible to characterize Bill's case as typical. In 1984, when his campaign peers were calculating their next moves and tying their futures to Hart's rising star, Bill was establishing Share Our Strength. He may have been watching the political headlines and the polls, but he was also watching what was happening a world away in Ethiopia where, through modern media coverage, the world got a first-hand look at the ravages of hunger and famine. As much as he had a job to do for sure-bet candidate Hart, Bill couldn't take his mind off the realities in Ethiopia. His calling was simply too strong.

What awoke in Bill was a recognition that a hunger emergency existed in the U.S. too, one that wasn't being addressed in a game-changing way. No one was taking full advantage of the resources, opportunities, and people who, working together, had so much potential to rid the world of hunger. So in 1984, in the basement of a row house in Washington, DC, Bill and Debbie Shore acted on their belief that everyone has a strength to share in the global fight against hunger and poverty.

Some 25 years later, their Share Our Strength activities have evolved to the point that his political campaign involvement and that dark May day in 1987 have become inconsequential memories. Instead of mobilizing voters, Bill became known for mobilizing tens of thousands to contribute their talents to philanthropy. Rather than creating a successful caucus, Bill has successfully created community and, through it, communal wealth far beyond the measures of votes or dollars. Bill's story isn't even about his calling so much as about a *collective* calling that he helped catalyze. And it's a story that proves those who pause to look around for something larger than themselves can change the world.

In his well-known book *The Cathedral Within,* Bill Shore likens many of today's leaders to the cathedral builders of old, all sharing a desire to create something that endures. The concept reminds me of a time-worn and inspiring parable.

One afternoon during the building of Chartres Cathedral in France, a visitor curious about its progress entered the nearly complete building. Once inside, he encountered a man covered in fine white dust from head to toe. "What are you doing?" he asked the man. "I am a stonecutter, carving statues for the chapels," the man replied. A little farther into the church, the visitor came upon a man brushing wood shavings from his work clothes. "What are you doing?" he asked the man. "I am building the pews that will line the aisles," said the second man. Shortly after, the visitor encountered a man gleaming with small fragments of glass on his coat. "What are you doing?" the visitor asked again. "I am a glass cutter. I am making the stained glass windows for the nave," he answered.

As the visitor reached the altar, he came upon an old woman sweeping up pieces of stone and wood and shards of glass. Although he assumed her answer to be predictable, the visitor asked her the same question he'd asked the others: "What are you doing?" Looking up, she answered, "I am building a cathedral to the glory of Almighty God."

Clearly, calling is something much, much deeper and longer lasting.

**The Entrepreneurial Triggers**
**Figure 8**

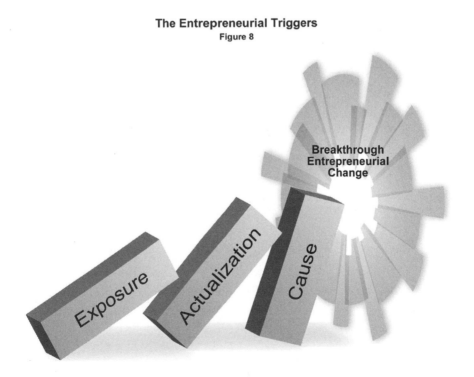

## *When to Pull the Trigger(s)*

Examining these three triggers is an exercise in assessing probable success on the entrepreneurial path. In virtually every case, at least one of these triggers gets pulled before entrepreneurs begin their journeys. As the successful entrepreneurial journey continues, all three eventually kick in and as they do, they play critical roles in developing the filter entrepreneurs rely on to keep them open but on course.

Conversely, until all three triggers are pulled, entrepreneurs are most likely to engage in ongoing battles within themselves, or their ventures, or to otherwise limit their successes. The more triggers that are pulled—and the sooner in the entrepreneurial journey this triggering occurs—the better the odds and speed of breakthrough entrepreneurial change and success.

When you pause to think this through, it makes sense. If you are walking the path for the *right* reasons, in the *right* direction, having the *right* faculties to manage and capitalize on what comes your way, you're likely to succeed. Indeed, entrepreneurship itself presents such a struggle that it doesn't make sense to compound its difficulty with confusion about what you're getting into, who you are, or whether you're pursuing something about which you feel absolutely confident.

Becoming familiar with these three triggers—exposure, actualization, calling—helps you know where you're walking on the entrepreneurial path. Applying discipline (addressed in Chapter 9) ensures that you can stay on the path toward lasting, meaningful change.

## Recommended Resources

### *Not Quite What I Was Planning*, edited by *SMITH Magazine*

Literary folklore has it that Ernest Hemingway was once asked to write a story in six words. Reportedly, he called his six-word memoir his best work. *SMITH Magazine* took the idea online and challenged its website visitors to write a story or memoir in just six short words. (It's an amazing exercise, one we'll talk about later in this book.) The results collected from hundreds of famous and obscure contributors opened my mind, both because of the submissions themselves and the way they challenge everyday thinking.

### *Atlas Shrugged* – Ayn Rand

It matters not your opinion of Ayn Rand, the self-proclaimed capitalist extraordinaire, and her philosophy on life. The way this lady could think and write will cause you to think in new ways. Her deep look at those who "contribute" compared with those who "take" is at once blunt and detailed. You come away from this book finding your own view of the world, with your role in it, challenged and transformed.

### *The Fountainhead* – Ayn Rand

Take all the comments about this author noted above, and direct them at the topic of creation—not the religious view of how we got here, but what we do with our time here, what we bring to the world today, and why. One thing you can't deny about Ayn Rand: she plumbs the soul of her characters and her topics. She does this here in what feels like a more personal journey than the purely philosophical *Atlas Shrugged*. In that sense, it provides a strong compendium to *Atlas Shrugged*'s view of exposure.

### *The Old Man and the Sea* – Ernest Hemingway

Much of this chapter spells out what triggers people to walk on certain paths, the entrepreneurial path in particular. Examining what makes others tick helps you learn about yourself. In this all-time favorite book of mine, I always learn something new about myself every time I read it.

# Contributors to Chapter 9

**Harry Weller** (See Chapter 3)
**Peter Senge** (See Chapter 4)
**Rafe Esquith** (See Chapter 5)
**Robin Mudge**
    Founder, Institute for the Digital Image
    Professor, American University
    Former BBC Executive Producer
**Ray Leach** (See Chapter 6)
**Jan Olsen**
    Founder, Handwriting Without Tears
**Eric Olsen**
    COO, Handwriting Without Tears
    CEO, No Tears Learning
**Alex Pinchev**
    President, International Operations, RedHat
**Gene Riechers**
    Co-founder, Partner, Valhalla Partners
    Founder, Former Managing Director, FBR Technology Venture Partners
**Siobhan Canty**
    President, Greater DC Cares
**Brien Biondi**
    President, Chief Executives Organization
    Former President, Young Entrepreneurs Organization
**Michael Simon**
    Founder, 3amLabs
    Founder, Former CEO, UpRoar
    Co-founder, Scala, Fathom Technology, and Red Dot
**Spencer Beebe** (See Chapter 1)
**John Wood** (See Chapter 1)
**Art Marks**
    Co-founder, Partner, Valhalla Partners
    Former Managing Partner, New Enterprise Associates
**Craig Burris** (See Chapter 7)

# Chapter 9: Fundamentally Focused on Discipline

*"There are certain things you have to do just to get to the poker table and play for the upside. The upside may be influenced by serendipity, but the basics are what matter and distinguish the players. It's amazing the probability shift you can make if you just cover the basics."*

- Harry Weller
Partner
New Enterprise Associates

Peter Senge, author of *The Fifth Discipline* and *The Necessary Revolution*, stated, "There are two extremes to how we perceive things get done: the cookbook and the complete unique experience. In between there are some principles that help you see and assess direction, progress, and the balance." Peter refers to a fundamental truth, whether it's about entrepreneurship, citizenship, or sportsmanship. While the presence of an entrepreneurial filter (as discussed in Chapter 8) matters greatly, lasting success has more to do with what entrepreneurs focus their filters on. Regardless of their specific pursuit, the most successful entrepreneurial ventures focus on achieving and balancing certain key fundamentals.

There's a difference between obeying the rules of a game and mastering the fundamentals that underlie the ability to play it successfully. Teacher and National Medal of Arts recipient Rafe Esquith (introduced in Chapter 5) echoed this reality that's often overlooked in a rush to get to the exciting stuff by saying, "You have to learn how to play the game first. If you plan to succeed, your focus should be on the fundamentals, no matter what you plan to succeed in." That is, if you come to know the underpinnings of what makes any game work—and master those fundamentals until they become second nature—it frees you to act with purpose, relevance, and impact, while mitigating randomness and avoiding taking action just for the sake of acting.

## Four Core Fundamentals

Experience shows that four fundamentals, practiced consistently and in balance, shape entrepreneurial success. They're the elements to which good judgment is applied and through which the balance between perspective and discipline emerges.

These core elements—value, strategy, investors, and leadership—were derived from hundreds of conversations with those who understand how these fundamentals drive everything entrepreneurs do. They shape how entrepreneurs make decisions and take action toward achieving their vision.

Let's examine each one of the four in detail.

**The 4 Fundamentals of Successful Entrepreneurship**
Figure 9

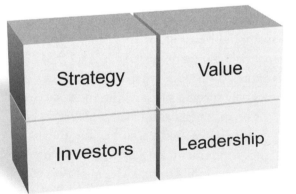

## First Fundamental—Value

The recognition, creation, and transfer of *value* define successful entrepreneurship. Robin Mudge, founder of the Institute for the Digital Image and former BBC executive producer, observed that "as human beings, our interest is ultimately in the *power* of the machine, *not* the machine or the operator." Similarly, the power of entrepreneurship lies in its ability to continually generate new and greater value.

Value explains *why* people choose to do anything. For entrepreneurs, value is used to communicate what they envision, to translate opportunity into action, and to attract others to their dreams. Ray Leach called it "the siren calling others to the entrepreneur."

Value sells, inspires, and guides. It provides the basis to measure progress. As Robin emphasized, "You achieve value when people actually use what you develop, gain benefit from it, and come to call it their own. Value happens when the audience embraces the vision and realizes its potential enough to choose to carry it forward."

In the long run, value binds the entrepreneurial ecosystem together. In the early stages of a venture, the idea of value motivates people. As an organization takes shape around an idea, its value becomes increasingly tangible, serving to keep people engaged and committed. But as value changes meaning (as it must) and the venture reorients its resources around that evolving meaning, the effect can be polarizing. That is, in pursing one form of value, those leading an entrepreneurial venture can develop tunnel vision and lose perspective. In essence, it can result in a narrowing of the definition of value. When that happens, the ability to see additional opportunities for creating value is closed off. Often, a venture's drive to generate profit causes the walls of value to close in. But the opposite can occur as well. Socially oriented entrepreneurs, for example, often disproportionately define a venture's value by its impact on a social condition. They ignore its ability to sustain itself financially in order to continue to be around to have that social impact over time.

The best ventures pursue a combination of several forms of value, not just one. And the best entrepreneurs invite an ongoing search for new forms, even as they remain focused on ensuring that their ventures deliver value, regardless of form. Optimally, value creation in the venture is simultaneously focused, flexible, and forward looking.

## Value in Action: Handwriting Without Tears

It's strange to think of products being created and sold without consciously intending to build a business or generate profit. After all, that's the default assumption as to why products are created and the value they'll bring. But it's only one interpretation of how a product can generate value. Jan Olsen's creations and her story serve as an excellent example of how creating and constantly expanding value—regardless of how it's defined—make an idea powerful.

In the 1970s, Jan developed a series of products and lesson plans to address the difficulties one of her children was having with handwriting. Jan wasn't looking to start a company; she was devoted to changing her son's life so his challenges wouldn't hold him back. But when she looked at the dynamic of teacher, tools, and student, she saw a much larger calling than helping her struggling child. Jan, an occupational therapist by training, knew this problem affected millions. Looking out into the status quo of that time, she saw resources and standards that were narrow in focus and limited in effectiveness. She observed teachers who had limited training trying to help kids with handwriting problems. Worse, she witnessed a system that assumed the *child* was the source of the problem. In Jan's eyes, catalyzing change became a foregone conclusion.

"The problem was in the teaching and the tools, not the child. Once the right problems were addressed, kids could write with ease. Learning to write dropped the hurdle blocking a child's progress and gave them a timeless life skill. More than that, it opened them up to infinite possibilities and replaced struggle with freedom. And the value of freedom," Jan concluded, "is universal, obvious, and deserved by every child."

When Jan described it, the connections seem logical, even obvious. But before her input, they weren't. Jan's advantage that allowed her to see what others missed was that she wasn't predisposed to one view of value. For school districts, budgets often drove the value of how and even whether to teach handwriting. For teachers, prioritization of curriculum and management of time dominated. But certain children, many children, and most especially *her* child were falling through the cracks. Where was *their* value? What defined true value for a child, not just in one subject, not just in school, but overall in life? And wasn't *their* value why everyone went to school in the first place?

For Jan, what began as a way to give her own child freedom turned into two decades of tutoring children one-on-one and sharing her tools and teachings with other OTs, educators, and students. Yet while the value of her products to individuals was incalculable, her reach was modest—small ripples, not yet waves.

In the late 1990s, another of Jan's children, Eric, joined the mission and assumed the role of activator to his mom's catalyst. He knew Jan's products had the potential to reach more kids, parents, and teachers than Jan could ever reach alone, which was, after all, the whole point.

To grow the vision and the opportunity, her small enterprise Handwriting Without Tears (HWT) needed to become a legitimate business, not a part-time operation run out of her garage. To be true to herself and those she served, Jan insisted that bettering each life that HWT touched take priority over profit. Yet the more people HWT helped, the more financially sound the business became—a natural outcome. As often happens, value begat more value.

Eric also recognized that this view of value gave their small operation an advantage over large, established competitors. Today, everything about the company reflects and supports that view. One of the best examples is that HWT fiercely adheres to a policy of hiring people attracted by the mission first and salary second. Despite the impression that we live in a money-driven society, you'd be surprised at the amazing talent that philosophy attracts and the loyalty to the vision it renders.

The philosophy, value equation, and even sales of the company have become infectious, bordering on viral. Almost a decade after launching as a "serious" business, HWT still doesn't have a dedicated sales force. Instead, it has cultivated a team of advocates for products within the communities it serves. These advocates can be called customers in the full entrepreneurial ecosystem sense of "customer." So evangelical are they that HWT developed a program so advocates can actively promote the products. Some advocates use this program to build businesses of their own; others do it out of love of the products and a passion for seeing their use spread; all believe in the vision of seeing children overcome their writing and learning difficulties to thrive.

Make no mistake, Eric ensures that a profitable business forms the undercarriage of the company. But profit functions within the context of the company's total values. Eric stated the distinction this way: "Profit is a barometer, not the driving force or how we define our success. Our ability to inspire people and help change lives is the best indicator."

## Second Fundamental—Strategy

When thinking of strategy, most often it's related to *strategic planning* in the form of business or administrative planning. Certainly entrepreneurs and their teams have to plan for progress as their ventures move forward. But it's the tail wagging the dog if the plan takes precedent over relevant actions that support the dream.

A clear separation exists between the fixed plan and the strategy that the plan supports. "It's important to look around you, always," said Alex Pinchev. As the founder of half a dozen ventures and in his current role as president of International Operations with software leader RedHat, Alex knows that the entrepreneurial journey never unfolds according to plan. Successfully executing a plan hinges on having the context to recall what you're after in the first place and the habit of constantly looking around to see what it will take to achieve it. That's strategy. As Gene Riechers, co-founder and partner of Valhalla Partners, refined it, "Planning and implementing the plan are the training and the tweaking. What matters more is the larger strategic process and the ability to react."

Strategy takes into account the fluidity of the entrepreneurial journey. "It's not a formula, but an ability to understand the limits of what you've set out to achieve and to maintain perspective," noted Siobhan Canty, president of Greater DC Cares. "You then seek to overcome those limits through a broad set of steps that are over and above what we typically think of as the plan."

In entrepreneurship, strategy fills several important functions. First and foremost, it offers an outline and a set of guidelines for the journey ahead. Far too often, that strategy, once developed, is assumed, set aside, or forgotten. But well-articulated strategy can serve as a powerful reference point, a filter, to what the venture is doing and why.

Once a clear outline is established, strategy serves a second and equally critical role as a means of communication. Entrepreneurship requires building a set of beliefs, an organization, a new set of habits, a following, and more. As that building process occurs, things change and many hands manage that change. Sometimes everyone is aware of each other's activities and sometimes not.

But if everyone buys into a common strategy, odds are their disparate contributions will hang together. In over a decade as CEO of the Young Entrepreneurs Organization and now head of Chief Executives Organization, Brien Biondi has seen the benefits of having a strategy and the consequences of its absence. "A good strategy has to be there to communicate, to keep the team on the same track, to accurately assess progress, and to consider new opportunities."

Strategy plays a third critical role by functioning as the criteria against which progress is measured. As founder of numerous ventures including UpRoar and 3amLabs, Michael Simon knows that "good strategy comes down to continually asking what's working, what's happening, what's possible. You have to look at customers, competition, internal execution with an ability to both critique and defend." Strategy reveals the details *within context*. As Spencer Beebe mused, "Nature provides a better model of this than business. Nature doesn't have a plan; it has a set of fundamental operating principles. The key is to be clear about where you want to go and be positioned to jump on new opportunities."

## When the Storm Hit: Strategy in Action at Room to Read

When you blaze a new trail to change the world seismically, you place yourself at the mercy of the forces around you, even as you try to tame those forces through planning. John Wood's experience is a good example.

When John established Room to Read in 1999, he looked out and saw a billion illiterate people trapped in poverty, in large part because of their inability to read. Of those, 120 million were primary school age children who weren't enrolled in school—sometimes for cultural and economic reasons but more often because schools and libraries didn't exist. John saw the need to address the detrimental force of illiteracy by giving children the opportunity to learn reading so they could gain an education. Reflecting John's vision, Room to Read's philosophy is this: "World change starts with educated children."

John set out to create a strategy to advance his audacious vision of reaching 10 million children. He estimated that Room to Read would have to create 25,000 schools and libraries to do that—a huge goal that would be the foundation of something larger. And he wasn't willing to let it play out slowly, so he needed an organizational model with "the scalability of Starbucks and the compassion of Mother Teresa."

To that end, John and his team mapped a rollout plan, country by country, school by school, month by month, year by year looking out over several years. Over its formative years, Room to Read made steady progress as the vision gave birth to a strategy and the strategy exacted a plan for making it real.

Entrepreneurial hurdles get amplified when taking on cultural and political barriers across borders while influencing mindsets and managing scarce resources. But even with those challenges, Room to Read was on track executing its long-term operating plan. Within five years, John and his team had rolled out programs in Nepal, Vietnam, Cambodia, and India. In 2004, they'd celebrated the opening of their 1,000th school. Still, on December 26, 2004, opening schools in Sri Lanka was several years away in the plan.

That's the day the tsunami hit Southeast Asia, including Sri Lanka. It didn't just wipe out libraries and schools, it wiped out towns and lives. Many of the economically depressed coastal areas lost even the little they had. They needed resources, of course, but perhaps more, they needed a foundation to build on after the media attention dried up and immediate humanitarian aid faded away.

John knew the Sri Lankan people needed hope. They also needed gathering points around which to rebuild their communities. And they needed tools that could provide long-term solutions, not just immediate ones. Within days of the devastation, John and his Room to Read team gathered to discuss what they would do. "We noted that Room to Read's move into Sri Lanka was planned for 2007. We had no money for going in there in late 2004. We had no employees on the ground nor a license to operate there. But we had a vision and a proven strategy, so my response was, 'Let's go.' We simply acted on the greatest need and played it out," John summarized.

Operating plans rarely allow for decisions like Room to Read made on December 26, 2004. They stubbornly demand execution, results, approval, sign offs, and compliance with rules. But used correctly, plans can and should serve something larger—the overall strategy.

Yes, strategies are meant to be clear in their intent and direction, but they can be flexible too. They're bent on delivery and action, but they can make room for opportunity and course correction. John's strategy allowed Room to Read to go into Sri Lanka when the need was acute. By December 2005—a year after the tsunami struck—it had opened 38 schools in Sri Lanka, thus providing 38 gateways to hope and healing in deeply profound ways.

### Third Fundamental—Investors

Success in entrepreneurship doesn't arise from a bunch of investors standing around with bags of money looking for a place to put them. Those are, however, popular impressions of both investors and the seeds of a successful venture. In truth, investors in successful entrepreneurship help create value and expect to receive value in return. The distinction in the impression and the care and feeding of investors around a venture are critical.

The Latin root of *invest* means "to surround or to envelope." That is really what investors do for the entrepreneurial venture. Together, a full spectrum of investors provides the nurturing environment in which the entrepreneurial dream can come to life. More than bringing something of value, true investors bring a commitment to help create more value. They back it by becoming personally invested in realizing the venture's success. Anyone else is more accurately thought of as a speculator.

It's a reciprocal and symbiotic arrangement. Entrepreneurial investors (including the entrepreneur himself or herself) are bound together by value needed, value perceived, and value desired. Their reasons for and the nature of their obligation are both altruistic and self-serving.

On the one hand, they see the potential for value that's greater than what they could achieve alone in pursuit of an opportunity that seeks to serve a greater good. That clearly contributes to the fullness of their commitment, one they justify with a sense of rightness and a feeling that parallels the entrepreneur's feeling of having "no choice" but to make things work.

Having said that, all those who bring their unique form of value—financial capital, intellectual capital, access, time, or technical skills—recognize that they're making an investment and therefore—as any investor would—expect to see a return. They may be different than our impressions of investors lead us to expect, but they are still investors who seek rewards, both tangible and psychic.

How does this dynamic factor into the venture's likelihood of success? And what increases the odds of maintaining common ground that keeps investors committed and the entrepreneurial ecosystem thriving? A recognition of them as investors in their own right—seeking a return on their own dream rather than a view of many supporting just one—goes a long way. As Siobhan Canty noted, "No entrepreneurs start with everything they need to be successful. The only way they get there is because people invest in them."

For whatever form of value they bring to a venture, every investor wants a piece of the dream being pursued. They want some kind of ownership, some feeling that what they're building aligns with their shared view of value, too. And each investor—beginning with but extending beyond the entrepreneur—should *want* the others to feel that way as they build a dream that betters humanity. As former managing partner of New Enterprise Associates, Art Marks, described, "If you ask someone to fund your trip, don't be surprised if they want input on the journey, your class of travel, your choice of companions, and a share of your prize."

## Of Volunteers and Investors: The Evolution of DC Cares

Greater DC Cares has always been a wonderful, admirable, and important organization, but not long ago, it found its importance and relevancy at risk. The problem and solution had everything to do with investors.

Inspired by a similar organization in New York City, DC Cares was established with the primary focus of creating and matching a database of volunteers with service projects in the Washington, DC area. To understand the world in which they operated, think of busy professionals who want to volunteer in their community but their schedules, odd hours, and narrow range of interests interfere with creating a fit that works for both sides. The same thing occurs at a group level, too, with a corporation wanting to donate funds or volunteer time to help the right organization in the right way and with maximum return. On the flip side, consider the number of organizations that need volunteers but don't have the resources to find them. If you can paint this picture in your mind, you have a sense of the world of opportunity DC Cares entered into in 1989.

The formation of DC Cares proved to be not simply a standalone new venture but an investment in the community. Without question, DC Cares provided a great match-up service that helped fill a gap. But over time, problems emerged. First, DC Cares came to be seen just as a clearinghouse for volunteers and the database that tracked them—only one piece of a puzzle. Second, that's exactly how every investor in the picture—volunteers, service organizations, corporate donors, and more—viewed every other investor—as puzzle pieces or resources engaged only for a specific need. The third and biggest problem was that those involved in this volunteer-service-funder universe saw themselves as working on different puzzles. Although their efforts overlapped, they didn't share a common picture of what they wanted to achieve.

Not surprisingly, every contributor had his or her own investors, too. At DC Cares, one was Siobhan Canty, who joined the organization in 1998 as program director. Although new to DC Cares, she was no neophyte to the world it was serving. Valuably, she brought a different view of this kind of community, honed by having lived in many parts of it.

As a community activist in the early 1990s, she'd seen an enormous disconnect between the philanthropic community and the actual needs of the communities they served, particularly in response to crisis. Later, working at the Community Foundation for the National Capital Region and then at the Center for Policy Alternatives allowed her to "infiltrate" and understand the philanthropic side. Then, as a social justice grantee of the Ford Foundation, she added knowledge from the recipient side of philanthropy. With her combined experiences, she understood the web that loosely held these social service factions together. Frustrated by the many narrow attitudes she encountered in social services, philanthropy, and volunteerism, she lamented about the wasted opportunities to create greater value.

Upon her arrival, Siobhan quickly concluded that DC Cares suffered from this same unintended tunnel vision. From the community's perspective and even in its view of itself, DC Cares was too compartmentalized. To have a lasting impact, all pieces of the puzzle had to come together under strong leadership—something as yet still missing at DC Cares and in that community. Perhaps the greater challenge—nobody was particularly asking for or blessing DC Cares to step into the void. Siobhan began from within her designated domain, but that didn't define the boundaries of what she felt she must change.

In her first two years at DC Cares, she filled the vacant shoes of the leaders who'd recently left. From then on, she became instrumental in putting forth a new vision that embraced all the investors in DC's social service community. She emphasized a fuller view of community and an appreciation of every investor and contributor to it. DC Cares's organizational strategy shifted toward maximizing the value of the entire community, not just the organization itself. She recruited others—internally and beyond—to see, think, and act in a similar way.

Officially, she had no such mandate beyond her own organization. Changemakers rarely do. But she used value and logic to help other social services organizations, corporations, donors, and volunteers recognize their overlapping goals.

In part, she did this by addressing all investors in ways that emphasized their commonalities rather than their differences. As a result, Siobhan catalyzed change in the larger environment, helping those within the Washington DC community articulate their various goals, change their model, and bring the puzzle pieces together, not by force but through the logic of emphasizing common ground.

As Siobhan said, "The only successful entrepreneurs are the ones who change others' minds." Doing so requires viewing all contributors as investors, ensuring they bring and receive value, and binding them together in a vibrant, like-minded ecosystem. Then it's no longer about any one player or agenda. It's about tapping into the power of many working together as one—with a shared vision and mindset that benefits all.

## Fourth Fundamental—Leadership

The fundamentals of the entrepreneurship come together through *value* by way of *strategy* fueled by the contributions of *investors*. Yet this coming together can only happen because of *leadership*.

It's natural to look to the catalyzing entrepreneur for leadership. But entrepreneurs are not leaders by default. Rather, their ability to succeed is constantly tested by their ability to evolve into leaders. And as a venture evolves, entrepreneurs must extend leadership out to others and transition it away from themselves, requiring yet a further maturation. "The entrepreneurs who fail are those who have an inability to transform themselves into leaders as the company grows," said Craig Burris, founder of *SmartCEO* magazine. "They are unable to take on new responsibilities, fall into too many habits, and can't reinvent themselves to keep the venture moving forward. Many are never able to let go."

Without the maturation and evolution of leadership, value can't be expanded and perpetuated over time. Responsibility for the fundamental of leadership must be shared by the entrepreneur with the ecosystem as much as they share pursuing a dream. It can feel like a humbling experience, but this process reveals a true entrepreneurial leader. As Craig said, "Successful entrepreneurs are incredibly generous. Their leadership recognizes that it's no longer all about them. It's about giving to others without expecting things to come back personally." What limits entrepreneurs from feeling like leaders? Ego and the fear of others not coming through. "This requires a lot of asking and searching and thinking about yourself, about the business, and what needs to happens over time," Craig added.

For entrepreneurship to create lasting success, it's essential for leaders to find a blend between ego and humility. Granted, entrepreneurs are known for their individualism, yet it's being able to compel others, respect others, and lead them in a grand task that matters more. It requires them to be confident enough to influence others, without having an ego so big that it blocks any willingness to participate.

As with all the fundamentals, striking the right balance is key.

## Lessons in Leadership: Rafe Esquith

The day Rafe Esquith learned he was to receive the American Teacher Award in 1992 was one of the greatest days of his career. But that day was also one of the worst days of his life.

One of the most remarkable teachers and human beings you may ever meet, Rafe has taught fourth and fifth grade students for more than 20 years at a Los Angeles elementary school. At the time Rafe joined the school, it had been known more for its economically depressed immigrant population and immense social problems than for anything like the remarkable achievements Rafe would bring, as recounted in his book *There Are No Shortcuts.*

When Hobart Elementary's principal challenged Rafe to leave a cushy Beverly Hills school to test his skills in harsh conditions, rather than laugh, scoff, or hide Rafe stepped forward. Still full of altruistic passion, he wanted to make a difference by reaching kids in ways that mattered. So, against logic and in opposition to the views of colleagues and education experts, he moved to Hobart and began teaching his kids Shakespeare. Shakespeare, you might ask? Yes, Shakespeare. Where most students would consider this a punishment, Rafe structured the reading and acting out of Will's plays as a reward and an awakening to the possible.

In his teaching, Shakespeare is but a centerpiece of Rafe's larger strategy to help kids learn for the reward of learning and stretch beyond everyone's expectations. His "no shortcuts" philosophy drives his students to voluntarily show up in the classroom at 6:30 a.m. and linger until 5:00 p.m. He encourages them to read Steinbeck and Malcolm X; he cultivates a love of the arts in music and other areas.

Pause for a moment to reflect not only on these achievements in general but consider them among people whose average age is 10. Rafe's method proves itself further as his students consistently score in the top 10 percent *in the country* on standardized tests, then go on to attend its best colleges.

Rafe bases everything his class does on a strong work ethic, respect, manners, and a view of their education as both a responsibility and a privilege. But on the eve of his American Teacher Award honor, Rafe realized that everything he was teaching had to apply to the leader as well to have a lasting impact. In the grander scheme, he was awakening to lessons of his own and in the harshest ways when he could have been basking in his moment of glory.

What exactly did Rafe learn? That even though he was "by position" the leader, he was failing the truest test of leadership. Worse, he was learning it through the feedback of some of his closest and brightest students. He declared, "The true measure of successful leadership is this: Can those you touch, those impacted by what you do, and those you lead *keep* the culture and the values you instill *beyond* the environment of your classroom and apply it in their own worlds, without you? Leadership is about teaching them how to aspire and achieve on their own."

Certainly, Rafe had led his students brilliantly through the trials and terrain of his classroom, but then realized he hadn't shown them how to carry that leadership forward. Not only were some of his students stumbling as a result, they also resented and blamed him.

Fast forward to being the first teacher ever to receive the National Medal for the Arts in 2004—an accolade hardly noticed by Rafe. Why? Because he now defines his greatest reward as watching his students succeed, on their own, after they leave his classroom. He himself has evolved to framing his goals in shared values—with the ultimate being nurturing a personal code of behavior and priority. "I've learned to let others make their decisions, to find their own codes," he concluded.

This leader has nurtured the key fundamental of leadership by letting it evolve in both his career and his life.

### No Lines, No Laps, No Lectures

From the non-prescriptive focus on discipline in this chapter, you'll see that *A Deliberate Pause* isn't a formula-driven book, just as entrepreneurship isn't a formula-driven exercise. However, there are things we must learn to break with if we are ever to maximize the power of entrepreneurship. Even the author of this book needed to be reminded of this fundamental lesson.

For half a dozen years, I have coached soccer for kids aged six to eleven. And for nearly three decades, I played the game myself and was coached by others. I became an avid fan. (Keep in mind that my exposure to soccer has been to *American soccer*, not futbol as it's played and taught in the rest of the world.)

In my growing-up years and my early seasons of coaching, I learned soccer from a place in a line between orange cones, and from running laps around the edges of a soccer field. A few years ago, I enrolled in a program for teaching coaches how to coach the next generation of players. I admit I had a certain mix of skepticism and even cockiness going into my first weekend of classes. I'd subconsciously concluded, as Woody Allen might have, that all I had to do was show up. The program would affirm what I already believed to be the fundamentals of soccer.

The instructor, Len Oliver, had a rare and proper mix of European soccer upbringing (his father was a hardscrabble Scottish immigrant), street smarts (he learned soccer on the tough streets of Philly), years playing in the first professional leagues in America in the era of the great Pele, and decades of coaching players of his own. His résumé and Hall of Fame credentials made him the right guy for the job.

But learning from Len was counterintuitive. You see, all of us, even those trained in soccer outside of America, thought we knew soccer. What we wanted from this program was affirmation, a few ideas for drills to do with our kids, and the formality of being accredited. What we got instead was a sharp lesson in the fundamentals of what was actually behind success in the game.

For example, when someone asked how to place our players into the right *eleven* positions on the soccer field, Len told us there are only *three* positions: you have the ball, you're trying to get the ball, or the ball is in transition. Nothing else matters. When discussing drills we'd use with our players, he first admonished us for calling them *drills*, told us they were *games*, and then mandated following a sacred set of guidelines beyond which little else matters—no lines, no laps, no lectures. Using that one statement, he'd effectively taken away the fundamentals in the way most of us perceived them.

Had this guy taken too many soccer balls to the head? He was crazy alright—that kind of magical crazy that of one who knows better than the rest of us armchair coaches how the game really works. While we sat weighing whether to ignore this guy or anoint him, Len was slowly peeling back—wait, let me rephrase that—*powerwashing* away our notions about how to teach soccer (or play it, for that matter).

"No lines, no laps, no lectures? How could this be?" I stubbornly asked. I grew up "in a line" not just in soccer, but in most of my education. I'd almost exclusively experienced the lecture format from pre-school to graduate school. "Without lines and lectures, how will our young players learn this game?" I kept screaming silently. On day two, Len showed us.

It was a cool late fall Saturday. On Len's field, two dozen kids aged five to seven were cobbled together from the families of various attendees of this coaching program. Most had never played the game and barely knew a soccer ball from a basketball. Len gave each a black-and-white quilted ball and said, "Follow me across the field. Whenever you want, ask me what time it is. When I tell you it's dinner time, I want you to run back to the place we started as fast as you can." He offered no further instructions and off they went.

For 50 yards, these little open-minded sponges in shorts and cleats followed Len, ball at their feet, curious about his new game. When they asked him "what time is it?" he'd stop and turn around mischievously to throw out a potpourri of responses: "It's two o'clock. It's four. It's 12:17." And so on. The kids laughed and steadily advanced with him across the field, all the while not thinking about soccer, learning, or their parents' agenda about coaching them. (Meanwhile, the adult attendees wondered what the heck all this had to do with soccer.) Finally, half a football field from their starting point, the kids asked Len "what time is it" once more. He turned slowly to them, made a monster face, and growled, "It's *dinner time* and I'm going to eat you!"

From start to finish, Len never once made reference to the ball or gave any instruction to keep it with them. He didn't show a single child how to dribble. He didn't put out one cone and ask them to practice dribbling around it. Yet every single kid, weaving through the obstacles of players in the mad dash back to the starting point, returned with a ball. All of them, regardless of age or ability, had dribbled back with their feet fully in control, not losing their balls once in the melee that ensued to get away from Len. In a few minutes of exposure to this exercise, through no prompting and coaching, he had done what every coach in my youth struggled for years to teach—dribble the ball, under control, at speed, head up. More than that, they'd learned this key fundamental that would become the foundation of anything else that was destined to make them successful: have fun.

Len's approach to teaching caused us to pause that day. And today, when any of us pauses, it's easy to see that everything around us is changing at an accelerated rate, even a breakneck pace. With change comes uncertainty. Uncertainty requires adaptability more than it needs structure, constraints, and firm boundaries. Change doesn't play by rules, so why combat it or harness it by learning a strict set of formulas? Shouldn't we be taught to think that way in the first place? Isn't it possible our survival depends on it? For without adaptability, the odds run against seeing opportunity and capitalizing on it, especially if we're bound by lines, laps, and lectures.

Len's way of teaching kids to play soccer respects resourcefulness. It forces quick and flexible thinking. It fosters learning through exposure and leaves room for the individual, the unknown circumstances they've yet to face, and the surprising ways they capitalize on both. All the while, Len conveys and strongly instills in them the fundamentals of soccer.

Similarly, in discussing the fundamentals of entrepreneurship, I didn't tell you how to play them out or give a lecture on how to define value, develop strategy, engage investors, or be a leader. At least in today's emerging environment—the one that characterizes entrepreneurship— you can't line up how-to steps and then run through the paces expecting a perfect or predictable result. But you can appreciate the role these fundamentals play, the value each contributes, and the balancing act that characterizes their interplay. *That* is the point of highlighting them in *A Deliberate Pause*. And *that* is the beauty and the privilege of thinking differently.

## Recommended Resources

### *Built to Last* – Jim Collins

Fundamentals tend to boil down to the classics. While I'm actually a bigger fan of Collins's lesser known books (like *Beyond Entrepreneurship*), this classic look at the best organizations shows what makes them sustainable. True, it takes a traditional management perspective, but every organization eventually has to learn how to run efficiently and over time. This provides one excellent perspective.

### *The Seven Habits of Highly Effective People* – Stephen R. Covey

I admit up front that I don't consciously organize my life around Covey's seven habits. But that's not the point of reading this book. I look at this famous book as a lesson in grounding. You may not agree with his form, but Covey offers a great conversation on how to arrive at your own way of living. I appreciate his discussion about the circles of influence most of all.

### *My Personal Best* – John Wooden, Steve Jamison

If you want to talk fundamentals, at some point, you're going to draw on a sports analogy. Where else do you hear fundamentals as consistently mentioned? This book is more than a list of quotations from the famed basketball coach, John Wooden. His quips provide insightful commentary on what's fundamental, not just to basketball but to anything in life.

### *The Richest Man in Babylon* – George S. Clason

This book drills down into one single fundamental more than any of the others here. After you read this parable about sound financial management, you may stop measuring the value of your venture or your life by money. But everyone—even you—can benefit from a sound financial base and discipline in this area.

### *Kaisha* – James C. Abegglen, George Stalk

How can you arrive at the fundamentals that work best for you or your venture? By comparing existing models. From there, you create your own fundamentals and expect to adjust them over time.

This book was one of the first comprehensive looks at the Japanese approach to the firm so popular in the early 1980s—and at that time, shockingly different to what was practiced in the U.S. (Remember "just in time" management?) This is a classic that many have forgotten.

## Contributors to Chapter 10

**Telaekah Brooks**
> Executive Director, Center for Entrepreneurship, Southeastern University
> Former Public Defender, Washington, DC

**Melinna Giannini** (See Chapter 8)

**Dan Moore**
> Chairman, Founder, Dan T. Moore Company, Soundwich, and Impact Ceramics
> Trustee, Cleveland Clinic Foundation
> Director, InvaCare and Hawk Corporation

**Peter Seligmann** (See Chapter 4)

**Scott Frederick** (See Chapter 5)

**Mike Devine** (See Chapter 4)

**Art Marks** (See Chapter 9)

**Philippe Sommer**
> Director of Entrepreneurship Programs, University of Virginia's Darden
> School of Business
> Founder, Former President, Alsacia & Sommer and WestMed Venture Partners

**John Wood** (See Chapter 1)

**Margarita Rozenfeld**
> Founder, YES! Circle and Incite International

**Oran Hesterman** (See Chapter 8)

**Peter Meehan**
> Co-founder, President, Newman's Own Organics

**Bill Cast**
> Founding President, Tri-State IPA
> Author, *Going South*
> Board of Trustees, Indiana University

**Dave Jilk** (See Chapter 8)

**Kevin Burns** (See Chapter 7)

**Bob Allen**
> CEO, Chief Storytelling Officer, i.d.e.a.s.
> Former Creative Entertainment Executive, Walt Disney Imagineering
> Apprentice Zen Teacher

**Dipak Jain** (See Chapter 2)

**Jan Bruce** (See Chapter 2)

**Robert Egger** (See Chapter 4)

**Guy Kawasaki** (See Chapter 2)
**Alice Waters**
    Founder, The Edible Schoolyard
    Author, numerous books, including *Edible Schoolyard: A Universal Idea*
    Founder, Chez Panisse restaurant and the Slow Food movement
**Donna Jensen Madier**
    Founder, LeGourmet, Startups.com, Vibrant Ventures
    Adjunct Professor, School of Business, University of North Carolina

# Chapter 10: Not to Be Deterred

*"For the true entrepreneur, the prospect of failure doesn't kill the entrepreneurial drive, inhibit free thoughts, or hinder the risk-taking nature of entrepreneurship."*

- Telaekah Brooks
Executive Director
Center for Entrepreneurship
Southeastern University

What entrepreneurs voluntarily face isn't unique, to them or to the times they live in. The Greek philosopher Heraclitus, known for his doctrine of change being central to the universe, once said, "Change alone is unchanging. This universe is the same for all." None of us is or ever has been immune to change; all of us depend on it to keep our universe moving forward.

More than to facilitate the creation of new entrepreneurial ventures, entrepreneurial thinking exists to help humanity manage—and better, capitalize on—change. Let's step out of our conversation about entrepreneurship for a moment and consider a powerful example of entrepreneurial thinking.

In the winter of 1933, America was in the grip of a great depression. As Franklin Delano Roosevelt's first inaugural speech given at that time attests—and as most of those he spoke to saw it—times were bad. "Values have shrunken to fantastic levels," described Roosevelt. "Taxes have risen; our ability to pay has fallen; the means of exchange are frozen and the withered leaves of industrial enterprise lie on every side. More important, a host of unemployed citizens face the grim problem of existence. Only a foolish optimist," FDR continued, "can deny the dark realities of the moment."

And then, in the next moment, it was as if the newly sworn-in president did just that—deny the darkness. He pushed confidently forward to show why the only thing people had to fear was fear itself. Where others saw failure, Roosevelt saw no failure of substance. "We are not stricken by a plague of locusts," he said. "Compared with the perils our forefathers conquered because they believed and were not afraid, we have still much to be thankful for. Nature still offers her bounty and human efforts have multiplied it. Plenty is at our doorstep."

These were bold words, ones that upon first hearing risked insult. In addition to harboring a perception of failure, most Americans at that time had also made great sacrifices. And now, here was Roosevelt suggesting that more sacrifices lay ahead. Then, seemingly piling on, he told a reeling nation that not only were the sacrifices worth the effort, but they were manageable and perhaps most unsettling, relative.

Was *he* the foolish optimist? No. Roosevelt had a vision and a plan of attack. And on that crisp morning in 1933, he was announcing his intention to employ it—for the betterment of all. Strip away the façade of the presidency, an inauguration, and a present-day notion of what Roosevelt accomplished over his dozen years as president, and you could just as easily have been listening to the words of an entrepreneur.

Consider the last three chapters in the context of FDR's viewpoint. In this third part of *A Deliberate Pause,* we have been focused on how entrepreneurship evolves from dream to reality—how entrepreneurs get things done. But beyond fundamentals (Chapter 9), besides the entrepreneurial filter (Chapter 8), and aside from constantly seeking balance between perspective and discipline (Chapter 7), how is it that entrepreneurial thinkers carry humanity further forward than others?

Simply stated, the limitations holding back most people serve as fuel for entrepreneurs. Two limitations in particular—failure and sacrifice—are seen differently by entrepreneurs, as the following discussion explores. That difference in view explains a lot about the fact that while the universe may be the same for all, it's the few entrepreneurs who move it forward.

## *The Foreign Language of Failure*

Understanding failure in the context of entrepreneurship presents a challenge in the form of a language barrier. Entrepreneurs have trouble talking about failure because they don't know the meaning of the word; it simply isn't part of their vocabulary. A distinction in the entrepreneurial mindset shapes the interpretation of everything around them, including the hurdles entrepreneurs face. Melinna Giannini offered insight saying, "Entrepreneurship is the willingness to be fascinated by a problem and to never give up on finding a solution." In that context, even the hurdles are relative. Where most see roadblocks, entrepreneurs see opportunities disguised in workman's clothing—a perpetual mindset filtering their interpretation of everything.

Entrepreneurs embark on their journeys believing what they seek is entirely achievable. They have confidence that, somehow, they'll manifest their vision—"like a good Viking arriving in a new country and setting his boat on fire," mused Dan Moore, chairman and founder of Dan T. Moore Company, Soundwich, and Impact Ceramics. "There is no return and no option but to start anew, survive."

Entrepreneurs have trouble talking about failure because doing so requires them to look at the world in a manner that's completely counter to how they speak, act, and think each day. Besides, it's unproductive and bothersome. They're working too hard in the proving grounds to ever stop and "register" failure—as a concept, as a fear, as a reality. Commented Conservation International co-founder Peter Seligmann, "Failure is pretty absolute, as if it's over and done. There are certainly a lot of things that don't go according to plan and provide an opportunity to learn and try again. But failure is different."

To the entrepreneur, failure is akin to giving up—something entrepreneurs who have "no choice" except to pursue their dreams simply will not do. Indeed, the thought of quitting never occurs to them. Commenting on the thousands of business plans his investment firm receives from entrepreneurs each year, Scott Frederick said, "I've never read a single plan that predicted failure."

## A Matter of Interpretation

Is it accurate to say that failure *doesn't exist* for entrepreneurs, or do they just linger longer than most in hopeful denial? Mike Devine cleared up this question by pointing out that "entrepreneurs reinterpret, look differently at, and redefine things to *keep* them from ending as failures. They're so determined and so open to evolving that they take what they're given—favorable or not—and make it work." Because entrepreneurs seek change and pursue what's often untried, they naturally assume they'll have to sort through the possibilities to find what works. That leaves them without the need or even the option of focusing on what *doesn't* work. To them, even *looking* for failure is an acknowledgment that failure is a possibility.

Art Marks, who partners with Scott Frederick at venture capital firm Valhalla Partners, acknowledged that entrepreneurs try ventures that are difficult and push the envelope enough to fail. But while others would call the stumbles, errors, or misjudgments "failures," Art noted that entrepreneurs would call them the natural "artifacts of trying."

Logically, entrepreneurs don't seek to fail. They don't expect failure and therefore they don't accept failure either. Rather, they focus on learning the most workable ways.

## The Necessity of Learning

Finding the "workable way" is purely and simply a learning process, one that comes to define and determine the role of failure—in *any* endeavor—based on how much you justify, modify, and reapply what you learn to reach the goal you're after. Taking the risk to establish newness or greatness assumes the potential for failure, but that doesn't make failure itself a cohort by default. The real trick is viewing the unwanted outcome as *something else* that can be used to advance and succeed. "What can I learn and how can it advance me?" That's the question true entrepreneurs focus on. The opposite question, "how will this be my undoing?" is one of submission, not mission.

Turning failure into *something more* requires recognizing it as a necessity for change and advancement. "It's the personal ability to 'come back' (from what others deem failure) that matters most," noted Philippe Sommer, director of entrepreneurship programs at the University of Virginia's Darden School. "It's the learning and refinement, the forward, then back, then forward again motion tied up in entrepreneurship that makes it unique in the first place and allows advancement to occur."

Consistently, contributors to this book referred to failure as *code* for learning and experience—a crude measure of what's *really* being looked at and for. While acknowledging that even the best entrepreneurs encounter bumps, they know catalysts of change also have a smoothing technique of learning and changing, redirecting and recasting. With practice, they foresee potential failures sooner than most, and quickly adjust or repair. This concept is often referred to as *fast failing* or *failing forward,* which means pausing regularly, learning, and advancing rather than coming to a complete (or permanent) stop.

This ability (or inability) to foresee possible failure eventually becomes a point of separation among entrepreneurs. And those who succeed in their entrepreneurial endeavors well know that the process is always and foremost about learning. The challenge becomes *learning enough fast enough* so they don't reach an irretrievable point of failure and stop. "Failed attempts teach you but they don't knock you out, even if they knock the wind out of you," reminded John Wood. "You don't have to die to learn a lesson." Neither does your vision of "what could be" have to die. Said Margarita Rozenfeld, founder of the entrepreneurial community YES!Circle, "The net effect is that it all works and fits *because I will make it work.* I expect to ride a roller coaster. But I also know that when I get back up, I will be standing higher than before. FAIL means From All I Learn."

"If you fail and don't learn, it's worthless," concluded Kellogg Foundation director, Oran Hesterman. "But if trying and failing become a profound learning, it can make all the difference."

### The Proving Ground

"Failure is part of the legend of entrepreneurship," said co-founder and president of Newman's Own Organics, Peter Meehan. It's the belief that "these people" experience dramatic crashes as often as meteoric rises. But while failure has relevance, "It can be taken too far, like the rest of the entrepreneurial stereotype."

Peter isn't implying that entrepreneurs dismiss failure as irrelevant or that it doesn't exist at all in entrepreneurship. Let's face it. Even if failure isn't part of an entrepreneur's vocabulary, the *possibility of failure* still exists around each entrepreneur. Bill Cast, author of *Going South* (appropriately a book about how failure can and did occur for one company), expanded this point by saying, "It's a known fact that failure is present. But its existence is not the issue. When entrepreneurs fail, what's most important to ask and understand is *why* they failed and *what* they learned." Pausing to ask and answer such questions separates the quick from the dead and often proves which entrepreneurial dreams will wither and which will shape the universe. It's the dynamic of taking action, falling short, pausing, learning, adjusting, and acting again that turns the possibility of failure into the proving ground of entrepreneurship.

Entrepreneurs and their ideas are neither static nor the sole source of change in the world. Like plans, the value of ideas has to be tested many times over. In truth, successful entrepreneurship is the result of many ideas from many sources overlapping, reshaping, extending, supporting one another, and sometimes even falling away. No successful venture ever looks exactly as its catalyst first envisioned it. In every way, entrepreneurship is an evolution requiring the entrepreneur to learn, adapt, and avoid the finality of failure time and time again.

## Natural Inflection Points

Entrepreneurs encounter natural inflection points as they strive to move forward. These are the moments—the opportunities—for entrepreneurial thinkers to pause, recalibrate their tactical approaches, and refine their filters. Taking conscious advantage of such moments is the test; they're the moments when a failure can become either the outcome or the lesson.

Xaffire's CEO, Dave Jilk, described these points as "passages"— moments that "cause you to think harder about your motivations and level of commitment. They have the potential to drain you. They test your ability to stick with it." They invite entrepreneurs to take a hard look within and come to understand themselves better than before.

But as he noted, "Most people can't stop and do this until after a so-called failure has occurred."

Yet that's *exactly* what defines a proving ground. It's the place where would-be entrepreneurs separate from *successful* entrepreneurs, and where those entrepreneurs who produce *lasting* outcomes distinguish themselves even further. Such a capacity to evolve requires perspective mixed with discipline and an ample dose of sheer determination. The test of a true entrepreneur is the ability to keep going when things seem worst—"and to go again with the same or more fervor than the last time," reflected Kevin Burns, founder of Sage Software. "Entrepreneurship never works the way it was written in the after-the-fact fabrication of PR spin stories. It's always the later attempts that work—not the first ones. Yet the ones that *didn't* work factor more into progress and advancement than the shiny final outcomes," he added.

Pausing and learning after a misstep elicits perspective, validates discipline, and often points out a need to adjust. "For the true entrepreneur, the prospect of failure doesn't kill the entrepreneurial drive, inhibit free thoughts, or hinder the risk-taking nature of entrepreneurship," Telaekah Brooks said. "It simply focuses it by causing more discipline, reality, and testing of the idea." It's a lesson Telaekah works hard to instill in future generations of entrepreneurs as executive director of the Center for Entrepreneurship at Southeastern University. "The likelihood of hitting the one spot you set out for each time is very low," said i.d.e.a.s. CEO, Bob Allen. Accordingly, the need to constantly sharpen your aim means you never fully exit the proving ground. "If someone spends a lot of time dreading failure, he or she probably won't enjoy entrepreneurship," Bob concluded.

### *Sacrifice in Entrepreneurial Undertakings*

Hand in hand with our impressions of entrepreneurs risking failure is our belief that they give everything to succeed—and not in the good way. It's frustrating and ironic that, often, those who are mistakenly called entrepreneurs perpetuate the misconception. Here's one story about how we can confuse the meaning of sacrifice in entrepreneurial undertakings.

Early in my career, I gained some of my first and most memorable exposures to entrepreneurs, both real and aspiring, working in venture capital and investment banking in Silicon Valley. Of all those I met during my time there, one man in particular stood out—the brash founder of an innovative semiconductor company. He tirelessly built his company to what seemed like an overnight success. His achievements were hard to ignore.

As an acknowledgement of his early and rapid accomplishments, the Silicon Valley entrepreneurial community honored him for his achievement with an entrepreneur of the year award. On the night of the awards banquet following introductions and accolades from many, the podium was yielded to this so-called entrepreneur for a brief word of thanks. Nearly *an hour later,* we were still listening to him expound on the greatness of his sacrifice and achievement, not to mention his own personal greatness.

In making his points, he showed clips from the movie *Top Gun* and quoted the likes of Patton, Nietzsche, Machiavelli, and Napoleon. His themes emphasized a single-mindedness and sacrifice required. He unashamedly bragged that others lacked this fortitude, taunting certain members of the audience that night outright. At one point, he even spoke with pride about sacrificing his marriage to a divorce during this period of building his venture. To him, it was a necessary payment for success—indeed, a key element of the sacrifice of entrepreneurship—as he defined it.

Audience members, including respected members of one of the oldest and most established entrepreneurial communities, didn't know whether to laugh or shake their heads. We waited and waited for the punch line that never came, at least not that night. Instead, it came approximately 18 months later when this man's company fell into disarray on its way to eventual oblivion. Today, few remember this person or his venture except perhaps in the context of that evening. His failure in no small way resulted from his poor understanding of "sacrifice" within the context of true entrepreneurship.

## The Uniqueness of Entrepreneurship

Before placing sacrifice in its proper context, let's honor the uniqueness of what entrepreneurs do. Clearly, they seek the exceptional, what many might call the impossible. They want to change the world as it is. They also want to reshape the way we think, believe, and act. They see that the world needs to be made better, knowing that it *can* be better, and their commitment is to make it so. And they're willing to undertake great sacrifices to arrive there. That's why we're not surprised at the image of an entrepreneur sleeping on a cot in the office, seemingly unable to leave work. Nor do we flinch at the stories of the entrepreneur who knocks on a thousand doors, receiving a thousand "no" responses, only to knock on a thousand more. If that's what it takes to find that one "yes" that allows them to move forward, so be it.

There's no question that the entrepreneurial investment is unique. But images we hold of entrepreneurs—the ones translated into impressions of total sacrifice—only tell part of the story.

As Kellogg Business School dean, Dipak Jain, observed, "The entrepreneurial mind is twenty-four-seven, always accounting for the risk and updating it. This is a big difference between entrepreneurs and others. Entrepreneurs are always 'on' and don't separate the rest of their lives from their ventures."

But that isn't the same as *giving up* the rest of their lives. While acknowledging that the sacrifice required in entrepreneurship is real and extensive, publisher Jan Bruce pointed out that "it's not really good or bad nor always at the extreme. It's different, both tougher and more liberating than most assume. You have a lot of freedom and you are a slave. You live with your venture always. But you continue to live." The venture—and the entrepreneur's investment in it—forms part of a much larger picture. Entrepreneurship can't be the only piece if you want the investment to produce a return worthy of its sacrifice.

### Finding the Right Balance

"Finding the answer to the right nature and level of sacrifice is the most challenging thing about entrepreneurship," more than one interviewee told me. How much should one *invest*? How much is right to expect in return? How should either sacrifice or return be spread out to others?

As with entrepreneurship overall, there aren't universal answers or a formula for all entrepreneurs or all times. But one thing is certain:

all entrepreneurs need to find the balance, not only *within* the venture they work so hard to nurture but *beyond* it.

The effort to strike a balance between perspective and discipline, between total control and shared control, and between the degree of sacrifice relative to the degree of expected return reflects the *art* of entrepreneurship. Even more challenging is maintaining that balance over time as the entrepreneur, the venture, and the overall dream evolve. Think of it as a series of transitions, each requiring a *re*balancing before, during, and after each transition.

Indeed, the need to strike a balance never abates. Some sense that and adjust to it, but there's never a guarantee. It isn't always even a matter of capability. "Choice" is something that doesn't happen only at the start of a venture; it comes in over and over. In that sense, concluding you have "no choice" must be reinforced by asking these questions again and again:

"Do I still want to do this?"

"Am I willing to make the investment required to do it well and right?"

"What must I give up and how does that stack up to what might be returned to me for my investment?"

These questions reflect the challenges of constantly searching for balance and other requirements for entrepreneurship to evolve, to advance, and to last. And they're highly personal questions. It comes as no surprise, then, that entrepreneurs distinguish themselves more by how they mature as individuals than they do by the scale, structure, or size of whatever they create. After all, entrepreneurs who are capable of having the greatest impact and achieving lasting success are not born; they are made through hard work. It's not about luck, it's about striving to be—as DC Central Kitchen founder, Robert Egger, put it—"tuned in."

Entrepreneurs read the signs. They're plugged into the zeitgeist. They see and feel what others don't. And it only *appears* to be sacrifice or luck. Therein lies the art. And from there comes the all-important balance.

## Anything Done Well Requires Sacrifice

Entrepreneurs want to do great things. By that criterion alone, they are much more like others who also want to do great things than representing some anomaly. Within that context, so are their sacrifices. "Without question, entrepreneurship does require a great degree of sacrifice to do it well," allowed Guy Kawasaki. "But so does doing *anything* well—being an actor, artist, doctor, athlete, or countless other things. If being great at what you do were easy, more would do it."

The choice to do something at a high level naturally requires trade offs, giving up something in the present to invest in the future. Sacrifice is the downside in the sense that the decision to do anything is a decision *not* to do something else. The "what you give up" factor is always under consideration. Add to that the fact that, in any effort to change the world, dreams can go unfulfilled or turn in directions that aren't anticipated or desired. Sacrifice plays a role in that, too, as part of the entry fee to the game of advancement.

In theory, the greater the effort, the greater the sacrifice, but in reality, once anyone commits to do something fully and well, the sacrifice is relative to the return sought. That said, there's a flip side to the sacrifice made to do something well that mitigates the downside. That is, one never sacrifices anything without expecting to gain something greater in return. Indeed, the two are linked. If you want change to take place and eventually make the world better, you have to be willing to make the investment. The potential to achieve the desired return allows the sacrifice to be viewed in that context.

## Always a Matter of Choice

Making a sacrifice isn't a requirement; it's a choice, just as entrepreneurship is a choice. Unlike most things in life, you're completely at will to walk on this entrepreneurial path. Entrepreneurship doesn't find *you*; you find and create *it*. In fact, you re-choose and reaffirm your choice over and over. Why? Because you keep concluding you have something important to offer to humanity.

Describing her world-renowned Chez Panisse restaurant where she gave birth to the Slow Food movement, Alice Waters told me this: "I've always run my venture seeking meaning and a sense of interest. If

I couldn't find meaning, I'd seek it out or leave the venture altogether." As a consequence, in every action she takes, she wants to reconnect to it. Continuing to take action—and to make the sacrifices those actions demand—is a choice driven by the meaning and level of interest that comes back to her.

It isn't a mystery why Alice loves what she does and has enjoyed success for a long time, not just with Chez Panisse, but in many undertakings. (See Chapter 11 for more about Alice and the scope of her creative contribution The Edible Schoolyard.) Staying in touch with the reasons and the rewards for her sacrifice makes all the difference. "Every year, I threaten to close the doors," she told me. And this threat isn't an empty one. Once a year, she goes through a cathartic process of reevaluating why the restaurant should stay open. She asks these questions: Why is this the best way to meet the mission and goals? Why is this the best use of the resources she's lucky enough to have brought together to manifest her vision? Why is another version of the vision not a better answer, a better use of her time? "I'm always figuring out what keeps that dialectic going—the push and the pull. I'm always looking for a way to change the conversation to get to something better, to have a greater impact."

In the process of asking questions, Alice finds the reasons that justify and reaffirm the sacrifices she's making, choosing once again to make them (or not). There isn't an endpoint as long as the reasons remain strong enough to press on. Every day offers a fresh opportunity to decide whether to ride the train for one more station or hop off and ride a bike.

As Alice continued, she made clear that it's not about the restaurant or the hard work. It's about *something more*. Chez Panisse doesn't define Alice or her vision; it's just a vehicle. She either invests her energy there or she places it where it has better use. It's less about sacrifice and more about progress and return in the larger sense.

That isn't sacrifice; it's conscious choice. The real sacrifice comes when you fail to take a deliberate pause to question and reconsider why to keep your doors open and, instead, blindly march on. Then again, maybe sacrifice isn't the right word for such passivity. Maybe a better word is stupidity.

## A Viewpoint of Sacrifice from the Trenches

Donna Jensen Madier knows well about personal choice in the context of lasting entrepreneurship. As founder of numerous ventures including LeGourmet, Startups.com, and most recently, Vibrant Ventures, she's lived the ups and downs of entrepreneurship multiple times. Still, she chooses the entrepreneurial path time and again, expecting and accepting the sacrifices her choices entail.

In 2006, Donna joined the Keenan Flagler School of Business at the University of North Carolina at Chapel Hill as an adjunct professor of entrepreneurship. In this role, she provides aspiring entrepreneurs with reality checks on what it takes to be successful. Describing the context in which she places sacrifice, she said, "The dedication and passion take over your life because you're breathing life into something and someplace where life didn't exist before. You lend your soul to it.

"The amount of love, passion, and dedication you put in, especially early on, goes beyond what you can imagine ahead of time. What you give of yourself is so far beyond what you give to a corporation. And much else is put on hold while you do it. There are hard times. There are no quick payoffs. Even when you get funded, you put it all back into the 'child.'

"You're working toward a payoff that's far away and often doesn't happen. Yet a true entrepreneur can't do otherwise." Clearly, true entrepreneurs don't see it as sacrifice in the same way most would. Rather, they're doing something they believe they *must* do. Just as the desire to make the choice becomes natural, even intoxicating, the sacrifice required simply becomes part of the process.

## Recommended Resources

### *Lincoln at Gettysburg* – Garry Wills

How does one measure, balance, and even leverage disappointment, failure, and sacrifice? There isn't one answer, of course, but studying Lincoln provides a good start. Gettysburg wasn't one moment filled with these elements; it was a culmination of many moments, both in Lincoln's life and in the Civil War. How Lincoln was able to nudge the country toward a "glass-half-full" mindset rather than a "glass-half-empty" one is worth reflecting on.

### *His Excellency* – Joseph Ellis

It's easy to overlook the most thoughtful and complex of human beings for the stories they've come to be known by. George Washington has been the poster boy of this kind of error for me. Ellis, a masterful writer and exhaustive researcher, set me straight. In addition to revealing the depth of Washington's character and how he overcame much to achieve what was assumed came easily to him, Ellis uncovered the truth about his peers, too. By the end of this book, you'll wonder why Washington's peers are considered some of the country's greatest heroes and why the Father of Our Country isn't given greater acknowledgment as a sage, leader, and powerful human being.

### *The Ecology of Commerce* – Paul Hawken

This is as much a book written by a man who couldn't be stopped as it is one of the earliest, most robust arguments for why environmentalists and businessmen must and can find a balance. It's amazing that several decades after its writing, we still argue about its well-articulated points rather than implementing them. The reason we'll eventually get there: Paul Hawken is not to be deterred.

# A Deliberate Pause
## The Buried Treasure Parable

There once was an old man who was worried about his talented but lazy grandson. The boy wanted great rewards but didn't want to work for them.

One day, the boy overheard his grandfather and his grandfather's friend talking about a fortune in gold that lay under an untended field nearby. The boy got excited about this and decided to clear the field of logs, refuse, and shrubbery so he could find the gold. After many days of effort, he had a beautifully cleared field but saw no sign of the gold.

With the field cleared, the boy's grandfather suggested that he plow the field to see what he might turn up that way. For days more, the grandson plowed the soil in search of gold. He left no corner unturned, yet in the end he had no gold, just a fully plowed field.

Frustrated by the lack of gold yet buoyed by his own efforts, the grandson next took his grandfather's advice to dig holes in search of the gold. So as not to miss any place where the gold might lie, the boy dug the holes in long straight lines. Still, he found no gold. But with all his efforts in the field, his grandfather's advice to plant seed made sense to the boy. So he planted seed, fenced in the field, watered the seed, and tended the plants that grew so he could protect his efforts until he could retrieve the gold.

At harvest time, as the grandson was loading wagons with fine vegetables from his crop, a man came by and asked if the vegetables were for sale. The boy agreed to sell and deliver them in exchange for the man's offer of a bag of gold. When the boy returned to his grandfather's house after delivering the vegetables, his grandfather said, "So you see, there was gold under that old field after all."

# Part IV:
*Reward and Reason*

# Contributors to Chapter 11

**Dipak Jain** (See Chapter 2)
**Will Murray** (See Chapter 2)
**Joel Peterson** (See Chapter 5)
**Peter Senge** (See Chapter 4)
**Dave Jilk** (See Chapter 8)
**Ray Leach** (See Chapter 6)
**Muhammad Yunus** (See Chapter 1)
**Alan Sorkin**
    Founder, CEO PARTS and six other ventures
    Author, *CustomerMaker*
    Vice Chair, San Diego Social Venture Partners International
**Margarita Rozenfeld** (See Chapter 10)
**Esther Dyson** (See Chapter 5)
**Doug Davidoff** (See Chapter 3)
**Laurence Gonzales** (See Chapter 2)
**Casey Golden** (See Chapter 6)
**Alice Waters** (See Chapter 10)
**Jeffrey Hollender** (See Chapter 1)
**Dan Pink** (See Chapter 1)
**Guy Kawasaki** (See Chapter 2)

# Chapter 11: Something More

*"In entrepreneurship, you have to keep in mind that you are building not for tomorrow but for many more years beyond. Successful entrepreneurship is about taking good steps that will allow others to take good steps and will eventually complete the work. It's not just about getting there."*

- Dipak Jain
Dean, Professor of Entrepreneurial Studies
Kellogg School of Management
Northwestern University

In Chapter 10, we learned that entrepreneurs don't register failure. What drives them is simply too strong and too important to allow it. More, we came to understand that the importance of what they do serves as a balancing force, even a justification, for what they sacrifice in order to realize their vision. In short, the entrepreneurial undertaking is so important that, in the minds of those who take it up, there is "no choice" but to achieve success.

That brings us to this challenging question: What exactly *is* success?

Like the meaning of entrepreneurship, we tend to think that we know (or should know). As a result, we are rather nonchalant in our use of the term and sparing in our efforts to understand what success really means. We casually insert "success" at the end of the sentence, saying, "Larry did what he did because he wants to achieve success." Statements like that presume that everyone knows exactly what it means to be successful. But do we? Surprisingly, success is a topic far too many of us never think about below the superficial.

Entrepreneurs who catalyze lasting change are not nearly as cavalier about success. It is something they are fully cognizant of, and always refining and adapting. And yet, success in their eyes looks far different than what most of us conclude success to mean—for entrepreneurs or anyone for that matter.

This chapter takes the discussion of success further than most would venture—below the surface, and into its relevance and meaning, as well as keys to achieving it. Exploring what success means in entrepreneurship requires that we undo much of what it's assumed to mean. Yet even as we strip away our misconceptions, we'll draw a strong connection between success and both value and human progress.

Not surprisingly, what leads to understanding success in entrepreneurship is a synthesis of everything addressed up to this point. But first, let's examine what success is *not*.

## What Success is Not

We tend to define success narrowly, vaguely, or on a one-time basis. A ubiquitous example of this tendency is limiting its definition to "getting rich" financially. But accumulating dollars is only a measure. It's but *one* measure, and often not even the best indicator of either progress or value.

Yet this isn't the end of the problems in defining success in dollars. Just as problematic, "getting rich" typically implies value accruing to a few and in a naturally time-bound way (e.g., "Joe Jones made a fortune when his shares in his venture were purchased by Mega-Company X on December 15, 2008."). This narrow view centers on *one*—one undertaking, one person, one time—a concept that runs counter to the things we know enable successful entrepreneurship.

### Money and Trappings Don't Equate to Success

For all of these reasons, dollars neither define nor measure success well. Still, it's worth examining this all-too-common view of success a bit further to make a key point.

Equating success with its trappings—money, fame, power—is in many places a cultural norm and cultural norms are powerful. Because such views of success are widely held, there is a tendency to assume they apply to everyone, including entrepreneurs. It gets to the point that we assume these trappings are what entrepreneurs seek, and become the primary motivators for what they do. But for true entrepreneurs, they have relative importance, if any at all.

"Most common definitions of success are really measures, proxies, and milestones—establishing the organization, accomplishing marketing goals, meeting revenue targets, and so on," said Conservation Impact co-founder Will Murray. "We often get distracted from our real understanding of success and refer to it in terms of the measures alone." The central goal of entrepreneurship—catalyzing lasting change—can be measured but isn't embodied in the measure itself. Such narrow references aren't meant to last.

The way in which entrepreneurs view success is one more example of how they view the world differently—and one more argument for adding entrepreneurial thinking to our patterns. Emphasizing the point, studies have repeatedly shown that most people—entrepreneurs or otherwise—who define success in dollars alone have a rude awakening when they actually become wealthy. Upon reaching their monetary goal, they almost universally report feeling *un*satisfied. In his book *Lucky or Smart?: Secrets to an Entrepreneurial Life*, author Bo Peabody put it this way: "No matter what anyone might tell you, all but the most hardened human beings want to believe that they will get up in the morning to pursue a goal greater than simply padding their pockets."[16]

## What Success Is

Perhaps that's why Joel Peterson teaches his students at Stanford Business School that they need "to look beyond the superficial" to truly understand success, how to achieve it, and what makes it stick. As Will and Joel know, those entrepreneurs with the highest likelihood of having great impact look at success in broad terms. Their capacity to do so is, in fact, a key point of separation for the best among them.

### Sense of Worth, Contribution to Society

Though we seem somehow to repeatedly lose the lesson, success as something more than money isn't a new concept. The father of modern management, Peter Drucker, in his book *Innovation and Entrepreneurship* wrote that total confusion exists over entrepreneurs and entrepreneurship, in part because we fail to recognize that, to them, success and value mean much more than the boundaries of pure economics and its measures allow. By Drucker's assessment, entrepreneurial value included a sense of the entrepreneur's own worth and the general contribution they feel they are making to society. Going further, he emphasized a difference between small business owners seeking purely economic return and entrepreneurs, pointing out that the latter consciously seek to create things that are new and different. In their eyes, both of these characteristics are directly relevant to the value of what they manifest. Although Drucker never undervalued the importance of capital, profits, or sound management, he believed that value isn't and shouldn't be bound by industry, market, or profit.

A fan of Drucker's and a sage in his own right, Peter Senge added to this view of value among entrepreneurs by saying "theirs isn't a definition of value or success limited to just the passion or the reward of the single individual either." The social, cultural, or environmental impact they have is regarded just as highly. When you consider entrepreneurship and the profound change sought as the reason for beginning in the first place, it quickly becomes impossible to limit success's definition to something as myopic as one person getting rich.

**A Continuum to "Something More"**
Figure 10

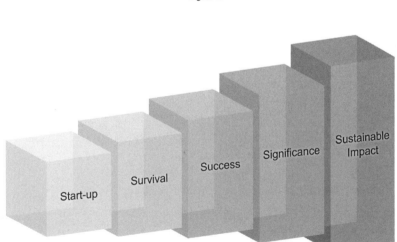

## Beyond Significance to Sustainability

Success by the more common definition of money or a single measure doesn't get anyone very far. Perhaps that's why a popular counseling theory talks about *significance* as an alternative term to *success*. By this theory, achieving significance involves reaching more people and addressing more needs, problems, and opportunities beyond adding to one's own bank account. At the very least, it adds a layer of nuance that helps mask a narrower definition of success.

But there's a problem with this focus on significance as it's most often manifested. Too often, attempts to create significance still come as a direct and tethered extension of one person and take the form of dollars and cents. Think of checks written to charities. Check writers simply execute a wealth transfer; they don't catalyze further creation of value, their own or someone else's. Consequently, that sense of emptiness remains.

Rather than mask popular definitions of success, we need to reach deeper. Rather than simply layer on, we need to dismiss our popular notions of success and see it through altogether different eyes. This isn't to say that transferring wealth has no value, just that it takes something more for humanity to truly progress.

Successful entrepreneurship is about that *something more*. Remember, what distinguishes entrepreneurs is their drive to catalyze lasting change. That means extending beyond *significance* to embrace a value known as *sustainability*—the key part of the successful change entrepreneurs make. And as you're about to see, sustainability takes hold when success is defined, personal, continuous, and connected.

## *Defining Success More Deeply—An Overlooked Necessity*

A central problem in *understanding* success happens to be the same problem encountered in *achieving* success: the failure to define it clearly in the first place. It's awfully hard to hit a target you haven't clearly defined. Shockingly, the failure to define success, even among entrepreneurs, is far too common and the crux of many failed entrepreneurial forays.

Without exception, entrepreneurs must be clear on what success is for them individually. Yes, it seems simple and obvious to *say* that.

Naturally, you have to know what success means; otherwise how can you tell when it occurs? *Not* knowing would be akin to *not* understanding that the object of soccer is getting that funny patterned ball into the net more often than the other team. (As a simplistic analogy, note the difference between the objective of "scoring more often than the other team" and "attaining a precise number of goals"—the difference between success and a measure of success.) Still, as Dave Jilk, CEO of Xaffire, noted, "The definition of success is something that many people don't think about." In its absence, they're targeting something that's vague or imagined, tilting at windmills. However, once success is defined, it allows everything else to come into view. It works as an added lens or filter to one's perceptions, decisions, and actions, and eventually to the outcomes achieved.

When you look at vast numbers of so-called entrepreneurs who haven't attained lasting change, you can't help but wonder if they lacked a definitive sense of purpose from the start. Vague notions of success don't get anyone very far. It needs to be clear *always*. Here's how Ray Leach described the meaning behind this maxim: "Entrepreneurs who hope to succeed have to have a clear definition of success when they begin their venture, of course, but also as they walk through their venture. It is the definition of where you want to end up and your means of filtering out what gets you there and what does not." (Picking up the soccer analogy, within the context of a game, a soccer team may at first define success as scoring more than their opponent, but over the course of a season, that definition must broaden to, at the very least, "outscore more teams than not.")

This fluid definition goes beyond rewarding only one person. "As you add partners, the definition broadens," Ray pointed out. "Your definition of success therefore has to be flexible and adaptable, but still anchored to what got you started in the first place. In total, it's a reflection of the ability to move through uncertainty."

## 16 Decisions Lead to Lasting Community Change

Defining success in the context of seeking seismic change clearly begins with a vision. Consider the vision Muhammad Yunus had before he lent his first dollar of micro-credit, before he founded the Grameen Bank or any of its affiliates, before others modeled his approach worldwide, and before he won the Nobel Peace Prize for his success to that point. *He set out to help the poor eliminate their own poverty.*

Grameen Bank has primarily focused on the poorest one billion of our species—those who, historically, had two life choices: starve or work for themselves. And of those two options, one—working for oneself—wasn't viable; a typically poor person in the third world could only turn to the local "5 and 6" to fund a small venture. (The local lender is called a "5 and 6" because he lends five pesos in the morning and expects a return of six pesos by evening—not a very viable or sustainable option for working for oneself.)

At the beginning, as Dr. Yunus sought to help the poor help themselves, he couldn't completely define what success would look like on the way to the ultimate goal of eradicating poverty. Yet he and others who joined him had a clear sense of purpose and immediate goals for what to do and how. They also knew the definition of success would morph, so they remained vigilant in their observations of what worked and what did not. Over time, they created a definition of *collective* success, one that every borrower and lending officer in every rural village or shanty could understand because each had a hand in shaping it. Eventually, they formalized their definition by calling it the 16 Decisions, which has evolved into vibrant descriptions of how all members of the Grameen community—regardless of their roles, activities, or rewards—choose to live.

The 16 Decisions include such measures as keeping their families small, minimizing expenditures, and looking after their health (collectively, Decision 6), educating their children while earning money to pay for their own education (Decision 7), and no longer taking or giving dowries or practicing child marriage (Decision 11). Certainly the Grameen community's definition of success touches on the philosophical, yet it's basic, too, for it includes the decision to *not* live in dilapidated houses (Decision 3) and to only drink clean water (Decision 10). The success that has evolved from these decisions has significantly changed the face of Bangladeshi society forever.

Statistical evidence adds credibility to this success story. Since 1983, Grameen Bank has disbursed an astounding amount of nearly $8 billion in increments of $100, give or take. Grameen borrowers actually own 95 percent of the equity in the banks themselves. Of those owners, 97 percent are women. More astonishing, the bank has a consistent 98 percent recovery rate of funds disbursed. No commercial bank in the world has ever been able to make this claim. Ironically, traditional banks never take on Grameen's borrowers as clients, though perhaps they should.

Think of how profound Grameen's success has become. The poorest of the poor—a forgotten third of the world's population—now own one of the most successful financial institutions in the world, one in which women once faced restrictions, but in the Grameen community, the women lead the way. And on that success, the poorest of the poor are now further refining their definition of success to include such things as achieving representation of the poor among the country's governing bodies, building business partnerships with multinational corporations, and changing health and education infrastructures at a country and regional level, well beyond a village-by-village approach. All of these advancements bring texture to the vision of *helping the poor to successfully eliminate their own condition of poverty.* From one vision comes many manifestations of success, *ad infinitum.*

With the Grameen example as a backdrop, here's what comes through loud and clear: by thoughtfully, completely, and perpetually *defining* success, the odds of achieving it clearly improve. The opposite proves just as true and just as important to recognize: *not* defining success might even ensure failure if activities don't have a clear direction and purpose. Said Alan Sorkin, vice chair of San Diego Social Venture Partners, "Many people clawed themselves to the top of the ladder of success only to find that the ladder was propped against the wrong wall."

## *The Inevitability of Making Success Personal*

Bringing disparate efforts together around a common purpose is critical to creating lasting change on a large scale. But as much as people must come together in entrepreneurship, ultimately teams are still collections of individuals. All of these individuals have their own reasons for participating, their own agendas to serve, their own paths to follow, and their own set of motivators shaping the way they view the world. So although it takes a collective effort to bring about change, for any accomplishment to be considered a success, it must pass through each individual's filter. Incite International founder, Margarita Rozenfeld, stated this point bluntly: "Success is undermined by running counter to yourself. It can't be determined by a societal measure, or someone else's definition, or a marketing image. It must be individually defined."

If the personal element is lost, then the drive to succeed—personal and collective—disappears, too. This occurs all too often among leaders of entrepreneurial ventures who experience early success but allow their vision to get lost in the drive to be disciplined in delivering that vision. Working with numerous entrepreneurs as an executive coach, Margarita understands the importance of striking a balance between community and individual goals, noting that the values, priorities, and goals of the individual can't become obscured or overshadowed if entrepreneurship is to succeed. After all, it's those personal elements that send individuals—entrepreneurs and otherwise—down the entrepreneurial path in the first place. It's these personal touch points that have the capacity to keep them going, despite the obstacles and demands encountered on that path. Indeed, at the heart of each person's ability to proceed is the need to remain committed to his or her own definition of success. If this personal sense of purpose and fulfillment gets lost, so does the motivation to continue and the desire to unite with others to achieve a shared goal of change.

When it happens, why does this personal element become lost? Because too many entrepreneurs get so caught up in their to-do lists that they lose perspective. This element reinforces a lesson discussed earlier—continuing to strike a balance between the *perspective* that determines ways to move forward and the *discipline* that accomplishes it. Every entrepreneur needs to be constantly in tune with this "dance of entrepreneurship," staying balanced or getting refocused. Most find it by taking a deliberate pause.

The personal fulfillment factor can't be undervalued as a source of staying power along the difficult path of entrepreneurship. Founder of Edventures Holdings and author of the bi-monthly *New York Times* column *Release 3.0,* Esther Dyson, put it this way: "Achieving success through something you are not proud of is hard to enjoy." Similarly, a venture that isn't satisfying is nearly impossible to sustain. As Imagine Companies founder, Doug Davidoff, noted, "Success is the ability to achieve greatness and the unlikely, while still being true to yourself."

## The Power in a Shared Definition of Success

If people fail to define success for themselves, what happens? Society, markets, or other people fill that void. Therefore, having a strong personal definition of success protects you, keeping you on course and maximizing your efforts. Better, it also allows you to have a strong hand in the collective definition of success because it fuels the drive to persist, thus providing a barometer of satisfaction and fulfillment. Imagine the outcome if everybody came to the entrepreneurial journey clear about where they stood and what they wanted individually *before* they joined forces. Clarity begets clarity. More than that, it empowers a collective choice to work toward a common goal.

All that said, the power of entrepreneurship lies in the "coming together." As Chapter 4 addressed, for lasting change to take root, having many hands joined in a common endeavor is necessary. When many are involved, the definition of both success and value in fact broadens and deepens, forming a continuum. That doesn't have to occur at the expense of individual definitions of success; it just means both individual and collective definitions are expected to evolve. Both need to be honored and a continuing balance struck. Thus, success—while initially defined at the individual level and ultimately filtered there as well—becomes tightly woven in with the concept of the entrepreneurial ecosystem and the power of community—each of which is ultimately comprised of individuals.

## Awakening to Seeing Value in New Ways

Every one of us knows value when we encounter it. We *sense* it; we *feel* it because it represents something that matters to us. It feels worthy of our investment. If we looked at value according to our sense of value rather than according to a monetary metric, suddenly the potential for value would know no limits.

Yet, through habit or social norms, we don't tend to regard value that way. Instead, we often dismiss our "sense" of value because if the value doesn't fit our expectations for form or measure, we assume it's a fluke, it's unsustainable, or, more harshly, it isn't valuable at all. As Grameen Foundation president, Alex Counts, commented in a presentation in October of 2008, "The tendency to dismiss success and the value that comes of it occurs everywhere humans congregate."

Value occupies a strange continuum from the ethereal to the narrow. It's the force that moves us from just an idea to real and lasting change, even as it's the tangible that everyone strives for. Value is the language and currency used to attract others into the ecosystem. It is concurrently *infinite* in its potential and potential form, and *finite* when seen only by a single metric validating progress. But it's admittedly hard to hold highly different thoughts in our heads at once. And so, as humans, we naturally come up with shortcuts, one being that if opportunity doesn't look like value as we already know it, we tend to dismiss it.

Part of our aversion to the appearance of new value on the one hand when we're capable of sensing value on the other relates to accepted social norms and metrics. But part of it goes deeper in a more primal way. Author of *Deep Survival* and *Everyday Survival,* Laurence Gonzales, explained why. "Humans in general," he said, "don't perceive the world in total, taking in all the data that's presented to us." Yet it's from the taking in of new data that entrepreneurs often discover new patterns, new sources, and new forms of value. "In contrast, most people work off of signals that call up mental models and maps we have stored. Those maps are based on our past experiences, what we know. Rather than stop and see what is really in front of us, we take in a signal, a small piece of the available information, which we then tie to our known experiences. Then we act according to those maps of what happened the last time." When that happens, we cap our ability to advance, which is truly our dominate desire as humans.

Just because we've accepted a programming format, that doesn't mean we lack the capacity to alter it. And altering it can be as straight forward as *choosing to see differently*, which often results from taking a deliberate pause. "It isn't intellectual knowledge that helps you survive or interact with new surroundings," said Laurence. "Seeing and seizing value depend on being awake." If we're asleep, it's hard to see the world as entrepreneurs do. By implication, it's hard to recognize, capture, and benefit from the value they discover if we can't see things in a fresh new way—for good or for bad—because of our programming.

Unless you actively open your mind and awaken to a larger idea of value, you could end up devalued, disadvantaged, or dead. Yet when you do, you're able to see *something more*.

### Forms and Flow of Value a Liquid Mosaic

Once you awaken your capacity to see value, it quickly becomes clear that value is a fluid mosaic. Its many forms combined make a whole that's larger than the sum of the parts. Therefore, tapping into the promise of successful entrepreneurship does not lie solely in that capacity to *see* new forms. Just as important is having the opportunity— perhaps even better, the mandate—to continually and actively *search* for fresh forms of value. *That* is what makes entrepreneurship truly powerful.

You have this skill inherently, but it must be exercised and developed over and over again so entrepreneurship and value can be manifested in many forms, even allowed to flow together. That's where the magic happens. So your goal becomes to perpetually expand value in form, in quantity, in impact. Seeing different forms of value and weaving them together so they can draw from each other, push each other, and embolden and strengthen each other—that's how value reflects the pure entrepreneurial vision that started things in the first place.

Even a small act can have value, generating a ripple effect that cycles and reinforces. You simply have to be awake enough to see it. The Small Act Network (see *The Rippling Value of a Small Act*) demonstrates this dynamic in action.

## The Rippling Value of a Small Act

In 2007, Casey Golden created Small Act Network, an undertaking that requires an open, expandable mind to understand. Its basic forms of value are quite simple, but they ripple so quickly into so many other forms that the mind swims with visions of how to expand into other avenues. As you will see, Casey hands out the matches and kerosene, then sets the imagination ablaze with numerous possibilities.

At first glance, Small Act Network appears to serve mainly as a simple landing page and search engine. Casey's premise is to make this page your jumping-off point for searching the Internet. But its premise belies its power. In reality, it is the starting point for relationships, community, and the rippling creation of value. Let me take you on a virtual tour to show you why.

Picture arriving at Small Act's home page and being greeted by the "Small Act of the Day" window. You're told about some seemingly small thing that someone did—something that had an impact on another person, on the planet, within a business, or similar. For the sake of a mental image, let's say someone submitted "plant a tree" as one small way to make the earth greener, cleaner, and more inviting. Imagine this "plant a tree" action moved you. Inspired, you then execute a small act of your own. Maybe you volunteer to help clean up in a wooded park in your community. Or you purchase a product from one seller over another because the first one pledged to plant a tree in your name for every $10 you spend. Or you reuse and recycle more of your paper in your office and home to save trees from being unnecessarily cut down. You think of countless other things you might do, all inspired by someone else's one small act. Now imagine hundreds of others doing the same, alone or in groups. They build a small act into much more, and suddenly it's not so small. You get the idea.

Why ever limit the ideas or forms of value that one small act could create? Casey doesn't.

He has added to the example of acting a specific *incentive* to act by communing at Small Act Network. If you use Small Act as your landing page and search engine, Casey gives away 50 percent of his organization's revenue to a designated beneficiary—a charity, cause, school, nonprofit group, etc.— every time the site is used. And *you,* the user, get to pick the beneficiary, either an existing one or a new one of your choice. To do all that, your cost is zero. This quickly shifts the key question from "what have you got to lose?" to "what else might you be able to gain, just by a small act?"

We're not done yet. Around the edges of this home page is a series of logos or display ads purchased by advertisers. If site visitors click through on an advertiser's logo and beyond, the advertiser tells more about how it supports causes of interest to the site users, and offers further ways for them to get involved. This works because advertisers get a rare chance to directly engage a potential customer in a trusted environment. In turn, those customers get to add power to their voices beyond their purchasing decisions. Even if you don't click on an ad or logo, the companies affiliated with them still put money toward your stated charity, but when you do click through, they may put forth even more.

Linked with Small Act Network are receiving organizations who get the dollars paid by the advertisers on Casey's site.[17] That means that the receiving organization doesn't only receive money; it gets diversity in capital sources. With that comes increased stability and flexibility for the organization itself.

Everybody wins in the sense that everybody is defining and then generating value on their own terms. People sharing information, people sharing ideas, people joining forces, people serving their own and one another's causes, and all doing so by choice. That's value.

### *Shared Value Creates Community*

Various forms and flows of value lead to values coming together at some point. So, too, do those creators of value.

Alice Waters creates community in that most comforting form—the one that centers around food. Many know Alice as the founder of the Slow Food movement, author of numerous cookbooks, and innovative founder, owner, and lead chef of her world-renowned Chez Panisse restaurant in Northern California. Less known but arguably far more important is her bigger vision: *to re-inspire the importance of community in our world and at the same time, change the education process in the United States.* To live her mission further, she recently started The Edible Schoolyard, perhaps her most innovative vehicle yet. Its goals are awesome and, for Alice, aren't optional. She feels she has "no choice."

Alice's Edible Schoolyard is a microcosm of the whole idea of community. In some ways, the concept is simple—that is, kids and teachers work together to establish a schoolyard garden from which they can harvest food to consume and share. But Alice's purpose runs deeper. She's bringing together disparate, often disconnected groups—merchants, consumers, students, politicians, educators, and more—and giving them reasons to work with and hear each other. As the kids grow vegetables in their educational program, they're learning about health, agriculture, cooking, retailing (because they sell some of what they grow to local restaurants and food sellers), and countless other topics. And their teachers go beyond having students assigned to them in school—they have young co-workers and collaborators who make decisions alongside them each day. More important, teachers and students alike touch every person in the community that forms around the Schoolyard program.

To get community members involved, Alice appealed to their individual senses of value. "When you engage a community," Alice said, "you have to make it in their best interest. The exchange of food is one powerful way to do that. It creates a bond. It's every day and common." Entrepreneurs sense points of common ground better than most. "That is the basis for community, when you're willing to sacrifice because it involves someone or something you really care about," Alice added. The caring component is powerful and valuable, even beyond words.

When asked about the value of the Edible Schoolyard program, Alice explained, "It can't be measured. It's profound. It's about school reform and priorities for learning. It's opening kids' senses. It's all the extraordinary benefits of learning by doing. It's putting money into the community by buying what they produce. It brings people together and back into the schools. It's giving kids something tasty to eat. It's endless. It's about beauty and meaning being brought back into people's lives. It gives purpose and application to every subject in the school. It's hard for kids to understand 'purpose' and this does it. It's teaching children to be environmentalists. It's preservation of culture. It allows every child to see and appreciate the world around them and to see that it is their world, too. It's dignifying farming and cooking. The benefits go on and on."

The program also teaches kids about the relationship of men to women, how to converse and live with others, and cooperate and define roles. "We don't tend to learn that any place," added Alice. "So what better place than in the kitchen or at the table?"

From one entry point, community and value build on each other. The result? A shared fingerprint of collective creation that's *their* dream, not only the dream of the catalyst. Calling what's achieved here success seems almost limiting. It's something far more.

### *Yet There's Still Something More*

The mind comes alive at the idea of ventures like Casey's or Alice's. Suddenly, success isn't narrow and value isn't finite or bounded. Everything is cast in the larger idea of constantly evolving humanity forward, irrespective of the vehicle, the time, or the catalyst. All these components play a part, but the reward of entrepreneurship becomes *something more* than any one person, time, or measure and so much more than what's typically attributed as success. Recognizing this— from the start or more often with time—drives entrepreneurs forward to realize value far greater than what most imagine possible. Like their vision, the reward they want humanity to realize, with or without them, is almost unbounded. As the possibilities and potential increase, the impact lasts longer and, almost by necessity, is passed along hand to hand, rather than being bound up or ending with one. In the process, individual success becomes relative to lasting change; significance means significance for all; one step becomes the first toward many; and sustainability is nearly assured.

As you see how entrepreneurs delineate the reward of what they do, you can also see the whole picture of entrepreneurship through shared eyes like those in the Seventh Generation community (see *In the Service of Community*).

## In the Service of Community

Seventh Generation founder, Jeffrey Hollender, has evolved in the direction of collective sharing and sees the process of evolution as lasting and ongoing. "I frequently ask myself who I need to become to provide value to the business," Jeffrey said. "If I'm the same person I was last year, I'm likely to become a restraint to the business and its vision. It's not in any way walking away from the essence and the heart and soul of who I am, but it's how to express that as the business grows and evolves."

Growth, in Jeffrey's eyes, is continuing to show others how to identify, define, and realize their own reward and reason, both within the entrepreneurial vision and beyond. "In the early stages, the business asks you to do a lot of stuff. Over time, you increasingly let go of most of that doing. Your role becomes supporting the development of all the doers around you. By holding onto it yourself, you can take up the space others need to do those things."

For Jeffrey as for Dr. Yunus, it's not all theory, nor is it all practice either. Their beliefs lie deep within their values. Those values form the base of the organizations they've created to carry their visions forward. Their values drive more value; they feel it deeply.

In Jeffrey's case, making sure value was deeply planted in Seventh Generation began even before the company chose its name. It comes from the Great Law of the Iroquois Confederacy, which stated, "In every deliberation, we must consider the impact of our decisions on the next seven generations." The Confederacy was a banding together of six tribes, also known as the League of Peace and Power and the People of the Longhouse. These six tribes realized that to achieve *something more* than what they could create separately, they had to work as one and live in one common longhouse. Rather than stone or wood, the walls of this metaphoric longhouse are forged of shared principles and beliefs. The tribes' leaders recognized that what each did affected the others. They had to choose whether to act in concert toward something larger—capturing and combining their potential—or to risk the ripples of their separate actions colliding with one another in their common pond.

Reflecting on the ever-advancing cycles of evolution for Seventh Generation, Jeffrey said, "If I had to choose between the questions of 'does the business need me to be an entrepreneur' versus 'does it need me to be a community builder,' I'd choose the latter. I still seek out new possibilities and I can have all the ideas I want. But if I can't get the buy-in of the community, I can't just impose my ideas on them. I have to respect the will of the community around what we're trying to do. It isn't *me* trying to do something more; it's *us*."

## The Spiritual Element of Being Human

Seeking betterment in life is innately human, even if we're out of practice with it. Because we want to make meaning and manifest value beyond our ability to create or enjoy alone, entrepreneurship becomes an extremely sincere reflection of our humanness. If we suspend the stereotypes that can devalue the term "spiritual," it's almost obvious to find that there's a spiritual element to successful entrepreneurship—something that speaks to those who walk the entrepreneurial path. Having "no choice" is, in a sense, a recognition and statement of an inability to go against oneself, or against the betterment of one's species. Something—perhaps at its heart a spiritual quest—tells the entrepreneur and all who follow that it isn't only who *he* is but who *we* are, and that this act of betterment is what we must do. Thus, entrepreneurs must move forward and evolve both for themselves *and* for human progress.

More directly than many, Dan Pink addressed the importance of spirituality in *A Whole New Mind*. While some hesitate to openly acknowledge its importance for fear of ridicule or lack of understanding, Dan pointed out that what he (and countless others) are observing as a force gaining momentum in the world today is not religion *per se*, but a core and deeply personal "concern for meaning and purpose in life, which is a fundamental part of the human condition."[18] More and more, entrepreneurs and people in general are seeking ways to manifest that purpose and improve the human condition, somehow and in some way through their life's work. Similarly, Guy Kawasaki—in his advice to me and to countless others in his books, webinars, speeches, and blog—is emphatic about how he believes entrepreneurs can have the highest odds of success. His sage advice: "Make meaning above all else; the rest will follow."

The frequency with which entrepreneurs and others interviewed for this book refer to spirituality should be a sign. It's both a window into their choice to catalyze a quest for something more, and a window into their souls as members of an exceptional species. In a manner of speaking, it's a reminder of who we are and what separates us. As Laurence Gonzales wrote, "Animals and natural forces are frank. Survivors therefore must have spirituality and humility. You hear things like that and at first they sound silly. But when you hear enough survivors [or creators] of impossible situations say it, you become a believer."[19]

A sense of spirituality may be something that lingers in the subconscious when entrepreneurs get going. It may be something that, at a societal level, they only feel comfortable talking about behind the closed doors of their offices, homes, or places of worship (where it both benefits and suffers from an over-narrowing of context). But it's present, always—perceived even when it can't or won't be named. And when those who embrace spirituality build it into whatever they do, it makes a world of difference.

Laurence has subtitled his *Deep Survival* book *Who Lives, Who Dies and Why*. What you quickly learn from his book is that *Who* refers not to individuals as much as to humans as a species. *Why* has a great deal to do with humans' ability to turn a new awareness into an opportunity to advance, rather than to come to an end. Let's examine answers to that critical question *Why* for ourselves and for the entrepreneurial universe in Chapter 12.

## Recommended Resources

### *The Alchemist* – Paulo Coelho

This is a simple yet deeply thoughtful story that teaches us how to do something more almost without us knowing it's happening. More than any other topic in *A Deliberate Pause*, the one of "Something More" in this chapter is the most personal. *My* "something more" may not be yours. We all must find our own purpose, or, as Paulo Coelho would say, we all must follow our own personal legend.

### *Man's Search for Meaning* – Victor Frankl

Where *The Alchemist* is allegorical and light, *Man's Search for Meaning* hits you right in the face. Although it's one person's reflection on his own unplanned experience in Nazi concentration camps, how he came to survive rises in importance above one person's story.

### *Presence* – Peter Senge et al

Peter and his co-authors go Frankl and Coelho one better. They provide the insight gained from their specific journey to finding something more, while offering reason and a framework for taking your own journey. This is a thinking book in the "big thinking" sense, thus it takes concentration to stay with it, but it's well worth the effort.

### *The Agony and the Ecstasy* – Irving Stone

How Michelangelo found reason and inspiration to lie on his back for four straight years and paint the ceiling of the Sistine Chapel is hard to comprehend. Stone tries to imagine what it was like, and describes it almost as stunningly as the artist painted the ceiling. No matter what, it's a great book. But it's also a way to climb inside someone else's head and see why this artist continued to do what others would have found impossible.

## Contributors to Chapter 12

**Bill Drayton** (See Chapter 3)
**Peter Senge** (See Chapter 4)
**Casey Golden** (See Chapter 6)
**Guy Kawasaki** (See Chapter 2)
**Gene Kahn** (See Chapter 2)
**Oran Hesterman** (See Chapter 8)
**Mike Morris** (See Chapter 8)
**Will Finnerty** (See Chapter 8)
**Bijoy Goswami** (See Chapter 2)
**Richard Tait** (See Chapter 1)
**Alice Waters** (See Chapter 10)
**Jeffrey Hollender** (See Chapter 1)
**John Wood** (See Chapter 1)
**Steve Mariotti** (See Chapter 2)
**Muhammed Yunus** (See Chapter 1)
**Robert Egger** (See Chapter 4)

# Chapter 12: The Power of Why

*"Entrepreneurs cannot come to rest until their vision is part of the very fabric of their world."*

- Bill Drayton
Founder, Ashoka
*U.S. News'* America's 25 Best Leaders, 2005

Why should we care about *why* entrepreneurs do what they do?

Peter Senge told me a story that I think answers this nicely. One of his colleagues moved himself and his work to Silicon Valley during the dot.com boom because, as he told Peter, he wanted to see what entrepreneurs were really like. After this man had lived and worked in various entrepreneurial communities for several years, Peter asked him, "Are entrepreneurs really all in it for the money and the fame?"

"Yes," replied his friend, "all the mediocre ones. The best are attempting to do nothing less than change the world." And that, of course, affects all of us—if someone is going to change our world, obviously we want to know how, but to then know how to react to their vision and intent, we ought to take an interest in *why*. In *A Deliberate Pause*, we have taken that interest to heart.

In Chapter 11, we spoke of the reward and reason behind the entrepreneur's undertaking, focusing mostly on the tangibles. But there's further to go if we are to fully understand why entrepreneurs succeed in achieving something more—beyond the personal or temporal—and strive at the level of advancing humanity. Without a doubt, there's a power inherent in why entrepreneurs act and persist. But to be frank, the power isn't about the motivation that starts us down the entrepreneurial path in the first place (reason) nor is it explained by what may result along the way (reward). The power is in the asking of the question *why* itself, and what happens during the process of doing so.

Here's a guiding thought as you read and reflect on this chapter: the critical difference between a question and a statement is that a question *demands that you think*. Just spitting out a statement is an act of staying still. In contrast, asking *why* is a conscious act—a choice—to advance. What I call the power of why is so simple that it's perhaps best seen through the eyes of a six year old.

## Really, Why?

Adults are curious, but only to a point. They're so busy, they won't stop to ponder everything they're told. More often than not, adults filter what they hear and then affirm, ignore, or accept.

As adults, if what we hear matches up with what we know, we're happy to affirm that truth. But if what we hear doesn't make sense, we have a choice that's usually filtered by determining how much effort we want to make. We may momentarily consider reasons for any disconnect that exists between what we hear and what we know, but we inevitably move on to either ignoring or accepting the disconnect.

My six-year-old daughter does not.

Like most youngsters, she exudes an abundance of entrepreneurial curiosity and a hunger for meaning. To her, only a few hard rules exist; the lines most adults operate within have either not yet been drawn or she hasn't fully accepted them. So with everything open to exploration, what she and her peers like to explore most is the question of why. *Why should they do what they are being asked to do? Why does the world work the way it does? Why should it have to work the way that grown-ups say it should?*

While I might expect an adult to ask me *why* once in a while, I can fully expect my daughter to ask me five or seven or even ten layers of *why* questions—that's all before she either accepts my reasoning as sound or is willing to back off until she can process what I've told her, usually with every intent of coming back at me again to learn more. Learning requires passion and choice. She is fully aware that both are available to her and embraces each. She searches for *something more* than the trite responses adults are prone to give. She wants the truth.

And for her, the truth must be something that has meaning and value, going deeper than most people over the age of six are willing to go.

Playwright Peter Brooks once wrote, "There are three truths: my truth, your truth, and *the* truth." Like six year olds, the best entrepreneurs search for *the* truth. Rather than simply be satisfied with what's known, accepted, or good enough, they thirst for *something more*, which is precisely what's being addressed in Part IV of *A Deliberate Pause*. Everything that lies before us may be *true*, but until we press further and ask *why*, we don't know it's *the* truth.

## *Where Asking Why Can Lead*

In tracing the entrepreneurial search for answers to bigger questions to its root, you're bound to get involved in a search for the answer to *why*. Presumably at the root is the entrepreneurs' pattern-recognition ability that allows them to identify what could be—a possible vision of the future. But more than that, asking *why* defines the person who employs entrepreneurial thinking. As Ashoka's Bill Drayton told us in Chapter 3, "Some people simply define themselves in bigger ways than others." In their search for *something more*, they orient themselves around things that really matter—not just to them, but to their world. Because they view themselves and their purpose in a big way, their potential for impact is naturally big, too.

Sure, it's easy to mistake the entrepreneur for the dreamer, but you now know there's much more to this change catalyst. Entrepreneurs also take action, convert others, and generate and transfer value. Yet it all begins with their need to ask and answer the question *why*. The power of why used by one can then radiate out to many.

## A Kind of Reawakening

Casey Golden, founder of Small Act Network, described to me the reawakening he experienced after leaving another company he'd co-founded but outgrown. He immersed himself in conversations for the following year within communities of entrepreneurs. Somewhere during that period of pausing, he heard strategic communications specialist and ethnographer Simon Sinek speak about the difference between the why-driven organization and the what-driven alternative.[20] As Casey recounted it, Sinek was describing people in general, not specifically entrepreneurs, but this distinction "clicked" with what Casey had experienced in the entrepreneurial universe.

Casey visualized his basic theory as a bull's eye. At the center of the bull's eye is the question of *why*; the next ring around it represents the question of *how*; and the outer rings encompass the question of *what*. When an organization begins with the question *why*, then everything within the organization—its people, their actions, the products or services they provide—is driven by the effort to answer that question. Naturally following from the *why* are the *how* and the *what*. These serve the *why*, not the other way around.

But far too many organizations reach a point of reversal when the *what*—perhaps a product or service—becomes such an important focal point that it dictates *how* and eventually *why* as well. When that happens, the power of why gets overshadowed, if not extinguished.

"A why orientation," said Casey, "is like the river that powers things forward. Any other way of operating is a pointless swim upstream against the current." In that sense, asking *why* provides a natural, efficient, and effective answer that can lead to *something more*. "It's human nature for people to want to be associated with the *why* of something, even if they buy the *what*," he added. Casey highlighted Apple and its loyal customers as one obvious and excellent example. Arguably, customers are drawn to Apple more for its vision, philosophy, and reasons behind its actions than they are to its products—an intentional outcome.

As described in Chapter 5, Apple has nurtured legendarily loyal customers for its products. Thanks to the efforts of people like Guy Kawasaki, these customers can be called evangelical followers. And while they endlessly gab online about the company's products, reading their comments reveals that they talk mostly about *why*—for example, why did Apple develop a certain product a certain way? Or why can't Apple do something different instead?

Apple's customers believe (and ample evidence can support this belief) that *they* are empowered, even obligated, to relentlessly pursue that question of why. That directly results from Apple's corporate culture that's so driven by the question of why. Its leaders have determined that *how* they make products and interface with customers should also be driven by a pursuit of *why*. Clearly, when culture takes hold of the power of *why*, the multiplier effect across individuals is stunning, even unstoppable.

## *Where the Power of Why Comes From*

San Francisco columnist Herb Caen once famously said, "There has to be another way if only because there has to be another way." Most would chuckle away this comment as quirky, even Yogi Berra-ish. Some, however, would call it a mantra. Asking *why* isn't a genetic right available to some and not to others, after all. Entrepreneurs don't hold sway over the ability to tap into its power. But the difference between entrepreneurs and most other people is that entrepreneurs make asking the *why* question a practice.

Eastern philosophy offers a concept of practicing something so often that you instill it into your being as a natural response or practice, a sixth sense. When that something becomes second nature, it's called *samskara*.

This term comes from the words *sam*, meaning intensely, and *kara,* meaning to do, and literally translates as "acting with intensity." But in common use, the meaning of samskara is more refined. It's a tendency to act, think, see and react in a certain way based on and conditioned by previous thought or action. In effect, this is what the best entrepreneurial thinkers create for themselves through practice— they make "asking *why*" a samskara, or conditioned response.

### Cultivating an Entrepreneurial Mindset

The power in asking *why* isn't found in a one-time or occasional exercise, nor is it a reaction to circumstances. Rather, it's a mindset. For the best entrepreneurs, asking *why* is their *modus operandi* for evolving the entrepreneurial venture every day, in every way, at every stage in its life. "When the vision feels so much like you that you get goose bumps, then you're ready to move forward," said Cascadian Farms founder, Gene Kahn. "Success in entrepreneurship is a conditioning process. You need to live with a vision for quite some time to be capable of making it real."

That means you have to practice and push to gain a clearer understanding of *why*, always determining what the answers can mean from a value standpoint. It's never happenstance or luck that brings you to the point of goose bumps or samskara. Our contributors have been consistent in that message throughout this book. "I attribute it much more to synchronicity," said Oran Hesterman, program director at the W.K. Kellogg Foundation. "There's a synchronicity that will feed our creativity if we learn how to hear it, see it, feel it, taste it, and trust it." Getting to that point takes time, but it's worth it. In fact, it's what makes the entrepreneur's filter work. Completing the thought, Mike Morris, president and founder of OceanOptics, added, "If you know your guiding principles, the details are easy. And if you *really* know them, you don't need to go back to some business plan document."

Everything that makes entrepreneurship work has its roots in this samskara. You can trace it back to how entrepreneurs come to see patterns that most of us don't, why they act in a *how* mode rather than with a *how to* approach. This practice is how entrepreneurs actualize, process, and leverage their exposure, and hear their calling. It's part of their ability to see and seek value; it's built into their search for *something more*.

Asking *why* causes you to dig deeply rather than skim the surface, bringing you to the realization that the answers to all the *whys* can't be found alone. That creates the need to build and overlap ecosystems, communities, ideas, and dreams. It's found everywhere in entrepreneurship as a constant thread, a lifeline. The power of why lies also in coming to know the possibilities *within* as well as the possibilities *out there*. Indeed, it comes in refining to the point that the two fuse.

### Tapping into the Power to Change

In March of 2009, Tiger Woods won his 14th major golf championship. To some it was, pardon the expression, par for the course. Tiger always seems to win and stay on pace toward his dream of bettering his idol, Jack Nicklaus.

However, to regard Woods's victory that day as "just another win" would be to miss important subtleties. He won it equaling the biggest final round comeback of his career, and did it on a barely-out-of-the-shop reconstructed leg. (Tiger had sat out for most of the previous year for reconstructive knee surgery.) A more thoughtful answer is that Tiger has spent a lifetime methodically reinventing the game, never being held back by what golf was in Nicklaus's day or what people expect it to be.

I read an article shortly after Woods's win that compared Tiger to the legendary Golden Bear. *Washington Post* sports columnist Thomas Boswell distinguished the two greats with precision and wisdom when he wrote, "Nicklaus tried to master the game. Tiger tries to redefine and expand it."[21]

Those few who have asked and answered *why* tap into an available power—the power to change something in the world around them. Entrepreneurship that lasts and maximizes the opportunity to better things is characterized by a rhythm of constant course corrections large and small. How would you know to make them if you didn't ask why? And if your practice of asking is perpetual, ubiquitous, and multifaceted, can there be any limit to what's discovered? Why should there be? After all, leveraging the power of asking *why* is the process by which the entrepreneurial venture evolves, creates value, and succeeds. The best entrepreneurs work a thousand times over to master this mindset in order to redefine and expand the world. They become conditioned to being constantly aware, adaptable, and oriented toward better.

A tall order? Maybe.

A well-hedged bet in the effort to achieve sustained success? Without question.

A key fundamental to entrepreneurial success? Definitely. And it really isn't so difficult if you develop this habit. You just have to get going.

## Get Going

"Okay, let's get going," I said abruptly to a class of juniors and seniors at Georgetown University. They'd never met me before and knew little about me. (I've had the good fortune to regularly step in for Will Finnerty, the class's professor, and guest-teach his highly sought-after beginners' course on entrepreneurship.) After that impersonal opener,

I continued by saying, "I'd like each of you to grab a piece of paper and take a few minutes to answer this question: *Why are you here?*"

Amazingly, all but one of the 50 or so students did exactly as I asked, without hesitation and without clarification. That one person quietly asked, "You mean why are we here in this *class*?" but I simply repeated my original question and he, too, went to work on it. Pencils and pens moved diligently. Occasionally, one or two students looked up to see if others were still writing. After five minutes, I told them to wrap it up. Then, without saying another word, I moved on to other topics for the day.

Later in the class, I came back to this exercise. In between, we had talked for close to two hours about specifics of entrepreneurs and entrepreneurship, including the catalyst role versus those filled by the many others that successful entrepreneurship depends on. We discussed how entrepreneurs do what they do and where they place their focus—similar to what you find in this book but at a faster fly-by pace. And then we came back to the initial question: *Why are you here?*

As they scurried to grab their papers, I told them these answers were for them alone. I didn't want to see their papers nor hear what was on them. Instead, I asked for a show of hands in response to the following: "When you answered the question, who answered it in terms of why you were here in this class today?" Most hands went up. "Who answered it," I continued, "thinking 'why am I here at Georgetown?'" A solid number of hands went up. I continued with several more options including in Washington, DC, in the U.S., and so on. Finally I asked, "Who answered the question thinking 'why am I here on this planet and in this world?'" Only two hands were up. In the context of entrepreneurship, how they answered the question was the key to how far the lessons of entrepreneurship would take them. And of all the things I taught them that day—perhaps of everything they'll ever learn about entrepreneurship—that question gave them the most meaningful insight. Indeed, it was the most powerful gift I could have given them about entrepreneurship—and about something more in life.

How they answered the question *why* was entirely up to them—their choice to take it and fly with it, or not. Behind the idea was to get going and keep going, asking *why* all the time, probing deeply, consciously, constantly. I'm certain that if these Georgetown students allow this experience to remind them of this principle, it will give them advantages far beyond the classroom.

### Open to Questions, Answers, Perseverance

Indeed, the opportunity and the advantage are available to everyone.

As Bijoy Goswami, founder of Bootstrap Austin and author of *The Human Fabric,* reminded me, that's particularly true of those in the United States for whom the opportunity and advantage have been available from birth or from citizenship, as the case may be. He noted, "The world is very noisy. There are all these distractions. The whole idea of life is to press on, not simply lie down and accept." Using a powerful tool like the question of *why* carries one forward. And as Bijoy said, "If you keep going, through all these veils, you get to this very clear perception of what is going on. Every time it seems you reach the end and can't go on, you do. It's a test. The whole thing is about being open to the answers and continuing to persevere."

Do you realize we can be reminded of the power of why and its availability at every baseball game, school assembly, or July 4th gathering? That's true, thanks to Bijoy's alertness and Francis Scott Key's contribution of the lyrics to our national anthem. "Have you ever noticed," Bijoy asked, "that the 'Star-Spangled Banner' ends in a question?" —*O! say does that star-spangled banner yet wave O'er the land of the free and the home of the brave?*— "I discovered this when I decided to become a citizen," Bijoy told me. "I took that process seriously. I wanted it all to be a step toward something. *America* is a question," Bijoy continued. "*Life* is a question. And every time we hear the 'Star-Spangled Banner,' the words can encourage us to live in a question.

"The Constitution itself is structured to allow us to evolve, to question. The genius of it all is that we don't know the answer but we can come up with our best, put it out there, see the feedback, and change it. And the Founding Fathers laid out the procedures to do that."

It's amazing that in listening to this nation's anthem, we get a free reminder about how humans do what they do and even why we're here in the first place. We'd be remiss not to leverage this powerful tool into a samskara. It's as simple as making a habit of asking the question *why*. And just think about what you could do with it. As Cranium's Richard Tait said, "Once you've changed the world, it's addictive."

## Why Embracing a Deliberate Pause Matters

Why is the world the way it is today? Why must it remain so? Why is the way I'm operating in that world what it is? Why isn't there a better form of the "good" we have or a better solution to the "not so good" we must contend with? Why does it seem like others don't see this? Of those who *do* see it, why isn't anyone doing anything about it? Of those who are doing something about it, why are they doing it the way they are or have been for so long? Why can't I be the one to change things? Why do I have to wait? Why am I not already doing something about it?

These very complex questions don't have easy answers, at least not ones that come in a single asking. Taken in total, they can feel overwhelming, exhausting, impossible to answer, and easier to ignore than pursue. What would a child say or do when contemplating such questions? Better yet, what did we say, think, or do as children when faced with an obstacle? How did we learn to act in our days in the sandbox, before the classroom, the cubicle, or the boardroom?

Let's pause for a moment in that thought stream and return to the sandbox to examine what we learned from sand, from water, and from our play.

Water is powerful, in part because it doesn't always move in a single direction or at a single speed. But it does always move forward. It has momentum. Obstacles or conflict doesn't put it off. It simply flows. Think back to when you were a child and you dropped a running hose into a sandbox. While the water came steadily out of the hose at a constant speed and direction, it didn't move through the sand that way. Whenever the water encountered an obstacle—a higher mound of sand, a toy shovel, a bucket, even your foot—its motion deliberately changed. With the hose still running, the water of course never came to a complete stop.

But it paused. It would be in motion even as it appeared hung up, all the while figuring out a way to advance. Sometimes it would pool, other times it would carve away at whatever had slowed it. Perhaps it would find a new way around, maybe more than one. Despite the slowing, the moving sideways, and the occasional backward motion, progress continued. And at whatever point the water found a new and better channel, it would break through and flood forward with all the same power and confidence it began with when it first was turned on.

As a child in that sandbox, you likely did the same. Your method of play was to "go with the flow." Water showed you what it could do and you simply went along with it, adjusting your play, your imagination, and even the landscape in which you operated.

You're acting in a similar way when you take a deliberate pause. You pause to reflect, with a willingness to consider a new direction. You incorporate whatever comes your way and search for how to fold in the new, the unexpected, even the serendipitous, so you can advance further than before.

### Entrepreneurs Habitually Pause to Reflect

If you've read this book from the beginning, you can't help but have assimilated the idea of a deliberate pause and noticed its importance. Entrepreneurs who habitually pause to reflect on what they do—asking why and assessing what they're doing and how to do it better—are hard to stop. Pausing to search for greater value, drawing others into the fold, helping them manifest that value, and continually reshaping the vision can lead to change that's sustainable and seismic.

Those who understand entrepreneurship embrace this pause, each in his or her own way, some consciously and others in synch with pursuing the question *why*. Recall Alice Waters who, even after three decades, consciously pauses each year when she considers closing her famed Chez Panisse restaurant. "I'm always looking for a way to change the conversation to get at something better, even if that means saying goodbye to this and reshaping something into a new form," she said. As with all who pause, it's not about coming to a complete rest or stopping. "Always, it's about trying to *start* something," added Alice.

This viewpoint echoes the element of perspective that starts each entrepreneurial journey in the first place—a factor that can't be sacrificed, can't be lost as the journey continues. As Alice put it, "The vision is really, really important. In this country (U.S.), we don't have enough vision. We are always trying to put Band-Aids on the parts. But we need to talk about the whole body and the big picture." Taking a deliberate pause allows people to reflect on that bigger picture, even while they're advancing.

Entrepreneurs incorporate a deliberate pause in their own ways. Jeffrey Hollender has worked to build an entire Seventh Generation culture around it. He expects the pause to be practiced at every level of the company and by all employees in their own lives as well. Only by working collectively, Jeffrey believes, can the true power in the pause be fully tapped. "We try to make people be more conscious," he said. "In the last few years, we've asked as a company, 'What does the world most need that we are uniquely capable of providing?' That has led us to things we weren't doing before and broadened the landscape."

As Jeffrey's statement shows, however, the practice of pausing isn't reckless or haphazard. It's not pausing for the sake of pausing; it's a far more conscious act than that. While entrepreneurs look out into the world at the possibilities, they are fully aware of their anchor. They filter what they *could* do through what they're already doing well. They question how to adapt in order to advance and not discard all the value they've built, yet all the while generating new things.

Jeffrey and his team know that even as they proactively explore the possible, they must "restrain the process enough that it doesn't become dysfunctionally disruptive to the business. It's a balance." It's also a practice.

Sometimes a tool can guide the practice. As an example, Jeffrey has shared with all his employees Peter Senge's book *Presence* as a centering tool. "So much of life inside a company is focused on what's visible," stated Jeffrey. "The hardest work and the greatest opportunity is a much less visible part—how we think about what we do and who we want to become." That "inner landscape" is beautifully articulated in Peter's co-authored book because it captures what's usually left out of the conversations. *Presence*—the book and the act—centers on knowing oneself, what's called the actualizing element of understanding oneself first in order to see how to change the world.

Learning how to know yourself is discovered by taking a deliberate pause. What becomes known about the self radiates out to what becomes possible by way of the entrepreneurial path. As stated in *Presence*, "If you want to be a leader, you have to become a real human being. You must understand yourself first. The cultivated self is the leader's greatest tool. It's the journey of a lifetime."[22]

## Pausing Regularly

Over the course of a lifetime, taking a pause regularly can be more deliberate or less. John Wood, after all, had to "leave Microsoft to change the world" with the founding of Room to Read, as his book fully acknowledges. Others like John consciously take dramatic pauses to inject ways to see differently and seek new paths. But even for those who make giant leaps for mankind by taking larger steps in new directions, they tap into a habit of pausing. For Steve Mariotti and the tens of thousands of students his National Foundation for the Teaching of Entrepreneurship touches, the seed takes the form of this mantra: *What question will your life answer?* Asking *why* may get you there, but *deliberately pausing to ask why* lends itself to grander answers.

"Like planting seeds," said Alice Waters, speaking of the decision to pursue the entrepreneurial path, "you really want your choices and actions to be right for the time, the people around it, and the place. You have to think, constantly. You have to do your homework and understand the concerns that allow you to see it right. You need to move slowly, not be a reckless planter. It happens too often that we go too fast. You learn a lot when you pace. You plant well and it thrives." It's the very thing that turns all those peach pits into orchards.

That's what a deliberate pause is all about. That's why entrepreneurship, when it works, does so mightily and uniquely. To advance as human beings on this planet, we simply cannot do without entrepreneurship, a force fueled by the conscious habit of asking *why* and made possible by taking a deliberate pause.

## Recommended Resources

### *Banker to the Poor* – Muhammad Yunus

In Books by Contributors in the back of the book, I've listed books by the people I interviewed for *A Deliberate Pause* so you can learn more about them. However, Dr. Yunus's first book stood out for me long ago and for all time, so I've included it here.

This story gives readers a view not only into Dr. Yunus's entrepreneurial thinking and the wonder of what he's achieved, but also a window into an unfamiliar world that's hard to comprehend. The success stories he tells truly reflect the power of *why* as Dr. Yunus asks it every day.

### *Begging for Change* – Robert Egger

Few perpetuate the power of a deliberate pause as fully as Robert Egger, as his engaging and inspiring story reveals. This book deserves much wider readership and greater marketing than it's received. Perhaps it's because Robert is just too busy building the foundation of his next volume in all the good he seeds.

# Contributors to Continuance

**Tom Szaky**
> Co-founder, CEO, TerraCycle
> Author, *Revolution in a Bottle*

**Nell Newman**
> Co-founder, Newman's Own Organics
> Co-author, *The Newman's Own Organics Guide to a Good Life*

**Peter Meehan** (See Chapter 10)

**Muhammad Yunus** (See Chapter 1)

**Ann Webster** (See Chapter 4)

**Edie Fraser** (See Chapter 1)

**Robert Egger** (See Chapter 4)

**Julie Kantor** (See Chapter 8)

**Casey Golden** (See Chapter 6)

**Jeff Sandefer**
> Co-founder, Acton School of Business and Acton MBA in Entrepreneurship
> Director, *National Review* magazine
> Founder, President, Sandefer Capital Partners

**Will Finnerty** (See Chapter 8)

# Continuance

*"We are one part of this movement. We don't plan to change the world on our own, but what we see is not only viable, it is the future. Our view is not the way people see it today. Therefore, part of our mission, a measure of our success, is to get people to believe it's possible."*

- Tom Szaky
Co-founder, CEO
TerraCycle

Someone once calculated it would take 14 billion 296 million fireflies to produce the brightness of the sun. It's not only that huge number that causes pause for reflection; it's the magnitude of doing it at all that staggers the imagination. So many life forms huddled together. And the audacity of the vision—to shine as brightly as the sun—is downright awe-inspiring.

Shining as brightly as the sun? Balderdash! Isn't that just absurd, ridiculous, far-fetched, and laughable, too?

Well, what about giving millions of people the chance to lift themselves out of poverty by lending them about $100 each? Is that ridiculous? And building more than 25,000 schools to teach 10 million children to read—isn't that far-fetched as well? And isn't it laughable to reshape transportation as we know it by renting cars *by the hour*?

Although these examples may seem ridiculous in the eyes of the *observer*, the *catalysts* of these exact ventures constantly dream about creating a better world.

Still, just as a lone firefly doesn't hold a candle to the power of the sun, a single spark doesn't equate to sustainable change. It takes many, many more—somewhere north of one and south of 14 billion. The impossible *is* possible in the right minds and hands. Yet getting from here to there comes from the power of entrepreneur*ship* rather than the magic of one mythical, all-powerful entrepreneur.

If you pause for a moment, you can see it. If you pause often, you can realize it.

## *Pausing to Reflect on Lessons Learned*

So what have you learned in your pause to read this book? I hope you've had your mind expanded, even a bit, causing you to see the world differently than you did before you began. With any luck, you now look at entrepreneurs less with awe and more with a wider view and a clearer understanding. I would feel an immense sense of accomplishment and progress if ideas like *value* and *community*, words like *perspective* and *discipline*, and questions like *why* meant something more to you as a result. I suggest summarizing our progress is now in order.

You may have begun this journey of *A Deliberate Pause* thinking everything boiled down to the entrepreneur. You might even have assumed that, by the end of this book, your greatest prize would be a better sense of these catalytic souls. It's even possible that, at this juncture, you're still figuring out for yourself who—of all the people you've met here—is the greatest entrepreneur? Not to worry. As you learn to think in a new way, these are hard questions to stop asking.

In the final analysis, though, it's not how grand the personality, vision, or venture is that matters. What *does* matter is the *change* that entrepreneurs help make real.

Just as having the discipline to see something through isn't enough to make that something last, perspective in and of itself isn't enough to realize the power of entrepreneurship. One bright mind, one great idea, one visionary won't change the world. Rather, a grand combination of factors must come together in a balanced way to evolve from a single idea to a seismic shift that betters humanity.

This process comes in far more textures than you might have assumed. Once you've awakened to this dynamic, it changes the conversation from irrelevant curiosities (such as "who is the best entrepreneur") to mind-opening questions. More deliberate questioners seek to understand what entrepreneurship is, who understands it, how deep the commitment is to leveraging entrepreneurship to create change, to what degree entrepreneurs can have an impact, how they can enable others to repeat the cycle, and much more. Substituting such expansive thinking for the traditionally narrow inquiry is like the difference between a thriving aspen stand and a single quaking aspen leaf.

Reading this book has, I hope, given you a deeper sense of entrepreneurship so that if you asked me "who among your contributors are entrepreneurs?" you wouldn't be surprised at my answer. I'd tell you that *it's those who realize they are the catalysts who must attract others to them into an ecosystem they build together.* Less than being about an entrepreneur, it's more about understanding what it means to be an entrepreneur who empowers others. Similarly, if you asked "who among your contributors is the most successful?" I'd say *I can look at the impact they're making and give you a progress report, but I can't tell you where their journeys will end.* From reading these chapters, you already know my answers aren't evasive; rather, they're reflective of progressive thinking and humbled by recognizing that the answer doesn't lie with one person, one book, or one time.

It's natural to seek an endpoint, yet in human progress, none exists. However, by pausing to read this book, I trust you've gained a richer view of what's possible. Nell Newman (see *Entrepreneurial Success from Every Viewpoint*) gives us an excellent overview.

## Entrepreneurial Success from Every Viewpoint

Nell Newman grew up with a passion for wildlife and a particular affection for falconry. "When I was about 13, I started reading about peregrines (falcons), how they could swoop down at up to 200 miles a hour. Then I learned that they were extinct east of the Mississippi because of the use of DDT." Pesticides used in farming were killing what she cared about; making a difference to her beloved falcon became her mantra.

After college, Nell worked with the Predatory Research Group at the University of California at Santa Cruz as a fundraiser. The organization was already helping stop the use of DDT and taking other actions to save the then-endangered falcons. Her team and others succeeded in protecting the birds so well, they rebounded from the brink of extinction. But would their accomplishments have a lasting impact? Unfortunately, down-listing them off the endangered species list immediately caused the funding that addressed the larger environmental and education issues to dry up. "Fundraising is hard enough," noted Nell, "but it's harder still when the world sees you as having achieved a success and doesn't see there's so much more to be done." This became a critical wake-up call.

Why wait for money to voluntarily come to the cause? Why depend on investor and donor whims? Why wait for anyone or anything to take up your dream at all? Wouldn't it be better to create an untethered source of income through a venture that reaches the everyday consciousness of millions, simply by giving them what they wanted anyway? An important lesson Nell learned about the environment from her mother, actress Joanne Woodward, was that changing the way food was grown could lead to a better environment and improve its taste, too. So Nell reasoned that if consumers had more organic options in the form of tasty foods that were also healthier for them, they would naturally support environmental issues with their purchases. In turn, that would help preserve the falcons and other wildlife. Why not merge all these paths?

By pausing to consider these questions, Nell saw a new way to address them. What she envisioned was Newman's Own Organics—a distinct company through which Nell could leverage her father Paul's fame and success to address these issues in a communal way. (Actor Paul Newman had already licensed his name to the Newman's Own line of conventional foods. Others in the food business did the manufacturing, putting his brand on select products. Why not take that value further?)

Along with this vision, she brought to Newman's Own Organics a deep sense of values, which in turn drove the company's focus and image. Wisely, she chose to partner with someone who shared her views and could help activate her vision, Peter Meehan. Typically, Nell came up with an idea; Peter harnessed it.

Today, unlike the original Newman's Own products made by other companies, Newman's Own Organics controls the development, sourcing, and production of every product it offers. This gives Nell, Peter, and their team the opportunity to influence many companies and communities beyond their own. In a way, they actually *infiltrate* the growers, manufacturers, packaging companies, and more as their shared values influence the decision-making across their multiple business partnerships.

But the value doesn't stop there. Newman's Own Organics also develops important relationships with its customers. Its packaging features homey stories laced with the company's beliefs that collectively say "come join the family."

And there's more yet. Newman's Own Organics' approach comes full circle in Nell's life. Taking a lead from papa Paul, she channels company profits into nonprofit organizations that support her passion for protecting the environment and its wildlife. Selected causes can count on Newman's Own Organics providing them with much-needed funding for the right reasons, in the right way, and over the long run. This remarkable approach is creating lasting change for people, for the environment, and for Nell's beloved falcons.

## Human . . .

Ultimately, two things separate human beings from other species: they can choose to advance, and they believe they must.

Similarly, what separates entrepreneurs from others is how they see unique ways to catalyze a change to advance others. It isn't an overstatement; entrepreneurs are found at the heart of all human progress. And far from popular belief, making a buck isn't what drives the successful ones. They do what they do because, as compassionate human beings, they want to advance all of humanity. In truth, they feel they have no choice.

An entrepreneur's ability to start something new is amazing, but it's the *outcomes* resulting from their pattern-recognition, boundless thinking, and intense beliefs that advance society and inspire us most. In the evolution of an entrepreneurial venture, the catalyst becomes a relative part of a larger phenomenon. Again, the Grameen movement catalyzed by Muhammad Yunus underscores that point.

In the winter of 2009, I had a chance to meet face to face a man I've greatly admired, Dr. Muhammad Yunus. We'd previously talked by phone for our interview—he in Bangladesh and I in the United States—but there's something extraordinary about standing in the same room with Dr. Yunus. Our meeting preceded a presentation he was giving in Washington, DC, directed not to a corporation, donors, or a partner organization, but to the public at large. Hundreds of people from countless walks of life came together for a brief few hours to pause, listen, and reflect.

When he walked on stage, a quiet calmness encircled Dr. Yunus and freely filled the 1,500-seat packed-to-capacity auditorium at George Washington University. "Gravitas" seems the right word to describe his power, inspiration, and humility, all combined in one man who could claim the title "hero" and is often described by it. Yet when Dr. Yunus speaks, his sincerity and his words reject this moniker.

Reflecting on the humbling power of his micro-lending programs that have played a pivotal role in raising tens of millions out of poverty, he remarked, "We do so little…just a loan, for example. They [the people who receive the loans] do the rest. It's amazing the capacity human beings have—enormous creativity, unlimited potential. Some don't know they have the gifts of creativity, entrepreneurship, or innovation. Most of all, we just want to awaken them."

His remarks expressed what's at the heart of making us human—to want to advance, not just ourselves but our whole species. The challenges facing society—poverty, degradation of the environment, economic depression, and more—are "artificial impositions on humans," as Dr. Yunus described them. But these challenges aren't innately human. And although we may inadvertently cause them, we do have the power to change them. As he stated that night, "Unlimited potential, *that's* innately human. We just have to call it out."

## The Human Touch of Entrepreneurship

"When people learn to pause and clear their heads, they are then able to look at their thoughts from a distance—to see if they are distorted, aligned, or even true. With that perspective, they can then begin to work on defining new patterns for acting, thinking, and feeling." When I heard Ann Webster say this, I felt as though she was reading *A Deliberate Pause* aloud. But in the most obvious respects, her world at Mass General, working as a psychologist with cancer and AIDS patients, is light years away from my world and the entrepreneurial universe. That said, how her statement aligns with the messages of this book isn't coincidence. The connection is natural—the bond of being human.

When I asked Ann what she wanted to instill in her patients through the mind-body program she teaches, she said to empower them to *make change* as part of what she calls "the third leg of the stool."

"One leg is pharma," she said, referring to the drugs her patients have to take. "The second is surgery or other procedures. But they can't stand on a two-legged stool, so I provide that third leg—the power *they* have *within themselves*, and the one thing they have control over."

Think about the setting her patients face—one person (the patient) learning to live with a life-limiting (even life-ending) medical condition, consumed by the logistics of treating the condition and managing other aspects of life. Then the patient is told by Ann, "I'm here to empower you to make change, in your world, in *the* world. I don't just want you to have a firm and complete stool, I want you to *stand* on it, see what you can see, reach higher." Hearing this at first must be overwhelming, if not off-putting, for the patient.

One of her patients represents what others must feel when faced with the reality of this "third leg." Ann described him as a man of lower income and moderate education who was less than warm to the idea of a mind-body program. In the first weeks of Ann's program, he bunkered in under his well-worn demeanor of being gruff, a bit obstinate, and highly skeptical.

Then one day, a different person came through Ann's door, seemingly transformed overnight. Animated and feeling light as never before, he was shaking his head in joyful wonderment. "I don't know what's happening," he burst out. "It's me alright, but something's changing."

He went on to describe how his view of everyone around him had been turned inside out—toward the positive. Suddenly he saw people differently—why they were in his life, what he thought of them, what they did for him, even what he could do for them. In his recast world, what was familiar took on a different pattern, shape, and meaning. Even as he was battling a terminal illness, he stood firmly on his stool, completely inspired, energized, and hopeful.

"Interestingly," Ann reflected across the whole universe of her patients, "through this quieting-of-the-mind process, people don't only see the world differently; they become more oriented toward other people and less focused on themselves." It is a profound observation. In the darkest moments, humans pausing to clear the distractions and limits of their patterned lives find themselves focusing less on bettering themselves and more on what they can do to make life better for others. "The feeling of contributing to humanity makes a big difference in their motivation to act—like a mirror being held up. A profound connection occurs as they start helping themselves by helping others. It taps into something that's innately human."

And then, as if erasing all lines separating her world of patients and mine of entrepreneurial thinkers, she said, "There's a general belief that people plod through life, and that it takes a coming-apart-at-the-seams to move them. But that isn't what happens. It's taking time out that makes the real difference, not the crisis. The crisis only implores you to take the time." The choice to pause is available to anyone, anytime, anywhere. And the power and magic that happens when we choose to do so can be each of ours as well.

## . . . *Progress*

It's hard to see powerful truths such as those spoken by Dr. Yunus and Ann Webster—or even recognize opportunities for betterment—unless we consciously, deliberately pause and look around. And it's in the pause that we face what's real and what's imagined, the fountainhead of our ideas, even our fears. That's when we make the choice to harness one or hide in the other. It's something we—all of us, the tall and the small (as Dr. Seuss might say)—make a point of doing. Why? Because a pause is central to who we are, whether we choose to use its power or not. Short and sweet, this is how humankind progresses.

Let me share a significant pause that happened in my life near the beginning of 2009. I had the privilege of co-hosting an event that introduced an important book by my friend Edie Fraser, one of the contributors to *A Deliberate Pause*. Her book, *Do Your Giving While You Are Living*, reveals the need to think about philanthropy differently. Its core message encourages everyone to get engaged in the practice of giving.

For those who noticed, there was an ironic juxtaposition between the message of the book and the timing of its release. The fall of 2008 marked the beginning of a steep and rapid decline—a recession—not only in the U.S. economy, but in economies across the globe. This recession was being compared to the Great Depression of the early part of the 20th century. In that depression, millions lost their jobs and saw their wealth evaporate in months, even days. A feeling of depression beyond the economist's definition enveloped the whole nation. Just as at the beginning of 1933 and FDR's inauguration, giving to others wasn't foremost in most people's minds on the day of our event.

But with her book and with each event promoting it, Edie was sparking a whole new conversation. In effect, she was advancing the importance of thinking differently. This conversation included Edie, six diverse guests who knew giving and change intimately, and an audience of interested readers. (Besides Edie, three of the six guests happened to be interviewees for this book—Robert Egger, Julie Kantor, and Casey Golden.) Approximately 125 people took a break from their responsibilities and looming worries to fluidly exchange ideas about how each of us could give more to others—today, tomorrow, and at any time.

What caused these people to pause and consider something that could have been easily dismissed? There was some connection, some deeper force at work, something innately human. A proverb from the best-selling book of all times put a finger on it this way: "Where there is no vision, the people perish."[23] Somehow, at some level, every one of us intimately felt this truth.

That day, no one left the room without having gained new perspective or inspiration. Each of us—expert and novice alike—had our minds and eyes opened to fresh meaning and possibility, all facilitated by a deliberate pause. By breaking with routine to think, to converse, and to consider different points of view, we had all advanced.

## Continuance for All of Us

With all the humility that comes with knowing you've read this far investing your time and thought in this conversation, I posit that you've learned a lot as you took this deliberate pause of your own. What I can't know is what new realizations you've come to, or what new thinking you will manifest as you build on *A Deliberate Pause*'s foundation. That's why this last chapter is a *continuance*, not a conclusion. I do know that the model set by Acton School of Business (see *Spread the Learning Beyond You*) presents a powerful example of continuance, something I now encourage you to look toward, too.

### Spread the Learning Beyond You

The story of Acton School of Business began nearly 20 years ago with Jeff Sandefer and a handful of other practitioners coming to the University of Texas at Austin to teach. Before his teaching career, Jeff had already built and sold a successful business. He wanted to share what he knew, the good and the bad.

However, it isn't too far afield to say that no welcome mat greeted Jeff upon his arrival in Austin. "The dean didn't even return my calls," remembered Jeff. "And the faculty wanted nothing to do with outsiders teaching." Claiming their domain, they didn't allow Jeff to teach at the graduate level where his lessons had the best fit in proximity to the school's graduate business program. So he taught what amounted to a graduate level course in the undergraduate school, one that word of mouth quickly filled with graduate students wanting more than what their academic professors could offer.

As Jeff had time to look around, he could see what the graduate students "slumming" in his undergraduate class were experiencing. "I realized that (the school) wasn't teaching them what it really meant to run an organization or start a business. At best, they were preparing people to exist in the middle, or be on the outside and consult." It wasn't about being innovative or thinking for themselves, but instead, just tinkering on the edges of what existed.

To remedy that problem, Jeff encouraged the recruitment of others like him—people from the outside—to come to UT Austin. (Jeff is the first to tell you that his impact is far from a product of his vision and his work alone.) Together, Jeff and his founding colleagues aimed to broaden the exposure of students, not just to business, but to true entrepreneurial thinking and success, applicable anywhere in life. This solution went over well with students but sunk like a ton of rocks with tenured faculty. As one dean commented in frustration about Jeff's purely academic colleagues, "These are great professors, but the students don't think so."

Students were hungry for what Jeff and his outsider colleagues were serving up—real and applicable lessons. They wanted to learn, not be lectured to. But eventually, the academics pressed their case and asked the dean to make Jeff and his colleagues step aside to let the "experts" take over. Jeff and his band went one step further. They quit *en masse* and formed their own graduate school, one designed not just to teach but to totally immerse its students in entrepreneurial thinking.

That's how the Acton MBA in Entrepreneurship and the Acton School of Business were born.

Naming the new school for 19<sup>th</sup> century figure Lord Acton was telling. Acton, the man, had dedicated his life to the advancement of liberty. Suspicious of power for the sake of power, he saw liberty not as a license but as the freedom due every man to do what was right. His inspiration was not only a clear message to traditional academia from which Jeff and his team departed, but also a message to its future students. Using Acton's name and repute was meant to "stand as a powerful reminder that power and riches are poor masters and that contributing something important—raising a loving family and defending our freedoms—is far better aspiration for a life of meaning."

In that vein, the Acton professors pushed their students first and foremost to connect with themselves. Their self-actualization was believed to be the filter to every fundamental and tactical skill Acton would teach, and every life path its students chose to travel in the world. "You'll never be truly successful as an entrepreneur," Jeff stated firmly, "if you don't understand yourself. The more I am in this, the more I see that to do otherwise is a fool's errand."

The Acton program proudly conveys to new and prospective students that all of them have a special calling to change the world profoundly. "The idea of a calling," said Jeff, "is figuring out what you do best, that thing you love to do that still serves others." The students' job, as learners and also as individuals, is to search for and find that calling. Acton's job is to create an environment in which they can do that, and then help them chart the path to achieving it. Acton supports the belief that even if you travel the entrepreneurial path and use the right tactical tools, the journey is pointless if you aren't oriented toward meaning.

Over the course of the program, students are required to keep a journal of their thoughts and progress. It becomes their personalized interpretation of what Acton lays out before them and what it means to them. Jeff called it a specialized "entrepreneurial tool kit."

"In our classes we don't make declarative statements," emphasized Jeff. "It's the questions they ask that are important, not the answers." By the end, every Acton graduate has developed his or her own framework and principles to guide the journeys that follow. "This is not like your father's or your grandfather's MBA," Jeff quipped.

What's amazing—and perhaps most important—about Acton's approach is that it seeks its own larger vision. Its leaders want to spread its principles to as many people as possible through as many institutions as practical. So for a fee of one dollar, they will provide Acton's entire curriculum to any institution that will incorporate all or part of it into its educational format. *One dollar.* Clearly, they regard their payback as something much greater than common currency. Their greater purpose? To expose more people to entrepreneurship and spread its principles far and wide.

Just as the job of the Acton School of Business is ongoing, the job of leveraging the power of entrepreneurship and the human potential—even the job of writing this book—isn't finished either. How do I know that?

In February of 2009, I had a chance to listen to author Malcolm Gladwell speak on his recently released book at the time, *Outliers*. Its subtitle is *The Story of Success*, but that wasn't what Gladwell focused on during his talk.

Gladwell began by sharing a *new* idea that had already helped him make better sense of his just released book. He told us that, rather than being about success per se, *Outliers* was really about human potential—specifically, why some people, even some societies, step up to their potential more than others. As he explained, this refined idea occurred to him *after* his book was published.

To Gladwell, realizing this shift in emphasis came as no surprise. "The hardest part about writing a book," he confessed, "is that even greater ideas come to you after the book has been published." The job never ends!

Similarly, in my Introduction, I described *A Deliberate Pause* as offering a framework rather than a formula or "the answer." Indeed, answers come through the application, advancement, and enhancement of meaningful thoughts that go far beyond one person or one book. Given that, the vision and responsibility to carry out an entrepreneurial dream don't lie in one person's hands. And that's where you come in.

You have the capacity to think and see a better way; you need only to pause and practice. The problems and opportunities we face as a species—more important, as a planet—are simply too great to decline being a participant in resolving them. So I encourage you to see the patterns. Act on them. Activate others. Create and transfer value from your actions. Act as though you have "no choice" except to make the world better.

As you do all these things, you join the ranks of other wise people featured in this book, those already out there having a momentous impact. You'll realize first-hand the unlimited possibilities spawned through an entrepreneurial mindset—and the lasting advancement to human progress that results.

Do it now. Pause. Progress.

## Recommended Pauses

Throughout this book, I've offered Recommended Resources of books that inspired my thinking with the aim to stimulate your own. In this Continuance chapter, I want to do *something more*.

The following recommendations present a variety of ways in which you can take a deliberate pause—ones I've found useful myself. However, please recognize that each of us finds our own ways to pause; what works for me isn't necessarily universal. So I encourage you to seek, to experiment, and to develop "pausing" as your own habit, whatever form it takes.

### What's Your Favorite Book of All Time and Why?

My list of recommended reading across these chapters came from an exercise I began while teaching Will Finnerty's entrepreneurship class. I challenged the students to look for the patterns across various works on leadership they had been reading and learning about. "What did they all have in common?" I asked, knowing there wasn't a right answer. It became a welcome exercise in slowing down to see more than the assignment or the class or what was immediately obvious.

To make things fair, I compiled my own list. I was amazed to see what my reading patterns had been and where I had migrated over time. It was also revealing to think about what I had taken away from each book. I became aware of these patterns and learned much about myself.

Look for the patterns!

### Write a Six-Word Story or Memoir.

Not too long ago, I was poking through a bookstore, not looking for anything in particular (another great way to pause!) and I came across a book titled *Not Quite What I Was Planning*. It was a collection of six-word memoirs submitted by all manner of people to an online magazine called *SMITH Magazine*. This idea was based on a literary legend that someone had once challenged Ernest Hemingway to write an entire story in just six words. (He is said to have called it his best.)

While at first this exercise seems limiting, when you do it, you'll find it powerfully revealing. How do you get down the essence of who you are in just six words? Which ones are the most important and why? How do you make it compelling to others? All of that and more—things entrepreneurs ponder—are wrapped up in this brilliant pausing exercise.

### Ask a Kid.

You've likely seen the email floating around about how kids described "love" or old footage of Art Linkletter's TV show, *Kids Say the Darnedest Things* (pull a few up on YouTube if you haven't), or some other example of kids taking an angle on life that's outside the norm. We tend to view this as entertainment (yes, it *is* entertaining), but don't squander the chance to see it as insight.

You want to see the world through different eyes? Just ask a kid. He or she will take even the hardest concept and cut through the fog to reveal its essence. When you stop laughing, you'll see anew!

### Travel Beyond Your Back Yard.

There's a negative expression floating around as we fight for our own space and our own way of living. It's called NIMBY—Not In My Back Yard. This expression arose from the fact that, while certain things (a cell tower, a dump, a new public building) may be necessary to advance the world, those who push for them don't want the burden of having them "mess up" their own world (or backyard).

But what if we flipped that around? What if you went looking in other people's backyards and invited them to look in yours? Then it wouldn't be hard to see things differently. One of the best ways to do that is to travel. Go to other places. See how others do and see things differently. Expand your comfort zone. Travel will help you refine how you view what you may have always overlooked.

### Attend an NFTE Event.

In *A Deliberate Pause,* I referred several times to an organization called the National Foundation for Teaching Entrepreneurship, or NFTE. To refresh your memory, NFTE takes entrepreneurship into the classroom in high schools where the life hurdles (poverty, single-parent or absentee-parent households, exposure to crime, and more) persist and chances for change are minimal. These classes open young people's minds to another way of looking at the world.

Over the course of a year, students in NFTE classes develop

business plans for ideas of their own. They research them, write about them, present them to panels of grown-ups, and even compete to move on to higher levels of validation where they can earn start-up capital. During that time, frightened and sometimes angry shells of children transform into confident, empowered human beings. To watch 14 year olds from any background present what they care about can be an exercise in mutual discomfort, but when NFTE students do it, their poise, confidence, and humanness lift your spirits like no other force. You truly regain your belief in the potential of all human beings.

Seek out an NFTE class, business plan competition, or event and experience it. As a result, you'll come to believe in your own potential more and possibly even take action.

### Stand on Your Dining Room Table.

You heard me correctly. Climb on up there and have a look around the room. I can't recall where exactly, but a long time ago, someone made me do this. It changed my perspective. Rooms—frankly, the whole world, whether walled in or not—look quite different when you adopt a vantage point that's far different from your typical paths through life. Try it! I guarantee you'll see something you've never noticed before.

### Read. Read. Read.

Too many of us do this too infrequently. Even those who do read don't do it fully engaged. In 2008, Simba Information, an organization that does market research on the media and publishing industries, found that 70 percent of those who buy a book get through only 30 percent of it. Many of us proudly admit we are headline readers, skimmers, or sound bite addicts. Read! Read completely. Read something you don't read or hear every day. Read for pleasure and to open your mind. Read about a topic you wouldn't normally address. Read something that takes hours or days, and not just the time you spend at the breakfast table, on the subway, or in the doctor's reception area. You'll be amazed how different your world looks when you've finished reading!

# A Deliberate Pause
## The Three Questions Parable

A certain king decided he would never fail in anything he might undertake *if* he always knew the answers to three questions:

1. What is the right time for every action?
2. Who is the most important person?
3. What is the right thing to do?

He sent word out to everyone in his kingdom that he would bestow a great reward on those who could provide the answers. "Wise" men flocked to him, each prepared with a different answer to his questions.

In reply to the first question, one insisted, "Your Majesty, to ensure you take action at the right time, you must schedule all actions days, months, and years in advance, and then strictly adhere to this schedule." "Nonsense!" another said. "You never know what will demand your attention. Only through daily attentiveness and being in the moment will you know the right time for actions."

When asked the second question, one of those "wise" men advised, "Do not expect *one* wise man to decide the right time for actions. A *council of men* would better serve this purpose." Others argued that councils require too much time to make decisions. Another pleaded, "Dear King, you must see the future then make your own decisions, thereby magicians are the most necessary to you." Still others advised him to call upon priests, doctors, or warriors.

To the third question—how might he know the right thing to do?—some men were certain the right avenue was science. Others said skillful warfare or religious worship. Never were the answers the same; never was the king content that he had *the* answers.

Dissatisfied, the King sent all the "wise" men away empty-handed.

But he still wished to find the right answers to his questions, so he set out from his castle to consult with a hermit renowned for sharing his wisdom with the kingdom's common folk. To disarm the hermit, the King dressed himself as a common man. When he reached the woods where the hermit lived, he dismounted his horse, instructed his bodyguard to wait for him, and walked the rest of the way to the hermit's hut.

The hermit, frail and weak, was digging in the soil with a spade when the King approached him. The King said, "I have come to ask you three questions: What is the right time for any action? Who is the most important person? And what is the right thing to do?"

The hermit didn't answer. He just kept turning the soil.

"Here," said the King. "Let me help you a while."

The hermit handed over the spade, and when the King had dug two beds, he stopped and repeated his questions. The hermit again gave no answer. Instead, he rose, stretched out his hand for the spade, and said, "Rest. Let me work a bit."

But the King refused to give up the spade and continued to dig. At sunset, he stopped his work and asked his questions once again. Instead of answering, the hermit said, "Look, there's someone running toward us."

It was a man bleeding from a serious wound. When he reached the King, the injured man fell to the ground. The King washed his wound and used his own handkerchief to bandage it. Once the bleeding stopped, the injured man asked for a drink of water, and the King fetched it for him. By now the sun had set, so the hermit and the King carried their patient into the hut and put him down on the bed. Exhausted, the King lay on floor next to the bed. There he slept until morning.

When the King awoke, the injured man was staring at him, his eyes shining. "Forgive me," he weakly said to the King.

"I do not know you, and I have nothing to forgive you for," replied the King.

"But I know you. I am your enemy. I swore to take revenge on you because you executed my brother and seized my property. I planned to kill you when you returned from seeing the hermit. But the day passed and you didn't return, so I left my hiding spot and got accosted and wounded by your bodyguard. Forgive me. I sought to kill you, and you saved my life. Now, if you wish, my sons and I will serve you as your most faithful slaves."

The King was glad to so easily make peace with his enemy and also gain him as a friend. "I will forgive you," he told the man. "And, as your friend, I will see that you are restored to health and that your property is returned to you."

Outside the hut, the hermit was on his knees sowing seeds in the beds the King had prepared the previous day. The King approached him and said, "I am ready to return home, but for the last time, please answer my questions."

"They have already been answered," replied the hermit.

Annoyed, the King asked, "What do you mean?"

"Don't you see? If you hadn't helped me yesterday, that man would have killed you. So the most important time was when you were digging the beds. I was the most necessary man, and to do good for me was your most important business. Afterward, when that man came to us for help, the most important time was when you were attending to him. If you hadn't helped him, he would have died and not made peace with you. So he was the most necessary man, and what you did for him was your most important business."

A sense of understanding softened the King's face. Seeing that, the hermit admonished the King to remember the answers to his three questions:

1. There is only one time that is important. *Now* is when we must act!

2. The most important person is the one you are with.

3. The right thing to do is to do good for those you are with. For that is what man was sent to Earth to do.

- adapted from Leo Tolstoy

# Endnotes

Introduction
1. "Americans Believe Entrepreneurs Will Revive Economy, According to Kauffman Foundation Survey." MarketWatch.com, Business Wire. October 1, 2008.
2. David Montgomery, "One Name Stands Alone in The Grand Scheme of It All." *Washington Post*. December 20, 2008, p. C1.
3. Ibid.

Chapter 1
4. Muhammad Yunus, *Banker to the Poor: Micro-Lending and the Battle Against World Poverty*. PublicAffairs Books, 2003, p. 41.
5. Joseph A. Schumpeter, *Capitalism, Socialism, and Democracy*. Harper Perennial Modern Classics, 2008.
6. Peter F. Drucker, *Innovation and Entrepreneurship*. Harper Business, 1985.

Chapter 2
7. Claro Cortes IV – Reuters, Conversations, Interview with Muhammad Yunus, "If you think poverty should not exist, let's work on it." *Washington Post,* February 10, 2008, p. M2.

Chapter 3
8. http://www.marksquotes.com/Founding-Fathers/Paine/
9. Laurence Gonzales, *Deep Survival: Who Lives, Who Dies, and Why*. W.W. Norton & Company, paperback ed., 2004,, p. 183.

Chapter 4
10. Peter M. Senge et al, *Presence: An Exploration of Profound Change in People, Organizations, and Society*. Currency Doubleday, 2005, p. 141.
11. http://www.MSC.org (Marine Stewardship Council)

Chapter 6
12. http://www.guykawasaki.com. (Guy Kawasaki's blog and more)

Chapter 7
13. Paulo Coelho, *The Alchemist*. Harper Collins, 1993.

Chapter 8
14. Laurence Gonzales, *Deep Survival: Who Lives, Who Dies, and Why*. W.W. Norton & Company, paperback ed., 2004, p. 15.
15. Daniel H. Pink, *A Whole New Mind: Why Right-Brainers Will Rule the Future*. Riverhead Books, paperback ed., 2006, p. 1.

Chapter 11
16. Bo Peabody, *Lucky or Smart?: Secrets to an Entrepreneurial Life*. Random House, 2005, p. 7.

17. http://www.smallact.com (Small Act Network)
18. Daniel H. Pink, *A Whole New Mind: Why Right-Brainers Will Rule the Future*. Riverhead Books, paperback ed., 2006, p. 221.
19. Laurence Gonzales, *Deep Survival: Who Lives, Who Dies, and Why*. W.W. Norton & Company, paperback ed., 2004, p. 220.

Chapter 12

20. www.sinekpartners.typepad.com (Simon Sinek)
21. Thomas Boswell, "Woods vs. Nicklaus is Worth Examining." *Washington Post*, March 31, 2009, p. D1.
22. Peter Senge et al, *Presence: An Exploration of Profound Change in People, Organizations, and Society*. Currency Doubleday, 2005, p. 180.

Continuance

23. *The Holy Bible, King James Version*, Book of Proverbs, 29:18.

# Acknowledgments

The people I'd like to capture in my acknowledgments are too numerous to count. The last time I ventured to do this was during a commencement speech in high school. Sure enough, despite my best efforts, I left someone out. If that happens here, I apologize in advance. I feel I have to try, however, if only to let all of you who should be acknowledged know how grateful and humbled I am by your help.

First and foremost, I must thank my contributors (sometimes referred to as my interviewees). You know how much you gave, and yet you have no idea how much you actually contributed, individually and collectively. I thank you all for your time, insights, and passion for entrepreneurship, and for allowing its value to be clarified and spread through *A Deliberate Pause*.

I offer my special thanks to those who "invested" in my project. You went the extra mile to help me advance it—all leading to another interviewee, a new idea, a partner, a better draft, and more. I'd especially like to thank David Ford, Julie Kantor, Ed Robinson, Ruth Taylor Kidd, Brad Whitehead, Larry Sloan, Will Finnerty, Carter Cast, Donna Jensen Madier, Mike Sutton, Martin Goebel, Lyles Carr, Doug Davidoff, Jason Berv, John May, Will Murray, and Bijoy Goswami. Your efforts to put me in touch with amazing people were exceptional, your recommendations were spot on, and your enthusiasm infectious and empowering.

Jim Blasingame, Julie Bick Weed, Sue Landay, Bill Landay, Perry Hooks, and Kathleen McGowan—I have to thank you all for your patience with a neophyte author. I gained more than you know from your insights, warnings, and general truth serum about what I was getting into.

To Andy Riedy, Casey Golden, Rebecca Carpenter, John May, Jim Wrathall, and especially Kai Robertson, you pushed me further than most, challenged my ideas, and made me think more deeply. Forgive my occasional frustration with you; you were brave, loyal, wise, and honest—just what one finds in true friends and good advisors.

To Sally Shepard, you stood out among so many generous others who knew so little about me but embraced my project with passion and professionalism. I thank you for paying forward kindness and betting on what you sensed over the phone to be important (thanks for connecting me with Nell and Peter, too!).

A number of people who weren't formal interviewees but important contributors offered me sage advice. Burt Kinerk, Penny Pickett, Brent Robertson, Steve Shapiro, Ken and Linda Schantz, and Marvin Cohen, I thank you all.

And to those who helped me deliver, kept me buoyed, and did more than their fair share of carrying this ball over the goal line: David Ford, I can't tell you how grateful I am to you in countless ways. You preceded me on this authorship path and offered me many signposts. You bravely if foolishly agreed, along with Kai, to be an early editor (my apologies along with my gratitude). You counseled me in numerous detailed and contextual ways. And you have been a great friend to me always.

To my "readers" who agreed to read this book cover to cover before full polishing occurred—Mark Garay, Jim Wrathall, and my father, Larry Robertson. I asked for your brutal honesty in addition to your time. I got those things, and more. You enhanced my thoughts and focused this work to make it so much better than it was before. You were my collective compass.

To the team at Handwriting Without Tears and especially Julie Koborg, Jeannette Haislip, Cindy Astlin, and of course Eric Olsen, I thank you for your sharp eyes, exceptional talents, and your offers to help me at every turn.

No one gets through the oh so important closing logistics of a project—the ones that occur behind the scenes and in the final hours, the ones that make all the difference—without a great manager. Margo Toulouse at Morgan James, you probably aren't thanked often enough, but I thank you so very much for all your help and your patience with my first run through the publishing process.

My special thanks to Ryan Helling and Rachel Lopez, two other unsung heroes at Morgan James. How you stretch your talents as far as you do within the constraints given you I'll never know. But I am so grateful for your skilled design and keen eyes.

Ella and Noah, your leaps were amazing! Thanks for pausing to help me capture one of the many things you do so well in life. You two are the brightest of lights in my life. The cover, the stories inside the book, and my life would not be half what they are without you. Shine on!

Sam Horn, you are a treasure and an honest and wise human being. Thank you for trusting your instincts with such little knowledge of me when we first met, for guiding me, for sharing my passion and even pointing it out, and perhaps most of all for leading me to Barbara McNichol.

And to Barbara, you may never know just how greatly I valued your partnership in the final phases of this journey. You are so much more than just an editor. As Sam counseled me to find in an editor, you helped take this book to the next level and led me to other talented souls, like Peggy Henrikson, my exceptional proofreader, who could do the same. Kudos to who you are—the person, not just the grandest of editors.

I also want to thank the magic of doing right by others, not for the reward you hope to gain, but simply because it's right. I believe that philosophy and practice had a lot to do with the publication of this book. One important manifestation of it was the chain of people who led me to publish with Morgan James. Edie Fraser, we met by serendipity what now seems like so long ago and formed a friendship—one based not on what we might gain from each other professionally, but instead on a belief in one another and what each of us was trying to accomplish in life. That eventually led to my help with your book, which in turn led to my privilege to get to know your co-author, Robyn Spizman. The trust built with her over the three years' incubation of *Do Your Giving While You Are Living* in turn led to Robyn's knowledge of and support for my book and her introduction of me to David Hancock and Morgan James Publishing. Good things happen when good people get together for the right reasons.

# Contributors to *A Deliberate Pause*

Listed on the following pages are the primary contributors to *A Deliberate Pause*. I say "primary" because many others aided me in ways both great and small.

Although the book frequently refers to more than 200 interviewees, fewer than 200 names are listed below for the following reasons. Several individuals asked that I not formally include their names because of their public roles in companies, government, or otherwise. However, they spoke freely with me, echoed the comments of those listed here, and allowed me to use the content of our conversations. Nearly 20 other people contributed greatly to *A Deliberate Pause*, shaping the content and providing feedback, but were not interviewed; therefore, they don't appear in this list. In addition, numerous informal and helpful interviews occurred. Because I didn't approach those individuals for the express purpose of research for this book and receive permissions, I felt I must leave off their names.

Therefore, this list includes only those official and consenting interviewees whose thoughts and experiences contributed formally to this book. Their accomplishments and affiliations are too numerous to list here. So, as with the contributor lists at the start of each chapter, I provide only a sampling of their roles and accomplishments—enough to give you a flavor for how they are relevant to this discussion of entrepreneurship.

As noted in the Introduction, the information provided for each contributor was accurate at the time of the interview and updated only if requested.

For simplicity, contributors are listed in alphabetical order.

**David Adamson.** Founder, Adamson Gallery and Adamson Editions; formerly with Corcoran Gallery of Art; adamsongallery.jimdo.com.

**Bob Allen.** CEO, Chief Story Telling Officer, i.d.e.a.s.; former Creative Entertainment Executive, Walt Disney Imagineering; ideasorlando.com.

**Patty Alper.** President, Alper Portfolio Group; Co-founder NFTE Adopt-a-Class; Radio show host "For Love or Money."

**John Altorfer.** Former CEO, PermaStarch; Assistant Secretary of Commerce under Richard M. Nixon; Founder, Pioneer Park Development Company.

**Patrick Von Bargen.** CEO, Center for Venture Education for the Kauffman Foundation; Founder, Executive Director, National Commission on Entrepreneurship; kauffmanfellows.org.

**Brad Barnhorn.** CEO, Global NutriFoods; Board Member, Happy Planet and Harvest & Rowe Restaurants; fundamentalcapital.com.

**Jeff Bede.** Partner, Chesapeake Capital; former Banker, Donaldson, Lufkin & Jenrette.

**Spencer Beebe.** Founder, Ecotrust; Co-founder, Conservation International; former Senior Executive, The Nature Conservancy; ecotrust.org.

**David BenDaniel.** Berens Professor of Entrepreneurship and Senior Fellow of Entrepreneurship and Personal Enterprise, The Johnson School, Cornell University; Co-author, *M&A, Joint Ventures and Beyond*; Co-founder, entrepreneurship@cornell program.

**Mike Bernstein.** Co-founder, Simply Bits, Leapscape, Nextrio, and MIDAK; leapscape.com.

**Jason Berv.** Founder, Executive Director, The Watershed School; watershedschool.org.

**Brien Biondi.** President, CEO, Chief Executives Organization (CEO); former President, Young Entrepreneurs Organization (YEO); ceo.org.

**Ryan Black.** Founder, CEO, Sambazon; Ashoka Award for Sustainable Agro-forestry; former NFL player, Minnesota Vikings; sambazon.com.

**Jim Blasingame.** President, Founder, Small Business Network; Founder, host, "The Small Business Advocate"; author, *Three Minutes to Success* and *Small Business Is Like a Bunch of Bananas*; smallbusinessadvocate.com.

**P.V. Boccasam.** Founder, President/CEO, Approva; Co-founder, T.I.E.; former Senior Executive, Microsoft; approva.com.

**David Boyer.** Founder, CEO, GlobalWatch Technologies; Co-founder, Troy Systems.

**Don Britton.** Founder, CEO, Network Alliance; Chairman, Netpreneur; networkalliance.net.

**Telaekah Brooks.** Executive Director, Center for Entrepreneurship and Chair, Department of Business Management, Southeastern University; Founding Director, Georgia Avenue Business Resource Center; southeastern.edu.

**Jan Bruce.** Publisher, Managing Director, *Body + Soul* magazine, OmniMedia; former Publisher, Managing Director, Walking Magazine; bodyandsoulmag.com.

**Kevin Burns.** Co-founder, Managing Principal, Lazard Technology Partners; Founder, former CEO, Sage Software; lazardai.com/technologypartners/.

**Craig Burris.** Founder, Publisher, *SmartCEO* magazine; smartceo.com.

**Bill Campbell.** Founder, CEO, CBEnergy; former Senior Vice President, Bechtel International.

**Mary Cantando.** Author, *The Woman's Advantage*; Member, Advisory Board, *Enterprising Women* magazine; womansadvantage.biz.

**Siobhan Canty.** President, Chief Executive, Greater DC Cares; dc-cares.org.

**Lyles Carr.** Senior Vice President, The McCormick Group; Washingtonian of the Year, *Washingtonian* magazine; Director, Greater Washington Board of Trade and Community Wealth Ventures; mccormickgroup.com.

**Bill Cast.** Founding President, Tri-State IPA; Author, *Going South*; Board of Trustees, Indiana University; indiana.edu.

**Carter Cast.** Co-founder, President, CEO, walmart.com; Co-founder, President, Blue Nile; President, CEO, NetShops; netshopsinc.com.

**Robin Chase.** Co-founder, Zipcar; named to *Time* magazine's *100 World's Most Influential People*, 2009; Massachusetts Governor's Award for Entrepreneurial Spirit; Founder, CEO, GoLoco and Meadow Networks; meadownetworks.com.

**Michael Chasen.** Co-founder, CEO, President, BlackBoard; *SmartCEO* magazine Chief Executive Officer of the Year, 2006; Ernst & Young Entrepreneur of the Year, 2000; former Consultant, KPMG Consulting; blackboard.com.

**Nick Cho.** Founder, Murky Coffee; murkycoffee.com.

**Duke Chung.** Co-founder, CEO, Parature; Contributing Author, *Inside the Minds; Fast Company* magazine's Fast 50, 2006; parature.com.

**Dwayne Clark.** Founder, CEO, Chairman, Aegis Assisted Living; Ernst & Young Entrepreneur of the Year, 2007; aegisliving.com.

**Jim Click.** President, Jim Click Automotive; Director, Compass Bancshares; Co-founder, Co-owner Tuttle-Click Automotive Group; jimclick.com.

**Charles Conn.** Founder, CitySearch; former Senior Executive, McKinsey & Company.

**Joe Cracchiolo.** Co-founder, Simply Bits, Leapscape, Nextrio, and RightFax; co-recipient, Ernst & Young Entrepreneur of the Year Award, 1996; leapscape.com.

**Noah Croom.** Principal, Goodwin Sports; former Staff Attorney, NBA; former General Counsel, Vancouver Grizzlies; goodwinsports.com.

**Doug Davidoff.** Founder, Imagine Companies; Co-author, *Parenting the Office*; imaginellc.com.

**Mike Devine.** CFO, Secure Software; former Partner, Arthur Andersen and Deloitte Touche.

**Matt Dorman.** Founder, CEO, Credible Wireless; crediblewireless.com.

**Cheryl Dorsey.** President, Echoing Green; Co-founder, Family Van; former Special Assistant to Secretary of Labor; echoinggreen.org.

**Bill Drayton.** Founder, Ashoka; named to *U.S. News & World Report's* list of America's 25 Best Leaders, 2005; former Consultant, McKinsey & Company; ashoka.org.

**Esther Dyson.** Founder, Edventure Holdings; Author, *Release 2.0*; Editor at Large, CNET Networks; *The New York Times* bi-monthly columnist; edventure.com.

**Robert Egger.** Founder, DC Central Kitchen, Campus Kitchens, and more; Author, *Begging for Change*; Co-founder, the Nonprofit Congress; dccentralkitchen.org.

**Karl Eller.** Founder, President, The Eller Companies; Author, *Integrity is All You've Got*; Founder, Combined Communications and Eller Outdoor.

**Mary Ann Elliott.** Founder, CEO Arrowhead Global Solutions; arrowheadsat.com.

**Ben Elowitz.** CEO, WetPaint; former roles with eHarmony, Precor, and Bain & Company; wetpaint.com.

**Jed Emerson.** Co-founder, Blended Value; Co-author, *Enterprising Nonprofits* and *Strategic Tools for Social Entrepreneurs*; Author, *New Social Entrepreneurs*; Managing Director for Integrated Performance, Uhuru Capital Partners; uhuru.com.

**Doug Epstein.** Co-founder, President, Evolve Sports; Founder, Washington, DC Office, former Managing Director, Katalyst Capital; former Consultant, Dean & Company; evolve-sports.com.

**Rafe Esquith.** Author, *There Are No Shortcuts* and *Teach Like Your Hair's on Fire*; Winner, National Medal of Arts 2004; Teacher, Hobart Elementary School; hobartshakespeareans.org.

**Brad Feder.** Cofounder, Simply Bits, Leapscape, Nextrio, and RightFax; co-recipient, Ernst & Young Entrepreneur of the Year Award, 1996; leapscape.com.

**Ed Feeney.** Feeney & Associates; Career Achievement Award, Applied Behavioral Sciences.

**Brad Feld.** Founder, Managing Director, Mobius Venture Capital and Feld Technologies; Director, Young Entrepreneurs Organization; Entrepreneur in Residence, Kauffman Foundation Center for Entrepreneurial Leadership; mobiusvc.com.

**Charlie Ferris.** Chairman, Federal Law Section, Mintz Levin; Chairman, Federal Communications Commission (1977-1981); former General Counsel to Senator Tip O'Neill; mintz.com.

**Will Finnerty.** Founder, The Finnerty Group; Professor of Entrepreneurship, Georgetown University; willfinnerty.com.

**Betsy Flanagan.** Founder, StudioStartup and Bright Minds; startupprincess. com.

**Gene Foley.** Former and First Chair, Small Business Association (SBA); Founder, Foley & Associates Financial Consulting.

**David Ford.** Co-founder, Kalorama Village; Author, *Blind in One Eye*; Vice Chairman, Aegis Senior Communities; former Partner, Mintz Levin; aegisliving.com.

**Gregg Fraley.** Author, *Jack's Notebook*; greggfraley.com.

**Mark Frantz.** General Partner, RedShift Ventures; former Technology Advisor to Pennsylvania Governor Tom Ridge; redshiftventures.com.

**Edie Fraser.** Founder, Business Women's Network and Diversity Best Practices; Co-author, *Do Your Giving While You Are Living*; Author, *Risk to Riches: Women's Entrepreneurship in America*; diversifiedsearch.com.

**Scott Frederick.** Partner, Co-founder Valhalla Partners; former Partner, FBR Technology Partners and Dean & Company; valhallapartners.com.

**Betsy Friedlander.** Principal, Willmott & Associates; Author, *How to Land Job Offers: The Art of Generating Job Opportunities*; willmott.com.

**Ching Ho Fung.** Co-founder, Performix; Board of Directors, BlackBoard and Parature; parature.com.

**Ken Getz.** Founder, Center for Information and Study on Clinical Research Participation; Author, *Informed Consent* and *The Gift of Participation*; former Consultant, Arthur D. Little and Corporate Decisions; ciscrp. org.

**Melinna Giannini.** Founder, President, CEO, ABC Coding Solutions (formerly Alternative Link); abccodes.com.

**Tom Gillespie.** Senior Director, In-Q-Tel; Co-founder, LaunchFuel; in-q-tel. org.

**Martin Goebel.** Founder, President, Sustainable Northwest; Co-founder, Conservation International; Advisor, Walton Family Foundation; sustainablenorthwest.org.

**Casey Golden.** Founder, Small Act Network; Contributing Author, *Do Your Giving While You Are Living*; Co-founder, Parature; smallact.com.

**Maria Gomez.** Founder, Mary's Center; Recipient, *Washington Post* Award for Excellence in Nonprofit Management; maryscenter.org.

**Laurence Gonzales.** Author, *Deep Survival* and *Everyday Survival*; laurencegonzales.com.

**Sandy Gooch.** Founder, Mrs. Gooch's Natural Foods Markets.

**Bill Gorog.** Founder, CEO, LexisNexis and US Order; Co-founder, Verifone; Deputy Director, President's Economic Counsel (Ford Administration).

**Bijoy Goswami.** Founder, Bootstrap Austin; Author, *The Human Fabric: Unleashing the Power of Core Energy in Everyone*; Co-founder, Aviri; aviri. com.

**David Green.** Founder, The Eye Fund and Project Impact; Ashoka Fellow, MacArthur Fellow; ashoka.org.

**Allen Grossman.** Professor of Management Practice, Harvard Business School; Author, *High Performance Nonprofit Organizations*; former President, CEO, Outward Bound; hbs.edu.

**Irv Grousbeck.** Director, Center of Entrepreneurial Studies, Stanford Business School; Co-founder, Continental Cable Vision; gsb.stanford.edu.

**Anil Gupta.** Research Director, Dingman Center for Entrepreneurship, University of Maryland; Author, *The Quest for Global Dominance*; Professor of Strategy and Organization, University of Maryland; anilkgupta.com.

**Rob Hagen.** CEO, Commerce 5; former President, CEO Aqueduct and ChannelWave Software.

**Travis Hardmon.** Executive Director, National Capital Child and Family Development Center; nccfd.net.

**Verne Harnish.** Author, *Mastering the Rockefeller Habits*; Founder, Young Entrepreneurs Organization; Founder, Gazelles; the Growth Guy columnist; gazelles.com.

**Kristi Hedges.** Co-founder, Principal, Shea Hedges Group.

**Oran Hesterman.** Program Director, W.K. Kellogg Foundation; Professor, Michigan State University; wkkf.org.

**Najlah Feanny Hicks.** Co-founder, President, The Heart Gallery of New Jersey; Contributor to *America 24/7* and *An American Journey*; Editorial and Corporate Photographer; najlahfeanny.com.

**John Holaday.** Founder, President, CEO, EntreMed; Founder, MaxCyte; Co-founder, Chairman, HarVest Bank; harvestbankmd.com.

**Jeffrey Hollender.** Founder, President, Chief Inspired Protagonist, Seventh Generation; Co-author, *Naturally Clean* and *What Matters Most;* Founder, Network for Learning; seventhgeneration.com.

**Gary Hoover.** Founder, Bookstop, The Reference Press, Hoover's Online; Author, *Hoover's Vision;* hooversvision.com.

**Dipak Jain.** Dean, Kellogg School of Management, Professor of Entrepreneur Studies; Co-author, *Marketing Moves: A New Approach to Profits, Growth, and Renewal*; Director, Deere & Company, Northern Trust, and United Airlines; kellogg.edu.

**John Jaquette.** Executive Director, entrepreneurship@cornell; cornell.edu.

**Charlene Drew Jarvis.** President, Southeastern University; 21-year member Washington DC City Council; southeastern.edu.

**Dave Jilk.** CEO, Xaffire; Co-founder, former CEO, Wideforce Systems and Feld Technologies.

**Judy Jobbitt.** President, George Mason University Foundation; Vice President, University Development and Alumni Affairs; gmu.edu.

**Craig Johnson.** Founder, Venture Law Group; Co-founder, Garage Technology Ventures; former Partner, Wilson Sonsini.

**Gary Jonas.** CEO, Founder, former CEO, TLC Laser Eye Centers; Practitioner Faculty, Johns Hopkins MBA program.

**Gene Kahn.** Founder, Cascadian Farms; Founder, Small Planet Foods; Vice President, General Mills Sustainability Council; changemakers.net.

**Julie Kantor.** National Vice President, Entrepreneurship in America, NFTE; Author, *I Said Yes*; Youth Entrepreneurship Program Leader, The Aspen Institute; nfte.com.

**Andy Kapit.** CEO, CodeRyte; Founder, April Family of Companies; coderyte.com.

**Guy Kawasaki.** Founder, Managing Director, Garage Technology Ventures; Author, *The Art of the Start, Rules for Revolutionaries,* and five other books; guykawasaki.com.

**Karen Kerrigan.** Founder, President, CEO, Small Business and Entrepreneurship Council; President, CEO, Women Entrepreneurs; Director, National Women's Business Council; sbsc.org.

**Raj Khera.** Founder, former CEO, GovCon.com; Co-founder, CEO, Mailer Mailer; mailermailer.com.

**Ruth Taylor Kidd.** Partner, Beyond the Bottom Line; former CFO, Ashoka; former CFO National Children's Museum and the Guggenheim Museum; beyondtbl.com.

**Judy Kirpich.** Co-founder, Grafik; grafik.com.

**Mary Knebel.** Co-founder, LaunchFuel; Senior Vice President, Marketing, alarm.com; alarm.com.

**Ray Leach.** CEO, JumpStart; Founder, former President, Capella Capital; Co-founder, Publishing Solutions; jumpstartinc.org.

**Reggie Van Lee.** Partner, Senior Vice President, Booz Allen Hamilton; dancer, Alvin Ailey Company; Author, *Megacommunities*; Board Member, Clinton Small Business Initiative; boozallen.com.

**Mena Lofland.** NFTE-certified Teacher of Entrepreneurship, Suitland High School (Suitland, MD).

**Rich Lyons.** Dean, Haas School of Business, UC Berkeley; former Chief Learning Officer, Goldman Sachs; former Sylvan Coleman Professor of Finance, Haas School; haas.berkeley.edu.

**Mary MacPherson.** Founder, m2works; former Senior Vice President Marketing, BlackBoard; former Executive Director, Netpreneur; Chairman, Mary's Center; m2works.com.

**Donna Jensen Madier.** Founder, LeGourmet, Startups.com, Vibrant Ventures, and BelleEscape; Adjunct Professor, School of Business, University of North Carolina; belleescape.com.

**Darius Mahdjoubi.** Visiting Scholar and Professor of Entrepreneurship and Innovation, Creativity and Capital Institute, University of Texas, Austin; utexas.edu.

**Steve Mariotti.** Founder, President, National Foundation for Teaching Entrepreneurship; Author, *The Young Entrepreneur's Guide to Starting and Running a Business*; nfte.com.

**Art Marks.** Co-founder, Partner Valhalla Partners; former Managing Partner, New Enterprise Associates; valhallapartners.com.

**John May.** Founder, Principal, New Vantage Group; Co-author, *Every Business Needs an Angel* and *State of the Art*; newvantagegroup.com.

**Mike McCaffery.** President, CEO, Stanford Management Company; former President, Robertson, Stephens & Company; makenacap.com.

**Rob McGovern.** Founder, CareerBuilder; Author, *Bring Your 'A' Game*; Founder, President Market10 (now jobfox); jobfox.com.

**Peter Meehan.** Co-founder, President, Newman's Own Organics; newmansownorganics.com.

**Andreas Merkyl.** Co-founder, Environmental Practice, McKinsey & Company; Co-founder, Core Resources; Principal, CEA Consulting; Chairman, Sea Change Investment Fund; ceaconsulting.com.

**Caren DeWitt Merrick.** Co-founder, Vice President Marketing, webMethods; Partner, Bibury Partners investment and advisory fund; former Director, AOL.

**Jeff Mitchell.** Tribal Leader, Klamath Tribes, Oregon.

**Dan T. Moore, III.** Chairman, Founder, Dan T. Moore Company, Soundwich, and Impact Ceramics; Trustee, Cleveland Clinic Foundation; Director, InvaCare and Hawk Corporation; dantmoore.com.

**Mario Morino.** Chairman, Venture Philanthropy Partners; Founder, Legent Technologies and Netpreneur; venturephilanthropypartners.org.

**Mike Morris.** Founder, President, OceanOptics; oceanoptics.com.

**Robin Mudge.** Founder, Institute for the Digital Image; Professor, American University; former BBC Executive Producer; interactive-pioneers.org.

**Gary Mulhair.** Former President, Pioneer Human Services; Co-founder, First National Gathering for Social Entrepreneurship; former CEO, Community Wealth Ventures; Chief Investment Officer, Global Partnerships; globalpartnerships.org.

**Will Murray.** Co-founder, Conservation Impact; former Director, The Nature Conservancy; Founder, Will Murray Company; willmurraycompany.com.

**Gary Myers.** Artist; gcmyers.com.

**Mary Naylor.** CEO, Founder, VIPdesk and Capitol Concierge; Executive Committee YPO (Young Entrepreneurs Organization); vipdesk.com.

**Cory Neal.** Film writer, producer.

**Kirk Neiswander.** Founder, The Entrepreneur's Edge; Professor of Entrepreneurship, Weatherhead School of Management, Case Western University; Senior Vice President, JumpStart; edgef.org.

**Nell Newman.** Co-founder, Newman's Own Organics; Co-author, *The Newman's Own Organics Guide to a Good Life*; newmansownorganics. com.

**Stephen O'Connor.** Founder, CEO, Group Publisher, New World Publishing; Business Development Director, AIG-Lincoln, Moscow; aiglincoln.com.

**Eric Olsen.** COO, Handwriting Without Tears; CEO, No Tears Learning; hwtears.com.

**Jan Olsen.** Founder, Handwriting Without Tears; hwtears.com.

**Joel Peterson.** Founder, Peterson Partners (venture capital); Adjunct Professor, Stanford University's Graduate School of Business; former CEO, Trammell Crow Company; gsb.stanford.edu.

**Rick Phalen.** Former CEO, Western Cities Broadcasting; Author, *Our Chicago Cubs*, *In Our Time*, and *How We've Changed Since 1950*; former radio station innovator.

**Alex Pinchev.** President, International Operations, RedHat; redhat.com.

**Dan Pink.** Author, *Free Agent Nation*, *A Whole New Mind* and *The Adventures of Johnny Bunko*; Contributor to *The New York Times*, *Harvard Business Review*, and *Fast Company*; former Chief Speechwriter to former Vice President Al Gore; danpink.com.

**Jared Polis.** Founder, bluemountain.com, proflowers.com, and numerous other ventures; Director, Watershed School (Boulder, CO); Ernst & Young Entrepreneur of the Year, 2000; currently a member of Congress, 2nd district, Colorado; jaredpolis.com.

**Eddie Poplowski.** Executive Chairman, Anderson Daymon Worldwide; Director, Aegis Living.

**Jim Quest.** Visiting Lecturer, Entrepreneur-in-Residence, Hotel School, Cornell University; Founder, Biocide; cornell.edu.

**Ken Ramberg.** Founder, JobTrak, GoodSearch; Board of Governors, Cedars-Sinai Hospital; goodsearch.com.

**Dennis Ratner.** Co-founder, Haircuttery, Bubbles, and Salon Cielo and Spa; CEO, Ratner Companies; ratnerco.com.

**Robert Reffkin.** NFTE graduate; former White House Fellow; former Consultant, McKinsey & Company.

**Dave Remick.** Founder, The Daily Briefing; Corporate Relations Manager, Greater DC Cares.

**Gene Riechers.** Co-founder, Partner, Valhalla Partners; Founder, former Managing Director, FBR Technology Venture Partners; valhallapartners. com.

**Arjun Rishi.** Founder, CEO, Enterprise Bleu; Co-founder, former CEO, Vastera; bleu.com.

**Sandy Robertson.** Founder, Robertson, Stephens and Francisco Partners; Lifetime Achievement Award in Entrepreneurship, Haas School of Business; Director, salesforce.com and Schwab Fund for Charitable Giving; franciscopartners.com.

**Ed Robinson.** Founder, President, Capacity Building Solutions; former Chairman, Community Wealth Ventures; capacity-building.com.

**Steve Rogers.** Gund Family Distinguished Professor of Entrepreneurship and Director, Levy Institute for Entrepreneurial Practice, Kellogg Graduate School of Management, Northwestern University; Author, *The Entrepreneur's Guide to Finance and Business*; Kellogg.northwestern.edu.

**Jon Roush.** Conservation Consultant; Board of Directors, Western Rivers Conservancy; westernrivers.org.

**Margarita Rozenfeld.** Founder, YES! Circle and Incite International; inciteinternational.com.

**Steve Russell.** Founder, Chairman, CEO, Celadon Trucking; Board of Trustees, Johnson School of Business, Cornell University; former President, Sea Train Lines and Hertz Trucks; celedontrucking.com.

**Carl Safina.** Founder, Blue Ocean Institute; Author, *Song for the Blue Ocean, Voyage of the Turtle,* and *Eye of the Albatross*; blueocean.org.

**Gene Samburg.** Founder, CEO, Kastle Systems; Ernst & Young Entrepreneur of the Year, 1999; kastle.com.

**Jeff Sandefer.** Co-founder, Acton School of Business and Acton MBA in Entrepreneurship; Director, *National Review* magazine; Founder, President, Sandefer Capital Partners; actonmba.org.

**Roger Sant.** Co-founder, Alternative Energy Source; Book about Roger: *Power to People: The Inside story of AES and Globalization of Electricity;* Chair, Board of Regents, Smithsonian Institution.

**Otto Scharmer.** Senior Lecturer, Sloan School of Management, MIT; Author, *Theory U: Leading from the Future as It Emerges*; Co-author, *Presence*; mitsloan.edu.

**Spencer Schock.** Founder, President, Schock Logistics; goschock.com.

**Peter Seligmann.** Co-founder, Chairman, CEO, Conservation International; Winner, Order of the Golden Ark; former President, The Nature Conservancy; conservation.org.

**Peter Senge.** Author, *The Fifth Discipline,* Co-author, *The Necessary Revolution, Presence*; Strategist of the Century by the *Journal of Business Strategy* 1999; Senior Lecturer, MIT; solonline.org.

**Jim Shaffer.** Author, *The Leadership Solution*; Founder, Jim Shaffer Group; former Partner, Towers, Perrin; jimshaffergroup.com.

**Baiju Shah.** President, CEO, Bioenterprise; former Consultant, McKinsey & Company; bioenterprise.com.

**Billy Shields.** Executive Vice President, Development, Sunrise Senior Living; former NFL player.

**Bill Shore.** Founder, Share Our Strength and Community Wealth Ventures; Author, *The Cathedral Within*, *The Light of Conscience,* and *Revolution of the Heart*; Director, Timberland; strength.org.

**Michael Shuman.** Author, *Going Local*.

**Wayne Silby.** Founder, Calvert Funds; Co-founder, Social Venture Network; calvertfoundation.org.

**Michael Simon.** Founder, 3amLabs; Founder, former CEO, UpRoar; Co-founder, Scala, Fathom Technology and Red Dot; logmein.com.

**Geoff Smart.** Founder, Chairman, CEO, ghSMART; Co-author, *Who: The A Method for Hiring*; Lecturer, Kellogg and Sloan Graduate Schools of Management; ghsmart.com.

**Philippe Sommer.** Director of Entrepreneurship Programs, University of Virginia's Darden School of Business; Founder, former President, Alsacia & Sommer and WestMed Venture Partners; darden.virginia.edu.

**Alan Sorkin.** Founder, CEO PARTS and six other ventures; Author, *CustomerMaker*; Vice Chair, San Diego Social Venture Partners International; svpi.org.

**Rick Sperling.** Founder, Mosaic Youth Theatre of Detroit; mosaicdetroit. org.

**Vikki Spruill.** Founder, Foundation Works and Sea Web; President, CEO, Ocean Conservancy; oceanconservancy.org.

**Reggie Stanley.** Senior Vice President, Chief Marketing Officer, Calvert Group; former Consultant, McKinsey & Company and Bain Consulting; Director, Echoing Green; echoinggreen.com.

**Jill Stelfox.** Co-founder, Chairman, CEO, Defywire; CFO, NobleStar Systems and Netafirm.

**Tracy Stone-Manning.** Executive Director, Clark Fork Coalition.

**Michael Strong.** Co-founder, CEO, Flow Idealism; Author, *The Habit of Thought*; flowidealism.org.

**Unky Sundt.** Former CEO, Sundt Construction.

**Mike Sutton.** Founder, Marine Stewardship Council (MSC); Director, Monterey Bay Aquarium's Center for the Future of the Oceans; Co-founder, Packard Venture Capital Fund; montereybayaquarium.org.

**Tom Szaky.** Co-founder, CEO, TerraCycle; Author, *Revolution in a Bottle*; teracycle.net.

**Richard Tait.** Co-founder, Grand Poo-Bah, Cranium; Co-founder, 13 Microsoft businesses including Sidewalk, Carpoint, Expedia; cranium.com.

**Velan Thillairajah.** Founder, Chief Executive Innovator, Enterprise Application Integration; former Team Member, NetworkSolutions and Kinetic Technologies; eaiti.com.

**Carlene Thissen.** Author, *Immokalee's Fields of Hope* and *Called From Silence*; carlenethissen.com.

**Rick Toren.** Founder, Chairman, CodeRyte; Founder, Promedco; coderyte.com.

**Karen Usher.** Founder, Chair, The Personnel Office; tpo-inc.com.

**Julian Waits.** President, CEO, Brabeion; archer.com/brabeion.

**Tom Ward.** Executive Director, Pillsbury Institute for Hospitality Entrepreneurship, School of Hotel Administration, Cornell University; cornell.edu.

**Danny Warshay.** Co-founder, Clearview Software and Health Business Partners; Founder, Managing Director, DEW Ventures; Adjunct Professor, Co-founder Entrepreneurship Program, Brown University; dewventures.com.

**Alice Waters.** Founder, The Edible Schoolyard; Author, numerous books, including *Edible Schoolyard: A Universal Idea*; Founder, Chez Panisse restaurant and the Slow Food movement; chezpanisse.com.

**Ann Webster.** Instructor in Medicine, Harvard Medical School; Staff Psychologist, Massachusetts General Hospital; hms.harvard.edu.

**Harry Weller.** Partner, New Enterprise Associates; nea.com.

**Brad Whitehead.** Co-founder, Core Resources and the Civic Innovation Lab; former Managing Director, McKinsey & Company; President, The Fund for Our Economic Future; futurefundneo.com.

**Tien Wong.** Co-founder, CyberRep; Ernst & Young Entrepreneur of the Year, 2001; CEO, Opus 8; opus8.com.

**John Wood.** Co-founder, CEO, Room to Read; Author, *Leaving Microsoft to Change the World*; former Senior Executive, Microsoft; roomtoread.org.

**Jim Wrathall.** Co-founder, ChildSecure; Senior Counsel, Senate Committee on Environment and Public Works.

**April Young.** Managing Director, Mid-Atlantic South Region Technology and Life Sciences Division, Comerica Bank; Advisor, DreamLabs, My Job Coach, and Credible Wireless; former Director, Potomac KnowledgeWay; comerica.com.

**Muhammad Yunus.** Founder, Grameen Bank and Grameen Companies; Author, *Banker to the Poor* and *Creating a World Without Poverty*; Winner, Nobel Prize for Peace 2006; grameen.com.

**John Zitzner.** Founder, E City Cleveland, Entrepreneurship Preparatory School; Founder, former CEO, President, The Bradley Company; ecitycleveland.com.

# Books by Contributors

The following is a list of books by many of the contributors to *A Deliberate Pause*. While I have compiled it to the best of my ability, it is possible that I have missed books written by contributors, listed here or otherwise. The contributors and the books are listed alphabetically.

**Bill Cast**
William Cast, *Going South: An Inside Look at Corruption and Greed, and the Power of the HealthSouth Message Board.* Kaplan Books, 2005.

**Duke Chung**
Aspatore Books Staff, with contributing authors including Duke Chung, *Inside the Minds: Software Leadership Strategies: CRM, Integration, ERP, & Storage Solutions CEOs Offer Best Practices & Keys to Success.* Aspatore Books. eBook.

**Doug Davidoff**
Doris S. Davidoff, Philip G. Davidoff, Donald M. Davidoff, and Douglas G. Davidoff, *Parenting the Office.* Pelican Publishing, 2001.

**Esther Dyson**
Esther Dyson, *Release 2.0: A Design for Living in the Digital Age.* Broadway Books, 1997.

**Robert Egger**
Robert Egger with Howard Yoon, *Begging for Change, The Dollars and Sense of Making Nonprofits Responsive, Efficient, and Rewarding for All.* Harper Business, 2002.

**Karl Eller**
Karl Eller, *Integrity Is All You've Got: and Seven Other Lessons of Entrepreneurial Life.* McGraw Hill, 2005.

## Jed Emerson

J. Gregory Dees, Jed Emerson, and Peter Economy, *Enterprising Nonprofits: A Toolkit for Social Entrepreneurs.* Wiley, 2001.

Jed Emerson, *New Social Entrepreneurs: The Success, Challenge, and Lessons of Nonprofit Enterprise Creation.* The Roberts Foundation, 1996.

J. Gregory Dees, Jed Emerson, and Peter Economy, *Strategic Tools for Social Entrepreneurs: Enhancing the Performance of Your Enterprising Nonprofit.* Wiley, 2002.

## Rafe Esquith

Rafe Esquith, *Teach Like Your Hair's On Fire.* Penguin, 2007.

Rafe Esquith, *There Are No Shortcuts.* Pantheon Books, 2003.

## David Ford

David Ford, *Blind in One Eye.* Self-published memoir, 2009.

## Gregg Fraley

Gregg Fraley, *Jack's Notebook: A Business Novel About Creative Problem Solving.* Thomas Nelson, 2008.

## Edie Fraser

Edie Fraser and Robyn Spizman, *Do Your Giving While You Are Living.* Morgan James Publishing, 2007.

Edie Fraser, *Risk to Riches: Women and Entrepreneurship in America.* A Special Report, National Federation of Independent, 1986.

## Betsy Friedlander

Betsy Friedlander, *How to Land Job Offers: The Art of Generating Job Opportunities.* Privately Published.

## Ken Getz

Ken Getz, *The Gift of Participation: A Guide to Making Informed Decisions About Volunteering for Clinical Trials.* Jerian Publishing, 2007.

Ken Getz and Debra Borfitz, *Informed Consent: A Guide to the Risks and Benefits of Volunteering for Clinical Trials.* CenterWatch, 2002.

## Casey Golden

Edie Fraser and Robyn Spizman (contributing authors, including Casey Golden), *Do Your Giving While You Are Living.* Morgan James Publishing, 2007.

**Laurence Gonzales**

Laurence Gonzales, *Deep Survival: Who Lives, Who Dies and Why.* W.W. Norton & Company, 2003.

Laurence Gonzales, *Everyday Survival: Why Smart People Do Stupid Things.* Norton & Company, 2008.

**Bijoy Goswami**

Bijoy Goswami with David K. Wolpert, *The Human Fabric: Unleashing the Power of Core Energy in Everyone.* Aviri Publishing, 2004.

**Allen Grossman**

Christine W. Letts, William P. Ryan, and Allen Grossman, *High Performance Nonprofit Organizations: Managing Upstream for Greater Impact.* Wiley, 1998.

**Anil Gupta**

Anil Gupta, *The Quest for Global Dominance: Transforming Global Presence into Global Competition.* Jossey-Bass, 2008.

**Verne Harnish**

Verne Harnish, *Mastering the Rockefeller Habits: What You Must Do to Increase the Value of Your Growing Firm.* SelectBooks, Inc., 2002.

**Jeffrey Hollender**

Jeffrey Hollender, Geoff Davis and Meika Hollender, *Naturally Clean: The Seventh Generation Guide to Safe & Healthy, Non-Toxic Cleaning.* New Society Publishers, 2006.

Jeffrey Hollender, *What Matters Most: How a Small Group of Pioneers Is Teaching Social Responsibility to Big Business, and Why Big Business Is Listening.* Basic Books, 2006.

**Gary Hoover**

Gary Hoover, *Hoover's Vision: Original Thinking for Business Success.* Texere, 2001.

**Dipak Jain**

Phillip Kotler, Dipak Jain and Suvit Maesincee, *Marketing Moves: A New Approach to Profits, Growth, and Renewal.* Harvard Business School Press, 2002.

**Julie Silard Kantor**

Julie Silard Kantor, *I Said Yes: Real Life Stories of Students, Teachers, and Leaders Saying Yes! to Entrepreneurship in America's Schools.* Gazelles, 2006.

## Guy Kawasaki

Guy Kawasaki, *The Art of the Start: The Time-Tested, Battle-Hardened Guide for Anyone Starting Anything.* Portfolio Hardcover, 2004.

Guy Kawasaki, *Hindsights: The Wisdom and Breakthroughs of Remarkable People.* Grand Central Publishing, 1995.

Guy Kawasaki, *The MacIntosh Way.* Harper Collins, 1990.

Guy Kawasaki, *Reality Check: The Irreverent Guide to Outsmarting, Outmanaging, and Outmarketing your Competition.* Portfolio Hardcover, 2008.

Guy Kawasaki with Michele Moreno, *Rules for Revolutionaries: The Capitalist Manifesto for Creating and Marketing New Products and Services.* Collins Business, 2000.

Guy Kawasaki, *Selling the Dream.* Collins Business, 1992.

## Reggie Van Lee

Reginald Van Lee, Mark Gerencser, Fernando Napolitano, and Christopher Kelly, *Megacommunities: How Leaders of Government, Business and Non-profits Can Tackle Today's Global Challenges Together.* Palgrave Macmillan, 2009.

## Steve Mariotti

Steve Mariotti with Debra DeSalvo and Tony Towle, *The Young Entrepreneur's Guide to Starting and Running a Business.* Three Rivers Press, 2000.

## John May

John May and Cal Simmons, *Every Business Needs an Angel.* Crown Business, 2001.

John May and Elizabeth O'Haloran, *State of the Art: An Executive Briefing on Cutting Edge Practices in American Angel Investing.* Batten Institute, University of Virginia Darden School of Business, 2003.

## Rob McGovern

Robert J. McGovern, *Bring Your "A" Game: The 10 Career Secrets to the High Achiever.* Sourcebooks, 2005.

## Nell Newman

Nell Newman with Joseph D'Agnese, *The Newman's Own Organics Guide to a Good Life: Simple Measures that Benefit You and the Place You Live.* Willard, 2003.

## Rick Phalen

Rick Phalen, *A Bittersweet Journey: America's Fascination with Baseball.* McGregor Publishing, 2000.

Rick Phalen, *Our Chicago Cubs: Inside the History and the Mystery of Baseball's Favorite Franchise*. Diamond Communications, 1992.

**Dan Pink**
Daniel H. Pink, *The Adventures of Johnny Bunko: The Last Career Guide You'll Ever Need*. Riverhead Books, 2008.
Daniel H. Pink, *Free Agent Nation: The Future of Working for Yourself*. Business Plus, 2002.
Daniel H. Pink, *A Whole New Mind: Why Right-Brainers Will Rule the Future*. Riverhead Books, 2006.

**Steve Rogers**
Steven Rogers, *The Entrepreneur's Guide to Finance and Business: Wealth Creation Techniques for Growing a Business*. McGraw Hill, 2002.

**Carl Safina**
Carl Safina, *Eye of the Albatross: Visions of Hope and Survival*. Holt Paperbacks, 2003.
Carl Safina, *Song for the Blue Ocean: Encounters Along the World's Coasts and Beneath the Seas*. Holt Paperbacks, 1999.
Carl Safina, *Voyage of the Turtle: In Pursuit of the Earth's Last Dinosaur*. Henry Holt and Company, 2006.

**Otto Scharmer**
Peter Senge, C. Otto Scharmer, Joseph Jaworski, Betty Sue Flowers, *Presence: An Exploration of Profound Change in People, Organizations, and Society*. Currency, Doubleday, 2005.
C. Otto Scharmer, *Theory U: Leading from the Future as It Emerges*. Berrett-Koehler Publishers, 2009.

**Peter Senge**
Peter Senge, *The Fifth Discipline: The Art & Practice of the Learning Organization*, Currency, Doubleday, 1990, 2006.
Peter Senge, Bryan Smith, Nina Kruschwitz, Joe Laur, Sara Schley, *The Necessary Revolution: How Individuals and Organizations Are Working Together to Create a Sustainable World*, Doubleday, 2008.
Peter Senge, C. Otto Scharmer, Joseph Jaworski, Betty Sue Flowers, *Presence: An Exploration of Profound Change in People, Organizations, and Society*. Currency, Doubleday, 2005.

## Jim Shaffer

Jim Shaffer, *The Leadership Solution: Connecting People to Strategy, Creating Teams that Act Like Owners Communications Tactics of Today's Top Leaders.* McGraw Hill, 2000.

## Bill Shore

Bill Shore, *The Cathedral Within: Transforming Your Life by Giving Something Back.* Random House, 1999.

Bill Shore, *The Light of Consciousness: How a Simple Act Can Change Your Life.* Random House, 2005.

Bill Shore, *Revolution of the Heart: A New Strategy for Creating Wealth and Meaningful Change.* DIANE Publishing Company, 1999.

## Michael Shuman

Michael Shuman, *Going Local: Creating Self-Reliant Communities in a Global Age.* Routledge, 2000.

## Geoff Smart

Geoff Smart and Randy Street, *Who: The A Method for Hiring.* Ballantine Books, 2008.

## Alan Sorkin

Alan Sorkin, *CustomerMaker: More Customers, Loyal Employees & Higher Profits.* Privately Published.

Alan Sorkin, *What Parents Must Know and Can Do About Teenage Alcohol and Drug Abuse.* Black Forest Press, 1996.

## Michael Strong

Michael Strong, *The Habit of Thought: From Socratic Seminars To Socratic Practice.* New View Publications, 1997.

Michael Strong and John Mackey, *Be the Solution: How Entrepreneurs and Conscious Capitalists Can Solve All the World's Problems.* Wiley, 2009.

## Tom Szaky

Tom Szaky, *Revolution in a Bottle.* Portfolio, 2009.

## Carlene Thissen

Carlene Thissen, *Immokalee's Fields of Hope.* iUniverse Star, 2004.

Carlene Thissen, *Called from Silence: The Father Sanders Novel.* iUniverse. com, 2009.

**Alice Waters**

Alice Waters, *The Art of Simple Food: Notes, Lessons, and Recipes From a Delicious Revolution*. Clarkson Potter, 2007.

Alice Waters, *Chez Panisse Vegetables*. William Morrow Cookbooks, 1996. (One of many cookbooks by Alice Waters and Chez Panisse)

Alice Waters, *Edible Schoolyard: A Universal Idea*. Chronicle Books, 2008.

Carlo Petrini and Alice Waters, *Slow Food Nation: Why Our Food Should be Good, Clean, and Fair*. Rizzoli Ex Libris, 2007.

**John Wood**

John Wood, *Leaving Microsoft to Change the World: An Entrepreneur's Odyssey to Educate the World's Children*. Collins Business, 2007.

**Muhammad Yunus**

Muhammad Yunus, *Banker to the Poor: Microlending and the Battle Against World Poverty*. PublicAffairs Books, 2003.

Muhammad Yunus, *Creating a World Without Poverty: Social Business and the Future of Capitalism*. PublicAffairs Books, 2007.